Multiple Authorship and the Myth of Solitary Genius

Multiple Authorship and the Myth of Solitary Genius

JACK STILLINGER

New York   Oxford
OXFORD UNIVERSITY PRESS
1991

Oxford University Press

Oxford   New York   Toronto
Delhi   Bombay   Calcutta   Madras   Karachi
Petaling Jaya   Singapore   Hong Kong   Tokyo
Nairobi   Dar es Salaam   Cape Town
Melbourne   Auckland

and associated companies in
Berlin   Ibaden

Published by Oxford University Press, Inc.,
200 Madison Avenue, New York, New York 10016

Oxford is a registered trademark of Oxford University Press

Library of Congress Cataloging-in-Publication Data
Stillinger, Jack.
Multiple authorship and the myth of solitary genius /
Jack Stillinger.
p.   cm.   Includes bibliographical references and index.
ISBN 0-19-506861-0
1. English literature—History and criticism—Theory, etc.
2. American literature—History and criticism—Theory, etc.
3. Creation (Literary, artistic, etc.)
4. Authorship—Collaboration.   5. Genius.   I. Title.
PR21.S75   1991
820.9—dc20   90-24273

9 8 7 6 5 4 3 2 1

Printed in the United States of America
on acid-free paper

Preface

The initial concern of this book is the relevance of the author in the interpretation, presentation, and evaluation of a literary work. At one extreme of opinion on the question, there are theorists who speak of the "disappearance," "absence," "removal," "banishment," even "death" of the author (Roland Barthes and Michel Foucault are examples): once the work is written—indeed, some believe even before it is written—the author gives it up entirely, ceasing to have any connection with its meaning or significance. The opposite extreme of opinion (as in the writings of E. D. Hirsch, Jr., and P. D. Juhl) invests the author with an importance approaching apotheosis or deification: the author, having wrought the work, is the only possible determiner of its meaning ever afterward.

It is noteworthy that both of these theoretical extremes share the concept of *an* author—singular—as creator of a text. In many cases such a concept does not accord with the facts of literary production; numerous texts considered to be the work of single authorship turn out to be the product of several hands. It may, therefore, advance our thinking to expand the question to include, in effect, *how many* authors are being banished from a text or apotheosized in it.

Acknowledged multiple authorship occurs all through literature and the arts: Beaumont and Fletcher, Gilbert and Sullivan, Gilbert and Gubar—famous examples come readily to mind. The multiple authorship examined in the present study is a special variety: *the joint, or composite, or collaborative production of literary works that we usually think of as written by a single author.* This kind of multiple authorship, when all the different forms of it are taken together, is also an extremely common phenomenon; a work may be the collaborative product of the nominal author and a friend, a spouse, a ghost, an agent, an editor, a translator, a publisher, a censor, a transcriber, a printer, or—what is more often the case—several of these acting together or in succession.

The relationship of multiple authorship to literary and editorial theory ought to be of interest to anyone who cares for logic and consistency in our thinking about literature. Most theories of interpretation and editing are based on the idea of a single author (the romantic "myth of solitary genius" in my title) as sole controlling intelligence in a work. We routinely refer to a single authorial mind, or personality, or consciousness to validate "meaning" or "authority"; where others besides the nominal author have a share in the creation of a text, we usually ignore that share or else call it corruption and try to get rid of it. But literary works can and frequently do have multiple authors, sometimes with divided and even conflicting intentions among them; if we recognize that fact, we may have to worry a little about the adequacy of our current theories. The reality of what authors actually do and how works are actually produced is often—perhaps usually—much more complex than our theories and practices allow.

The organization of this book, probably self-evident in the Contents, is briefly outlined at the end of Chapter 1. I began thinking about the topic in the early 1970s, while I was investigating Keats's texts—making numerous discoveries about the transmission and publication of Keats's poems and at the same time reading up on textual theory and the relation of authorial intention to scholarly editing—for *The Texts of Keats's Poems,* which I published in 1974, and my edition *The Poems of John Keats,* which came out four years later. (I should have begun thinking about it a dozen years earlier, when I first worked on the early draft of Mill's *Autobiography* and had clear evidence in my hands of Harriet Mill's revisions of her husband's manuscript.) At an early stage I was much influenced by James Thorpe's *Principles of Textual Criticism* (1972), whose first chapter, "The Aesthetics of Textual Criticism" (originally published in *PMLA* in 1965), listed and discussed a great many examples of multiple authorship, including a number gleaned from Frank Luther Mott's histories of American magazines. Philip Gaskell's *From Writer to Reader: Studies in Editorial Method* (1978) presented an excellent model of using chapter-length case histories to illustrate variations of a common phenomenon (the complexities of textual production) and a recurring problem (how best to edit a work—to which Gaskell, on the basis of his examples, proposes a variety of solutions). As in Gaskell's work, my examples here are offered not primarily to construct a new theory of authorship or production, but to suggest that even the most sophisticated of the theories we already have are much too simple to deal with the variety and complexity of the historical circumstances.

This book is itself the product of multiple authorship, for I have had many helpers in the course of my research and writing. My greatest obligation is to my colleague–wife, Nina Baym, with whom I have been collaborating, in her works and mine, for more than two decades (I correct her punctuation and typing errors; she corrects my thinking). Other colleagues at Urbana who contributed valuable information and suggestions include Robert Carringer, Margaret Dickie, John Dussinger, Dale Kramer, Michael Shapiro, Charles Shattuck, John Stubbs, Mark Thomas, and Leon Waldoff. Among friends and colleagues (and an occasional relative) elsewhere, I wish especially to thank Lauren Berlant, Robert Murray Davis, Norman Fruman, Beth Lau, Paul Magnuson, David Miall, Ronald Primeau, Mark Reed, Donald Reiman, Ann Robson, Peter Shillingsburg, Tom Stillinger, Susan Wolfson, and Frances and Leo Zippin. I am also much obliged for the encouraging responses of audiences who listened to preliminary accounts of some of my discoveries (and provided criticism and suggestions afterward) at Agnes Scott College, the University of Georgia, Penn State, the University of Illinois, and the Society for Textual Scholarship. Earlier versions of Chapters 3 and 4 and part of 9 appeared in *Victorian Studies* 27 (1983): 7–23, *Studies in Romanticism* 28 (1989): 3–28, and *TEXT* 5 (1991): 283–93. I am grateful to the editors and publishers of these journals for permission to use the materials in revised form here.

Urbana, Illinois   J. S.
October 1990

Contents

*Multiple Authorship and the
Myth of Solitary Genius*

1

What Is an Author?

There has been much discussion, in theoretical writings of the last two decades, of the "disappearance," "absence," "removal," "banishment," even "death" of the author. Roland Barthes's famous phrase "la mort de l'auteur" began life in 1968. Michel Foucault, an author apparently alive enough to look across town and see what Barthes was doing, addressed the Société française de Philosophie in the following year on the "recent absence" of the author, how it came about, and some of the consequences that result when we think, if we can, of literary works as authorless (or, more precisely, as having abstract "author-functions" rather than real-life historical authors).[1] Ignoring (and ignorance) of authors had of course become more and more common in practical literary criticism of the 1930s, 1940s, and 1950s, as explicators focused on "the text itself" and attempted to disqualify everything extrinsic to the work, including the person (or persons) who created it. On more philosophical and political grounds, literary theorists—especially those writing under the influence of Barthes and Foucault (and of earlier writers like Nietzsche and Freud who influenced Barthes and Foucault)—have increasingly treated literary texts, and frequently all writing together, as autonomous, separate from any idea of authorship and, as one of the results, separate from any idea of determinate meaning. At both the practical level, where ignoring the author has often produced readings totally at odds with whatever one might imagine of the historical author's range of possible intentions, and the theoretical level, where the disappeared authors keep reappearing (between the lines, as it were, and in many lapses of rhetoric in the theorizing), the explicators and theorists have been doing some strange things. Let us examine for a moment what it is that they think they have banished. Toward the end of this chapter, and then in the rest of the book, I shall narrow the focus to a consideration of, in effect, *how many* authors are being banished from a text. Here at the outset I wish to inquire more generally into our common ideas of authorship,

3

especially concerning the identity of authors and the relationship of authorial identity to our experience and understanding of texts.

1

In ordinary usage, everybody knows what an author is: "the writer of a literary work (as a book)," according to a standard desk dictionary; "one that originates or gives existence"[2]—gives existence most frequently to words in a text. We are in touch with authors practically all our lives, though usually, at the beginning of our experience, without awareness of authors as such. Small children do not think of nursery rhymes, folktales, and fairy tales as having authors (probably our earliest unconscious ideas of authorship involve a parent or babysitter or teacher singing or telling a story). Quite soon, however, children begin making connections between stories and the authors' names attached to them. The authors' identities make an impression because the child is conscious of reading, or wanting to read, other stories by the same author. That is why one sees a whole shelfful of Dr. Seuss books in a home, or a row of Beatrix Potter or Richard Scarry or A. A. Milne. In early schooling, our experience of authors is a mixture of responses. Some authors provide lively stories, interesting information, or funny jokes, while others are offensive or boring. In the long run, only a few of the authors we read deserve full attention or get our unqualified admiration; but pleasurable or not, our experience with authors is rich, complicated, and long-lasting.

If we live and work in an academic environment, we are literally surrounded by authors. In my own English department at the University of Illinois, some nine poets, novelists, and short-story writers constitute the creative-writing faculty; I see one or more of these authors in the halls practically every day. But the "noncreative" (as it were) English faculty—another sixty or so professors—are authors as well; I am a member of this latter group, author of, among other things, the present chapter on authorship. Last December, when the Modern Language Association held its annual meeting, there were more than seven hundred separate sessions in the convention program: a handful of distinguished poets and novelists read from their poetry and fiction, and a large group of lesser authors—2500 English and foreign-language professors— read scholarly papers, or responses to papers, in which the subjects, even in the most rarefiedly theoretical of the sessions, were almost always still other authors. For three and a half days the convention hotels were buzzing with authorship.

But what, even supposing that we read authors' works all our lives and become professors and attend the MLA meetings, do we really know about authors? A high proportion of the authors we care most about are dead—not metaphorically, in the sense of Barthes's "la mort de l'auteur," but literally, as, for example, Chaucer or Shakespeare or Keats—and nearly all those who are alive are constantly out of sight (they live and write in other towns, other countries). And some theorists, worrying about the difficulty of interpreting a piece of writing, believe that it would make no difference if the author were present to answer questions about it anyway; the author's answers would merely complicate the problem, because they too (in common with all other utterances without exception) would require interpretation.[3]

Obviously we must go to their writings for the most essential information about authors. But it is just as obvious—or has been at least since Henry James (or one of his personae) discussed point of view in his prefaces—that there are nearly insurmountable problems in sorting out the differences between a historical author (for example, Henry James, 1843–1916) and the author's created narrators and characters, even when, as frequently happens, the narrator or character has the same name as the historical author. Indeed, there is a voluminous literature on narrators, points of view, voices, personae, masks, and the like.

James himself was a pioneer, in both practice and theory, of the basic ideas that authors are separate from their characters, that characters have limited knowledge, and that stories can be presented from multiple points of view. Wayne Booth, in *The Rhetoric of Fiction* (1961), has labeled and studied a variety of author's voices in fiction, dramatized and undramatized speakers, reliable and unreliable commentary, "authorial silence," and impersonal narration. Roland Barthes, in a paper originally published in 1966, more simply enumerates three standard concepts of narrator: the historical author who created the work (and exists—this was two years before Barthes's "La mort"!— independently of it); an "omniscient, apparently impersonal, consciousness that tells the story from a superior point of view, that of God" (this narrator is both inside and outside the characters at once); and a point of view limited to "what the characters can observe or know."[4]

In poetry, theorizing about dramatic speakers and situations is nearly two centuries old. Both Wordsworth in his preface to *Lyrical Ballads* and Coleridge in *Biographia Literaria* are well aware of poetic ventriloquism. Keats in his letters describes the chameleonlike adaptability of the poet's sympathetic imagination, and Emily Dickinson remarked to Thomas Wentworth Higginson: "When I state myself, as the Representative of the Verse—it does not mean—me—but a supposed person."[5] Patrick Cruttwell, in a frequently cited essay published nearly three decades ago, identifies four kinds of authorial self-presentation—the direct, the masked, the mythologized, and the dramatized—according to the distance between "person" and "maker" (that is, between the speaker in a work and the author who created it). More recently Ralph Rader, studying "The Dramatic Monologue and Related Lyric Forms," has similarly presented four types of situation: the expressive lyric (where the speaker and the historical author are one and the same); the dramatic lyric (where the speaker is a fictional creation, and we view the world through the speaker's eyes); the dramatic monologue (where the speaker is again a fictional creation, but we view the world from outside the speaker); and the mask lyric (where the speaker is an actor, a totally artificial self, and we see no world at all but only symbols).[6]

   Some critics hold that it is always the author who is speaking in the voice(s) of a work, but nevertheless an author assuming "poses," frequently with ambiguity, irony, and related modes of indirectness. Others believe that an author never writes anything—even a routine business letter or a note to a friend—without to some extent dramatizing, and therefore fictionalizing, the authorial self. It is no wonder that critics and theorists alike have wished to get rid of the authors. When the historical authors are dead or otherwise inaccessible, and the speakers in their texts are fictitious characters who have limited knowledge, are sometimes evasive, and frequently tell lies, there does seem to be a rather embarrassing circularity in going to the texts in order to recover the authors in order to interpret the texts.

   ## 2

In spite of their elusiveness, however, the real (historical) authors of our books and poems have continued to interest not only general readers but large numbers of teachers, scholars, and critics. The biographical study of authors that, in England, got seriously under way in the late eighteenth century (Johnson's *Lives of the English Poets* [1779–81] is the most prominent landmark) quickly became the principal method of writing about literature during the Romantic period, when the personalities of the poets and the essayists were thought to be central in their works and there was widespread discussion of such topics as inspiration, originality, creativity, and genius.[7] The biographical approach continued strong through the Victorian period and became a large element in the formal study of literature when English departments and curricula were instituted in colleges and universities toward the end of the nineteenth century.

By the early decades of the twentieth century, biography had actually *replaced* the works as the main focus in lectures, "critical" essays ("appreciations"), and even literary histories. The famous lectures on the Brownings by the Yale professor William Lyon Phelps inspired thousands of students to make a sentimental pilgrimage to Florence. The Princeton professor Charles Grosvenor Osgood, in *The Voice of England* (1935), the most widely used single-volume literary history in the later 1930s and 1940s, explains in his preface that, since "literature was created by men and women," he has "tried . . . to humanize the greater figures in English Literature" and has, "with the distinguished encouragement of Dr. Johnson, inclined to 'the biographical part of literature,' a leaning confirmed by many years' experience in the teaching of literature." Osgood's six hundred pages of agreeably readable humanization recount the lives in detail and the works hardly at all: *Paradise Lost* receives just a page of descriptive commentary (beginning "*Paradise Lost* is the greatest single poetic achievement in the language"); *The Rape of the Lock* is summarized in four sentences (concluding with the remark that the poem is "an imperishable treasure of fun and wit that never stale, and of beauty that never fades"); *Hamlet* and *King Lear* and Keats's odes are merely mentioned by title.[8]

Osgood's book typifies the approach that the New Critics, beginning in the later 1920s, set out to oppose by shifting the focus from the author to the text and from biography to explication and critical analysis. I. A. Richards had made an appalling discovery at Cambridge University, in a series of experiments that he wrote up in *Practical Criticism* (1929): his students' literary experience was so narrowly confined to "the biographical part of literature" that they could not read and understand a poem; when texts were detached from the authors' names and presented simply as "Poem 1" and "Poem 2," the students had no ability or methodology for recognizing or assessing differences between the work of Shakespeare and that of (in one of Richards's examples) Ella Wheeler Wilcox. There followed, then, several decades of renewed interest in the works themselves, with authors (and frequently historical contexts, sources, influences, generic and linguistic traditions, and much else) relegated to a dim background or ignored altogether. Among several consequences there arose a serious problem in the interpretation of works—the question of whether meaning is primarily a matter of authorial intention or the critic's inference (extraction, synthesis, "translation," "conversion") based on the statements, images, tone, and many other particulars of the text at hand. W. K. Wimsatt, Jr., and Monroe C. Beardsley, in their extremely influential essay "The Intentional Fallacy" (1946), argued strongly in favor of the latter view, that both the meaning and the value of a literary work exist (and must be determined) independently of the author's original intentions. Their position seemingly received the official support of the Modern Language Association when Northrop Frye repeated it in his MLA-sponsored essay "Literary Criticism" in 1963:

> We have to avoid of course the blunder that is called the intentional fallacy in criticism. The question "what did the author mean by this?" is always illegitimate. First, we can never know; second, there is no reason to suppose that the author knew; third, the question confuses imaginative with discursive writing. The legitimate form of the question is: "what does the text say?"[9]

Frye's essay, as exemplification of the several-decades-long "text itself" tradition, was answered at book length by E. D. Hirsch, Jr., in *Validity in Interpretation* (1967),[10] and Hirsch in turn provoked (and continues to provoke) much subsequent debate on all sides of the question. Then, almost in the midst of the arguments over Hirsch's book, a third possibility for the principal locus of meaning was introduced and promoted by Walter Slatoff, Norman Holland, Stanley Fish, Wolfgang Iser, David Bleich, and other critics sensitive to the realities of readers interacting with texts—meaning as a construct in the individual reader's mind. Thus reader response, or reception theory, offered yet another reason for slighting the authors.

But in spite of all the theoretical controversy over the relevance and place of the author, a great deal of literary study as it is routinely carried on from day to day continues to be fundamentally biographical in approach. The preponderance of critical interpreters are still trying to recover, explain, and clarify the *author's* meaning in a text, and thus are engaged in biographical work; and so too are the preponderance of textual scholars, trying to recover, preserve, purify, and re-present a text according to the *author's* intentions. Both kinds of work involve reconstruction of the life and mind of an author, and they are judged successful to a greater or lesser degree according to the amount of information that the scholar can discover about these essentially biographical matters. The same is true of the commonest subdivisions of critical and scholarly activity— such things as investigation of how an author wrote and revised a work; recovery of the circumstances of the transmission of a text, publication, and original and subsequent reception; consideration of an author's reading and education; study of comments that an author makes about a work (or about writing in general) in letters, journals, diaries, recorded conversations; relationship of details in a work to details of the author's life (and to the lives of people among the author's acquaintance); relationship of a work to other writings by the same author and to writings by other authors; study of an author's language and its sources; study of an author's ideas and their sources (and their relationship to ideas of the author's time and earlier); study of the historical, political, social, and cultural contexts that, although beyond an author's control, are channeled through the author into a work. All these (and more) are compassable under the general heading of biographical study. Indeed, apart from abstract theorizing about literature, it is sometimes difficult to think of a type of literary research or critical activity that is *not* fundamentally biographical in this large sense that I am proposing.

3

If literary study is structured by biography, then to remove biography from our purview is, in effect, to do away with literary study as we know it. But I wish also to suggest that continuous and prolonged interest in biography is not unreasonable. I shall use a short poem by Keats, *Sonnet to Sleep,* to make several points about how biographical knowledge produces textual knowledge and understanding. Here is the version that appears in the most recent scholarly edition of Keats's poems:

Sonnet to Sleep

O soft embalmer of the still midnight,
  Shutting with careful fingers and benign
Our gloom-pleas'd eyes, embower'd from the light,
  Enshaded in forgetfulness divine:
O soothest Sleep! if so it please thee, close,   5
  In midst of this thine hymn, my willing eyes,
Or wait the Amen ere thy poppy throws
  Around my bed its lulling charities.
Then save me or the passed day will shine
  Upon my pillow, breeding many woes: 10
Save me from curious conscience, that still hoards
  Its strength for darkness, burrowing like the mole;
Turn the key deftly in the oiled wards,
  And seal the hushed casket of my soul.[11]

Let us suppose for a moment that we could divest this poem of
its authorship and examine it, in the manner of one of I. A. Richards's experiments, as an anonymous "Poem 1." If we know something about poetic structures, we would not need the title to see that
it is a sonnet and that it is an apostrophe addressed to a personified
abstraction, Sleep, who is depicted as an embalmer, a closer of eyes,
and someone (or some thing) who can save the speaker from "curious conscience" by locking his soul in a casket. If we know certain
facts of literary history, we can place this sonnet in a long tradition
of poems invoking sleep, relating it to and comparing it with similar
apostrophes by Statius, Sidney, Daniel, Drummond of Hawthorn-
den, Thomas Warton, Wordsworth, and Hartley Coleridge[12] (although, when we place it this way, we are of course relating it to
authored poems). We can observe that the poem's two sentences
coincide with the commonest internal structure of the sonnet form—
the division into octave and sestet—but also that the rhyme scheme
(abab cdcd bc efef) deviates from the standard patterns by repeating
a "b" rhyme at the end of line 9 and a "c" rhyme at the end of 10,
giving in effect a structure of three quatrains (1–4, 5–8, 11–14) with
a pair of retrospectively rhymed lines between the second and third
quatrains. The theme and argument are straightforward enough—
"Come, Sleep, and save me . . ."—but if we examine the literal
meanings clause by clause, we get a rather silly statement in the
latter half of the first sentence (5–8), where Sleep is given the choice
of closing the speaker's eyes immediately, in the middle of the poem

(in which case the speaker will not finish it), or waiting until later (when the fourteen lines are completed).

In this hypothetical situation of unknown authorship, I think we would mainly be impressed with the musical qualities of the lines (the standard devices of alliteration and assonance and the pleasing variation of vowel sounds); we would note the richness and abundance of the images (there are more than two dozen of them in the fourteen lines); and we might award bonus points for general thematic seriousness provided by the associations of sleep with narcosis and death (embalming, closing of eyes, "forgetfulness," "poppy," sealing of the soul), the handful of religious terms ("divine," "hymn," "Amen"), and perhaps also the ominously nonspecific after-recollections of the daytime world ("many woes," "curious conscience") that the speaker is willing to accept a deathlike state in order to avoid. No doubt we would admire the poem, imperfect as it is in rhyme and logic, but probably we would not, in its guise as "Poem 1," strongly insist on its inclusion in the standard anthologies, even supposing that such anthologies had room for anonymous poems.

Now see what happens when we (re)introduce Keats as author and examine the sonnet in the context of his chronologically arranged poems (where it is placed between *Song of Four Fairies* and *Ode to Psyche*) or in the context of his letters (where it is copied, along with two sonnets *On Fame* and *Ode to Psyche*, in the 14 February–3 May 1819 journal letter to George and Georgiana Keats in a section dated 30 April) or even among the Keats selections in the *Norton Anthology of English Literature* (where it appears between *La Belle Dame sans Merci* and, again, *Ode to Psyche*). Keats wrote *Sonnet to Sleep* in the spring of 1819, probably toward the end of April, not long after he drafted *The Eve of St. Agnes* and *La Belle Dame* and perhaps just a few days before writing what we take to be the first of the great odes of that year, *Ode to Psyche*. His original draft of the sonnet (a twelve-line version that he abandoned without finishing) survives on a flyleaf of a volume of *Paradise Lost* now at Keats House, Hampstead; and we have, or can reconstruct, the two principal versions that followed—an earlier text that existed in a notebook or copybook that Keats was keeping at the time, and a later text that Keats wrote in a lady's album in June 1820. The sonnet was first published in a newspaper in the west of England, the *Plymouth and Devonport Weekly Journal,* on 11 October 1838, seventeen and a half years after Keats's death. It did not become generally known to readers until its second publication, a decade later, in the first major biography of the poet, Richard Monckton Milnes's *Life, Letters, and Literary Remains, of John Keats* (1848).

One immediate result of connecting the sonnet with its author and attending to some of the routine details of textual history is a consequence of the last set of facts just mentioned: Keats himself never published the poem. This is not a unique or even special situation in the Keats canon; there are no sonnets (and just nine shorter poems of any sort) in Keats's famous volume of 1820— *Lamia, Isabella, The Eve of St. Agnes, and Other Poems*—and only a few pieces, fourteen in all, appeared separately during his lifetime in periodicals like the *Champion,* the *Examiner,* the *Indicator,* and *Annals of the Fine Arts.* Thus a great many other poems besides *Sonnet to Sleep* first saw print posthumously. But a valid critical point may nevertheless be made: the sonnet's irregularity of rhymes in lines 9–10 (or 9–14 more generally) and the mild silliness of statement in the second quatrain (5–8) are much more tolerable— are perhaps even interesting in their own right—when we know that the poem was a work still in process or one that was only provisionally complete. Keats shared the sonnet with his brother and sister-in-law; allowed two close friends, Charles Brown and Richard Woodhouse, to make copies (this was standard procedure with Keats's poems at the time); and selected it, instead of a number of other poems, when the lady asked him to write some lines in her album a year later. But none of these distributions in manuscript indicates that he considered the piece finished. Right off, we gain a fact that improves our reading of the sonnet: its status as an unpublished poem among Keats's writings.

Another fact deriving from biographical context is the experimental character of *Sonnet to Sleep.* It is well known that in the spring of 1819 Keats expressed dissatisfaction with the two standard forms of the sonnet. As he explained in his journal letter at the end of April or the beginning of May, just before copying the sonnet *If by dull rhymes our English must be chain'd:*

> I have been endeavouring to discover a better sonnet stanza than we have. The legitimate [the Italian or Petrarchan] does not suit the language over-well from the pouncing rhymes—the other kind [the English or Shakespearean] appears too elegaic—and the couplet at the end of it has seldom a pleasing effect—I do not pretend to have succeeded.[13]

If by dull rhymes, the second sonnet *On Fame* ("How fever'd is the man"), and *Sonnet to Sleep*—written within a few days of one another—represent three different kinds of departure from the standard schemes. Critics beginning with H. W. Garrod in 1926, observing that the first fourteen lines of *Ode to Psyche* rhyme very much like an Italian sonnet and that the ten-line stanza used by Keats in *Ode to a Nightingale, Ode on a Grecian Urn,* and *Ode on Melancholy* consists of a Shakespearean quatrain followed by an Italian sestet, have argued quite reasonably that some of the formal characteristics of Keats's great odes, dating from late April 1819, are the immediate results of his experiments with the sonnet form.[14] The role of *Sonnet to Sleep* in this development cannot, by itself, have amounted to much; but Keats's interest in the sonnet form at the time has to be taken as an additional element of the history of *Sonnet to Sleep,* and one that (again) enhances our understanding of some of its peculiarities.

The language of the sonnet, rich as it is even in the limited context of "Poem 1" anonymity, gains many additional meanings and overtones when the words are associated with their historical author.[15] Because it was Keats who wrote the poem, "embalmer" in line 1 more certainly has the primary meaning of "one who makes balmy, or fragrant" but also has the secondary meaning connected with corpses and funerals (we respond to the same pair of meanings in "embalmed darkness" in the fifth stanza of *Ode to a Nightingale,* written just a month later, and cannot help having the nightingale lines retrospectively in mind when we read *Sonnet to Sleep*). "Soothest" in line 5, which would be a puzzler if encountered out of context, is for Keatsians a familiar usage meaning "smoothest," "softest," "most soothing" ("jellies soother than the creamy curd" occurs in *The Eve of St. Agnes* 266, and "sooth voice" in *The Fall of Hyperion* 1.155). "Conscience" in line 11, rather than carrying the modern idea of "moral sense," is more likely to mean "consciousness," "reflection," "awareness" (the primary meaning in Hamlet's "Thus conscience does make cowards of us all," 3.1.82). Such "consciousness" is a recurring mental state in the poems, regularly depicted as undesirable, for which Keats uses special meanings of "think" and "thought"—for example, "Alas, I must not think" (*Endymion* 4.303), "Where but to think is to be full of sorrow" (*Ode to a Nightingale* 27), "tease us out of thought" (*Ode on a Grecian Urn* 44), "Why do you think?" (*Lamia* 2.41). "Casket" in line 14 does not mean "coffin" (an American usage dating from 1870) but instead denotes a small chest or jewel box (as in *The Merchant of Venice* and several times elsewhere in Keats's poems).

The religious terms with secular meanings in lines 4–7 ("divine," "hymn," "Amen," perhaps also "charities" in 8) are almost a kind of signature in Keats's poetry; the knowledgeable reader will necessarily relate them to the many similar instances in other poems—"temple," "altar," "incense," "shrine," "oracle," "prophet," "pieties," "choir," "priest," "fane," and "sanctuary" in *Ode to Psyche* (to cite just examples from the odes); "requiem" and "anthem" in *Ode to a Nightingale;* "sacrifice," "altar," "mysterious priest," "pious morn," and "eternity" in *Ode on a Grecian Urn;* "rosary," "mysteries," "temple," and "shrine" in *Ode on Melancholy.* The narcotic state hinted at in lines 7–8 ("poppy . . . lulling charities") is another recurring motif in Keats's poems, as in "poppied warmth" in *The Eve of St. Agnes* (237) and the images of "drowsy numbness," "hemlock," "dull opiate," "Wolf's-bane," "nightshade," and "shade [coming] too drowsily" in the opening stanzas of *Nightingale* and *Melancholy.*

The main statement or theme in *Sonnet to Sleep* is also substantially enlarged through biographical contextualization. When we read it as an anonymous production, the poem invokes sleep as a means to escape (be "saved" from) consciousness of daytime reality—the "shining" of the "passed day" that, if allowed to have its effect, will "breed many woes" in the wakeful speaker's mind at night. When we connect it with its historical author, the sonnet becomes one more manifestation of Keats's structuring concern in the poems of 1818 and 1819 and gains thematic complexity through cross-reference to other works among his writings. If we ask what, in Keatsian terms, is meant by the "many woes" of the "passed day," a provisional answer might refer to the worldly jostling of the epistle *Dear Reynolds, as last night I lay in bed,* which, like *Sonnet to Sleep,* worries about the "shadow[ing]" of "our own soul's daytime / In the dark void of night" (70–71); or to "The weariness, the fever, and the fret / Here, where men sit and hear each other groan" that the speaker wishes to escape in the third stanza of *Ode to a Nightingale;* or to the "heart high-sorrowful and cloy'd, / A burning forehead, and a parching tongue" that the speaker associates with reality in the third stanza of *Ode on a Grecian Urn.*

A list of such connections could be extended to include virtually all of Keats's poems that we care most about, because they all turn on the same formal contrast between a defective actual world of mutability, natural process, and death and an ideal world of stasis that has neither nature nor death in it. The irreconcilability of natural and ideal becomes the linguistic, emotional, and ideological crux. Narratively, the poems represent the usually fruitless attempt of a protagonist to escape undesirable reality—Endymion pursues a goddess in another world, Madeline looks for perfect love in a dream (*The Eve of St. Agnes*), the ode-speakers search speculatively for permanence in the ideal worlds of nightingale and Grecian urn, Lycius quests misguidedly for unperplexed bliss through union with a snake-woman (*Lamia*), and so on. *Sonnet to Sleep* does not explicitly mention mutability or natural process, and it aligns death more with escape from reality than with woeful reality itself; but the Keatsian context immediately connects the simple contrast of sleep versus the bad effects of the passed day to similar problems and contrasts in other poems.

Likewise, the sonnet's relationship to its literary precursors becomes more significantly a part of the artistic configuration when we know that it was Keats who did the reading and made the choices. The most often cited source is King Henry's apostrophe to sleep in *2 Henry IV* (3.1.5–31):

> O sleep! O gentle sleep!
> Nature's soft nurse, how have I frighted thee,
> That thou no more wilt weigh my eyelids down,
> And steep my senses in forgetfulness? . . .

In addition to "soft," "weigh my eyelids," and "forgetfulness" in these opening lines, Henry's invocation has in common with Keats's sonnet the images and ideas of "hush'd," "perfum'd chambers," "lull'd," "Seal up," and "stillest night." Some passages in Burton's *Anatomy of Melancholy* (part 2, section 2, member 5, "Waking and Terrible Dreams Rectified") mention "sweet moistning sleep" (Keats's draft of the sonnet has "sweet-death dews"), the idea that "our speeches in the day time cause our phantasy to work upon the like in our sleep," and Morpheus's "ivory box." Many readers connect Keats's image of "burrowing like the mole" with Hamlet's "old mole, canst work i' th' earth so fast?" (1.5.162). For predecessor of the penultimate image in the sonnet, "Turn the key deftly in the oiled wards," there is a passage that Keats underlined in his copy of Cary's Dante (*Inferno* 13.60–62):

> I it was, who held
> Both keys to Frederick's heart, and turn'd the wards,
> Opening and shutting, with a skill so sweet. . . .[16]

We do not need Keats's authorship to observe similarities between *Sonnet to Sleep* and passages of Shakespeare, Burton, and Dante. But one can hardly ignore the fact that these three writers were, along with Spenser, Milton, and Wordsworth, the most significant influences operating on Keats's mature poetry (Shakespeare was "presider" from *Endymion* on; Burton provided the plot for *Lamia* and ideas and images throughout the poems; Dante was a principal source for *The Fall of Hyperion*). He owned copies of their works, which he read, reread, and marked with underlines and annotations that are well known among the materials of Keats scholarship. The biographical context of these echoes of earlier writers is one more source of pleasure in the sonnet for those of us who read for pleasure. For others, Keats's affiliation with a particular set of precursors allows us to see the construction of poetic tradition at work.

My point here is that knowledge of Keats's authorship greatly enlarges the scope of our understanding and appreciation of *Sonnet to Sleep:* its status as a private poem (unpublished and probably regarded as unfinished); its character as an experimental piece in a development that led shortly afterward to Keats's major achievement in the odes; the special Keatsian meanings and associations of the language and images; the numerous thematic connections that can be made between the sonnet and Keats's other works of the most fruitful period of his career; the relationships of the sources of the sonnet to the body of Keats's sources more generally. Conversely, a reading of the poem without such knowledge is comparatively impoverished. Like the New Critics earlier, the author-banishing theorists are deceiving themselves if they really believe that one can dispense with authors while still retaining an idea of the literary. Indeed, this is probably why the most self-consistent of them also attack the notion of literariness and give their attention to subliterary works—comic strips, James Bond novels, exchanges with waiters in restaurants. But to interpret even these, something like an author is necessary. A handful of theorists, realizing this necessity, have proposed an "implied author" (Booth), an "author-function" (Foucault), an "apparent artist" (Walton), a "postulated author" (Nehamas).[17] But such constructs hardly seem necessary for *Sonnet to Sleep* when the historical Keats is available and we have so much information about the composition, chronology, language, themes, and sources of his work.

4

Since we are so knowledgeable about Keats, it may seem a step backward at this point to raise the question of who wrote *Sonnet to Sleep*—that is, who was responsible for the words that we read and the lesser textual components (punctuation, capitalization, spelling, word-division) that guide our comprehension. There really should be no reason to doubt Keats's authorship: we have three manuscripts in his handwriting—the abandoned draft written in the volume of *Paradise Lost* at Hampstead, the version that he included in his journal letter of April 1819 (at Harvard), and the copy that he made for the lady's album in June 1820 (in the Berg Collection of the New York Public Library)—and we can reconstruct the substantive details of a lost fourth holograph from copies made by Brown and Woodhouse. Keats is always *thought* to have been the sole author. But actually Keats wrote only most of the words—not all of them—and in the course of revision, transcription, and publication, the sonnet underwent numerous changes.

The following diagram shows the transmission of text from one version to another and the relationships among the various manuscripts and early printings:

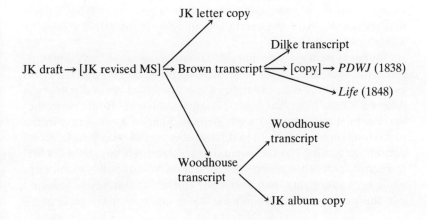

JK letter copy

Dilke transcript

JK draft → [JK revised MS] → Brown transcript ⇆ [copy] → *PDWJ* (1838)

→ *Life* (1848)

Woodhouse transcript

Woodhouse transcript

JK album copy

With the exception of Charles Wentworth Dilke's transcript (which reproduces its source, Brown's transcript, exactly), every one of the manuscripts and printings here is textually or critically important. Keats's incomplete draft has the intrinsic value that any major writer's beginning efforts at a work would have—we can admire the lucky hits and false starts alike (these are the *real* origins of a poem now read by thousands in the *Norton Anthology*)—and it also contains a piece of specific information about the development of the theme: the contrasting daytime reality did not enter the poem until the next stage of composition (there is nothing in the first draft about "the passed day" or "curious conscience," merely the straightforward desire for sleep to come, "shut the hushed Casket of my soul . . . turn the Key round . . . And let it rest"). The holograph version in Keats's journal letter, which is a copy of the same lost holograph from which Brown and Woodhouse took their texts (the "revised MS" shown in brackets in the diagram), is of course authoritative in its own right. Brown's transcript was the source not only of his friend Dilke's copy but of the first and second printings of the poem, in the *Plymouth and Devonport Weekly Journal* in 1838 (via a lost intermediary copy also shown in brackets) and Milnes's *Life* of Keats in 1848; Brown's manuscript actually served as printer's copy for the text in the latter work. Woodhouse's initial transcript was the source of the third extant holograph version, when Keats borrowed Woodhouse's book of transcripts, as Woodhouse notes, "to select a small poem to write in an Album, intended to consist of original Poetry, for a lady" in June 1820. Woodhouse's second transcript (copied from the first) is valuable for its information about the order and authority of certain changes that Woodhouse and Keats made in the text of Woodhouse's first transcript. And the extant album copy is the latest version in Keats's own hand.

What is perhaps most notable about this array of textual materials is the fact that, again with the exception of Dilke's transcript, every single version to the right of the bracketed revised holograph differs not only from that central original source but from every other version in the diagram as well. Brown changed Keats's text in the process of copying, and so, in different ways, did Woodhouse. Keats himself, in writing out the poem a year later from Woodhouse's first transcript, entered a change of wording in Woodhouse's manuscript while he was copying, and also made further alterations as he wrote out the new version. Woodhouse then made changes in Brown's manuscript when he compared Brown's text with his own. And *all* the printed texts have further changes from their manuscript sources.[18]

The first published version, in the *Plymouth and Devonport Weekly Journal*, is one of eleven short poems by Keats that Brown, who was then living in Plymouth, contributed to the newspaper in 1838 and 1839. Entitled "Sonnet.—to Sleep. / (From the Unpublished Poems of John Keats)," the newspaper text reproduces much of the punctuation of Brown's extant transcript (punctuation that we may assume was largely Brown's in the first place, since Keats regularly left such matters to his friends) but has other punctuation that is completely new (Brown's text, with a semicolon at the end of 8, is a single sentence of fourteen lines; the newspaper text, with periods at the end of 4, 8, and 12, divides the sonnet into four sentences). It incorporates in line 8 a word that Woodhouse had added in pencil in Brown's transcript (the revised "lulling," which Keats had substituted for "dewy" in both his album copy and Woodhouse's transcript, and which Woodhouse had then inserted above "dewy" in Brown's manuscript), and it also has two unique substantive variants: "Around my head" instead of "bed" in line 8 (perhaps a literal-minded "improvement" rather than a misprint) and "the passed day will rise" instead of "shine" in line 9 (probably a misguided attempt to amend the rhyme scheme). This first published version is thus technically authored by at least three people—Keats, Brown, and one or more persons who worked as editor and printer of the Plymouth newspaper.

The newspaper had very few readers outside Plymouth in 1838, but Milnes's *Life* of Keats, published ten years later, which in successive editions and reprintings served as the principal biography of the poet through the first two decades of the twentieth century, had a much larger audience. Milnes's text of *Sonnet to Sleep* is a slightly repunctuated rendering of Brown's extant transcript (which was printer's copy), substantively identical with the transcript except in line 8, where, just as in the newspaper text, Milnes or his printer took over Woodhouse's penciled "lulling." In line 12 someone introduced a punctuation error of substantive proportions, placing the comma after "strength" (instead of after "darkness") and thereby making "darkness" rather than "curious conscience" the molelike burrower. So Milnes's text also has at least three authors—Keats, Brown, and Milnes or his printer. In this century, when H. W. Garrod based his Oxford text of the sonnet on Milnes's printing of 1848, he made further punctuation and spelling changes, and accordingly the Oxford version, which was the standard scholarly text of the sonnet from the later 1930s to the later 1970s, has at least four authors—Keats, Brown, Milnes or his printer, and Garrod.

Up to a point, this is routine textual information—all (or nearly all) writers are repunctuated and sometimes mishandled in such ways. In the sense in which I have been most recently using "authorship" here, I am myself part-author of the text of the sonnet given at the beginning of section 3, because my *Poems* of 1978, taking Keats's album manuscript as copy-text, has editorial additions and changes in punctuation in lines 6, 10, 11, 13, and 14, an unauthorized capitalization in line 5 ("Sleep"), and reductions of Keats's capitals to lowercase in lines 13 and 14 ("key," "casket"). If there are errors, misjudgments, misrepresentations in such treatment of a text, it is a certainty that subsequent editors will find them out and correct them. That is the basic business of textual scholarship.

But there are some more interesting situations where the "nonauthorial" authorizing (as it were) is different both from routine tidying (as in Brown's transcripts and my *Poems*) and from the common types of textual corruption—situations where someone other than the nominal author is essentially and inextricably a part of the authorship. The text of lines 11 and 12 of *Sonnet to Sleep* in Woodhouse's transcripts and Keats's album copy is one of them. Here is the wording of the three copies made from Keats's lost holograph (Keats's letter text, Brown's transcript, and the original state of the first of Woodhouse's two transcripts):

> Save me from curious conscience, that still lords
>   Its strength for darkness, burrowing like a mole. . . .[19]

At some point between the writing of his first and second transcripts (and before Keats borrowed the first transcript to make the album copy in June 1820) Woodhouse, possibly puzzled by the phrase "lords / Its strength for darkness" and doubtful of the suitability of "lords" as it stands in juxtaposition with the next image, "burrowing like a mole," deleted "lords" in his transcript and penciled in "hoards" above the original word. (His second transcript, copied from the first, shows "hoards" from the beginning but no sign of the revised "lulling.") Seemingly Keats approved of Woodhouse's change, because he appropriated the word from Woodhouse's transcript when he wrote his final version in the lady's album:

Save me from curious conscience that still hoards
Its strength for darkness, burrowing like the mole. . . .

At this point in the development of the text, "hoards" (along with
the surrounding words in the phrase "that . . . darkness," which
take on much of their meaning from the verb) becomes an integral,
rather than a corrupt, element of the text, and Woodhouse, with
Keats's approval, becomes author of the effects of parts of lines 11
and 12.

Woodhouse's contributions to the poem are not insignificant.
Many subsequent readers have been dissatisfied by the linking of
"lords" (the reading long established in Garrod's Oxford text) with
the idea of "burrowing like a mole," and, once the alternative
"hoards" became known, there arose a small controversy over both
the proper wording and the proper interpretation of the lines. A
series of letters in the London *Times Literary Supplement* in 1941
begins with an inquiry from C. Archer, who considers "lords"
"clearly the worser reading." The opinions of H. B. and M. B.
Forman are conveyed by Laurence Binyon; R. W. King quotes L. C.
Martin's "ingenious but unconvincing" paraphrase of "lords . . ."
("is master of its power to exploit the darkness"); E. H. W. Meyerstein cites parallel uses of "lords" elsewhere in Keats (*Endymion*
3.1, "There are who lord it o'er their fellow-men") and in Spenser
and Chatterton; H. W. Garrod, citing another line of *Endymion*
(2.891, "all the revels he had lorded there"), attempts to support
"lords" on both textual and critical grounds, with grandiose paraphrase—"Conscience marshals, arrays, disposes, proudly and boast-
fully, its power for darkness"—and the pronouncement that "lords"
has "an added something that makes it poetry"; Meyerstein writes a
second letter expounding "lords" in "the sense of rearing up,"
"standing on . . . hind legs"; and so on. Though dissenting opinions
are interspersed, the main tendency of the letters is to defend
Keats's single authorship even at the cost of accepting a combination
of lordly order, pride, boastfulness, rearing up, *and* the under-
ground (and one might think relatively humble) secrecy of molelike
burrowing.[20] Nowadays we prefer "hoards"—it is the reading in
Miriam Allott's edition of 1970, John Barnard's second edition of
1976, and my own of 1978 (and thence the reading in the *Norton
Anthology*)—and in so doing, whether we know it or not, we are
preferring a text coauthored by Keats and Woodhouse.

5

Because it is a short poem and we know a great deal about the circumstances of its composition and the history of its text, *Sonnet to Sleep* may serve as a miniature example to illustrate two things that do not necessarily sit well together. The first is the importance of historical authorship to our reading, understanding, and appreciation of a literary text. The second is the fact that for many works, when the circumstances of composition are investigated in detail, the identifiable authorship turns out to be a plurality of authors: in any text ever printed, "Keats's" *Sonnet to Sleep* has at least three and sometimes as many as four or five authors. Keats is of course responsible for the lion's share—the subject, form, structure, and nearly all the individual images and sentiments—and Woodhouse for, as it were, the mole's: the specific image at the end of line 11 and its consistency of relationship with the preceding and following images. But a careful explication of the poem from beginning to end will examine a collaboratively produced work, no matter how disproportionate the shares.

I wish to claim that such multiple authorship—the collaborative authorship of writings that we routinely consider the work of a single author—is quite common, and that instances much more extensive and more impressive than *Sonnet to Sleep* can be found virtually anywhere we care to look in English and American literature of the last two centuries. If *Sonnet to Sleep* does not, in the long run, seem to make much difference in the totality of Keats's writings, then consider the example of *The Eve of St. Agnes,* which is an essential Keats item on everybody's reading list for the second half of the Romantic period. *The Eve of St. Agnes* as we know it, even more than the *Sonnet to Sleep,* is a collaborative product, a patching together of Keats's original and revised manuscript texts with editing and revisions by both Woodhouse and Keats's publisher John Taylor (a patching together in which some of the editorial changes were made by the publisher against Keats's wishes).

The frequency with which this kind of multiple authorship turns up, once one starts looking for it, is rather strikingly at odds with the interpretive and editorial theorists' almost universal concern with author and authorship as single entities. I have therefore gathered in this book a series of representative examples to call attention to a relatively neglected aspect of literary production and to form a basis for some generalizations and further study.

Chapters 2 and 3 develop in minute detail the circumstances of

two quite normal situations of multiple authorship: the collaboration
of a young writer with friends and publishers who want to help him
succeed (Keats with Woodhouse and Taylor in *Isabella* and several
other longer works) and the collaboration of a well-established writer
with a powerful intellectual partner who happens also to be a spouse
(John Stuart Mill with Harriet Mill in "Mill's" *Autobiography*).
Though some may think I have gone too far in elevating Keats's and
John Mill's helpers to the status of *collaborators,* Woodhouse and
Taylor between them were responsible for the title of *Isabella,* for
most of the punctuation and other accidentals throughout, and for
some of the wording of about 60 of the 504 lines (roughly 1 line out of
every 9 in the poem), while Harriet Mill significantly altered the style,
tone, characterizations, and numerous particular details of her husband's *Autobiography.* Neither Keats nor John Mill is practicably
separable from the contributions made by others to these works,
because each writer was interactively involved with collaborators at
several different stages in the development of the text.

Chapters 4 and 5, also concerned with nineteenth-century writers,
take up two other standard modes of composite creativity: the author
revising earlier versions of himself (Wordsworth in *The Prelude,*
among other works) and the author interacting collaboratively with
sources and influences (Coleridge in *Biographia Literaria*). In the first
instance, all the "collaborators" have the same name (young Wordsworth, middle-aged Wordsworth, old Wordsworth) but are considered, even by the poet himself, to be separate identities; in the second
instance, the author would gladly suppress the facts of collaboration so
as to evade charges of plagiarism. Though there are exceptions, Wordsworth scholars generally have been uncomfortable with the complexity
of their poet's extensive self-collaboration, while Coleridge scholars
continue to go to great lengths to avoid confronting their author's
unacknowledged borrowings. In these chapters, as in some of the others, my focus is partly on discrepancies between the actual circumstances of production and the imagined circumstances that critics have
depicted—and then sometimes rather desperately clung to—in their
interpretations, evaluations, and editorial theorizing.

The next three chapters treat works and situations mainly of the
twentieth century. Chapter 6 reexamines the famous and controversial case of *The Waste Land,* with a principal interest in the reactions
of Eliot scholars to the fact, widely publicized beginning in 1971, that
Ezra Pound was responsible for altering or canceling 350 to 400 of
Eliot's lines—roughly half the lines in the manuscript—and for chang-

ing the character of at least some parts of the poem rather drastically; a secondary interest lies in possible parallels between the well-documented collaboration of Eliot and Pound in this work and the much more problematic collaboration of Coleridge and Wordsworth 120 years earlier. Chapters 7 and 8 consider collaborative elements inherent in the production of commercial literature—best-selling novels side by side with "canonical" fiction in Chapter 7, plays and films of varying degrees of "seriousness" in Chapter 8.

The final chapter, attempting some summary statements about the relation of multiple authorship to theories of interpretation and editing, suggests that critics and textualists may need to adjust their theories. Real multiple authors are more difficult to banish than mythical single ones, and they are unquestionably, given the theological model, more difficult to apotheosize or deify as an ideal for validity in interpretation or textual purity. The better theories may turn out to be those that cover not only more facts but more authors.

2

Keats and His Helpers: The Multiple Authorship of Isabella

In the spring of 1818, a year before the initial composition of *Sonnet to Sleep,* Keats wrote the second longish narrative poem of his career. The first, *Endymion: A Poetic Romance,* drafted in April to November 1817, revised in January to March 1818, and published as a separate volume toward the end of April 1818, tells the story of a shepherd prince's search, unsuccessful until the final twenty lines of the poem, for reunion with a goddess whom he has met, and fallen desperately in love with, in a dream. The second, ultimately titled (by the publishers) *Isabella; or, The Pot of Basil,* written mainly in late March and April 1818 and published in Keats's final volume, *Lamia, Isabella, The Eve of St. Agnes, and Other Poems* (1820), tells the story of a young woman who, after learning that her absent lover has been murdered and buried by her brothers, exhumes his body, severs the head, carries it home to plant in a pot of basil, and then goes mad and dies.

Some of the differences between the narrative methods, styles, and explicit themes of the two poems are attributable to Keats's having only a brief general source for the earlier work, hardly more than the "Endymion" entry in Lemprière's *Classical Dictionary,* but a relatively lengthy and detailed scenario for the later one, the tale of Isabella in an English translation of Boccaccio's *Decameron* (fifth "novel," fourth day). Other differences, however, especially in tone and descriptive detail, are the result of Keats's rapid maturing and a "little change" that he told his brothers had "taken place in my intellect lately" while he was revising and recopying *Endymion.* Scholars have connected this change with a new approach to "romance" in the abstract and seen it as producing, in *Isabella,* a self-consciously modern, ultimately realistic, even antiromantic retelling of Boccaccio's sentimental story, which Keats's narrator characterizes as "the gentleness of old Romance, / The simple plaining of a minstrel's song" (*Isabella* 387–88).[1]

A decade of minute investigation into Keats's texts—working out relationships among the extant manuscripts, identifying the sources of the earliest printings, and assessing the relative authoritativeness of competing versions—has fashioned a clear picture of how Keats's poems got into print and, what is of special concern here, the extent to which others besides Keats entered into the production of the works in matters that we formerly attributed to Keats alone. This more sharply focused view of Keats the poet—Keats become "Keats and his helpers" in my chapter title—ought to be of interest to biographers, literary historians, and students of the history of publishing, and it has, in common with a number of other instances of writers and their helpers in subsequent chapters of this book, implications for several kinds of literary theory. Among more substantial works, Keats's *Isabella* is a useful beginning example, because we have a virtually complete set of documents with which to trace its development from original draft through publication in the version that has been the standard ever since 1820.

1

Keats originally undertook *Isabella* as part of a joint project with his friend John Hamilton Reynolds to publish a volume of versified stories based on the *Decameron*. He drafted the first six stanzas at home in Hampstead in February 1818, while he was still revising *Endymion*, and the remainder during the next two months in Teignmouth, on the Devonshire coast, where he took over the care of his consumptive brother Tom, who had gone down in December seeking improvement from the milder climate. Three-fifths of Keats's draft is extant, in fragments usually of a stanza or two apiece, in libraries in Texas, Massachusetts, Pennsylvania, New York, Scotland, and Switzerland. The next version following the draft, the only other manuscript in Keats's hand, is a revised fair copy, now in the British Library, that Keats wrote in the summer of 1818 in a notebook later given to his brother George, who filled it up with transcripts of Keats's poems to take back to America. The other extant manuscripts are three transcripts by Richard Woodhouse, the latest of which served as printer's copy for the published text of 1820.

Woodhouse, a lawyer seven years older than Keats, was a close friend and a legal and literary adviser to Keats's publishers John Taylor and J. A. Hessey. He had met Keats the year before, had become one of the poet's regular circle of friends by the spring of 1818, and, convinced (like others in the circle) that Keats was a genius who would ultimately attain major status among the English poets, had begun his collection of "Keatsiana"—unpublished poems and letters by Keats, variant readings to the published texts, datings, sources, biographical facts, and interpretive commentary. The surviving items of this invaluable collection include interleaved and annotated copies of Keats's *Poems* and *Endymion,* in the Huntington Library and the Berg Collection, respectively; a scrapbook of letters, poems, and miscellaneous biographical materials in the Morgan Library; three notebooks of poetry and letter transcripts in the Harvard Keats Collection (routinely referred to by Keats scholars as W^2, W^1, and Woodhouse's letterbook); and some smaller collections of copies, also at Harvard, that Woodhouse and his law clerks made for two of Keats's other friends, Joseph Severn and Charles Brown.[2]

Woodhouse's first transcript of *Isabella,* which is in shorthand, is a part of the contents of the Morgan scrapbook; the other two transcripts, which derive from the shorthand copy, are in the W^2 and W^1 notebooks. It is not perfectly certain that Woodhouse made the W^1 transcript directly from W^2; it repeats some of the peculiarities of the W^2 text, but incorporates others that occur elsewhere only in the shorthand, and the best explanation may be that Woodhouse used both of the earlier transcripts together as his source. If we may assume (as seems reasonable according to Woodhouse's known practice elsewhere) that W^2 was the primary source of W^1, the relationships among the existing texts of *Isabella* from draft through first publication make a simple straight-line diagram:

$$\text{JK draft} \rightarrow \text{JK fair copy} \rightarrow \underset{\text{shorthand}}{\text{Woodhouse}} \rightarrow W^2 \rightarrow W^1 \rightarrow 1820$$

Even if we were not specially focusing on other people's contributions to the wording of *Isabella,* the routine textual information given so far tells or implies a good deal about the precariousness of the transmission of Keats's writings. Woodhouse's system of shorthand, based on William Mavor's *Universal Stenography* (1779 and many later editions), preserves most of the consonants of the words that are being recorded but very little else; some of the consonants are ignored (as being understood or else recoverable via the copyist's memory of the original), and nearly all the vowels and the various particulars of punctuation, capitalization, and other "accidentals" of the text are regularly left out. The shorthand symbols for "sng," for instance, could, in Woodhouse's practice, represent "snag," "snug," "sing," "sang," "sung," and "song"; the context would of course be a help to interpretation, but in *Isabella* line 78 both "Sang" and "Sung" make sense at the beginning of the line—and Keats in fact wrote "Sung" in his revised manuscript, Woodhouse expanded his shorthand as "Sang" in W^2 and W^1, and the 1820 printer set "Sang" from W^1. Two other examples of the kind of ambiguity possible in such a system occur in *Isabella* line 382, where Woodhouse's shorthand for "trvl," from Keats's "travel" in the fair copy, became "travail" in the longhand transcripts and the 1820 text (rightly in this case—Keats's "travel" is merely an alternative spelling of "travail"), and line 471, where Woodhouse's shorthand for "st," from Keats's "sat," became "set" in W^2 and W^1 (but then ended up correctly as "sat" in 1820). These are small matters, to be sure—Woodhouse did get most of Keats's words right, or, when he changed them, changed them on purpose. But the fact remains that, owing to this peculiar sequence of copyings, where the text of Keats's manuscript was transmitted through a more or less punctuationless shorthand, the "accidental" features of the resulting standard text of 1820 are from beginning to end mostly Woodhouse's rather than Keats's.[3]

My second point concerning precariousness is simply that this is the way Keats wanted it. There is plenty of evidence that, beginning early in 1819, he regularly handed his manuscripts over to both Woodhouse and his housemate Charles Brown for transcribing and then considered their transcripts rather than his own holographs the principal finished versions of the poems before publication. It is not known when he gave away his draft of *Isabella* to Joseph Severn, the friend who later cut it up and distributed it, with inscriptions, in stanza-size fragments; but Keats never valued his drafts as texts once he had made a fair copy, just as, in general, he disregarded his own fair copies once Brown and Woodhouse had made their more painstaking and better punctuated transcripts. George Keats took the fair copy of *Isabella* back to America, along with Keats's draft of *The Eve of St. Mark,* a late holograph fair copy of *Lines on the Mermaid Tavern,* and transcripts of *The Eve of St. Agnes,* four odes, and some other short pieces (transcripts, it is worth noting, that George in most cases had made from Brown's copies, not from holographs), at the end of January 1820. Two months later, when Keats and Brown were assembling the poems for his volume of 1820, the *only* revised texts of *Isabella* available to them were in transcripts.

More important, for present purposes, is the evidence concerning Woodhouse's and others' substantive changes in Keats's text of *Isabella.* J. H. Reynolds, the first of Keats's helpers working to improve the poem, read the fair copy in October 1818, shortly after the appearance of the *Blackwood's* and *Quarterly Review* attacks on *Endymion,* and commented in a letter to Keats on 14 October:

> As to the Poem [*Isabella*] I am of all things anxious that you should publish it, for its completeness will be a full answer to all the ignorant malevolence of cold lying Scotchmen and stupid Englishmen. . . . When I see you, I will give you the Poem [that is, return the manuscript], and pray look it over with that eye to the *littlenesses* which the world are so fond of excepting to (though I confess with that word altered which I mentioned, I see nothing that can be cavilled at).[4]

We do not know which word Reynolds suggested altering. Of the five single-word revisions that Keats made above the line in the fair copy— "noise" for "sigh" in 14, "olive" for "forest" in 168, "smiling" for "laughing" in the manuscript text of 199, "Sick" for "Pale" in 213, and "rage" for "weep" in 314—the best guess might be that in 168, where the original "forest trees" (afterward changed to "olive trees") constitutes a redundancy that "the world" of Scottish and English reviewers might well (in Reynolds's view) have deemed objectionable.

The more extensive work of Keats's helpers that I wish to focus on, however, really begins with Woodhouse's initial copying of the poem from Keats's revised manuscript, when he not only introduced substantive changes in half a dozen lines of his shorthand transcript but marked words, lines, and stanzas in Keats's fair copy and, what might be considered strangest of all, actually penciled suggested revisions for several passages on the opposite (that is, facing) versos of Keats's leaves. In the W^2 and W^1 transcripts he altered still other lines in the process of copying and again penciled suggested revisions above, beneath, and opposite the texts, along with Xs and queries here and there in the margins. Keats himself read through the W^1 transcript before it was given to the printer, making further changes in wording, sometimes in response to Woodhouse's markings and queries. The publisher John Taylor's hand is also discernible in the W^1 transcript, clarifying some of the revisions, arbitrating between Keats's and Woodhouse's phrasings, and occasionally entering other revisions on his own.

The results of this editing and revision are substantive changes between Keats's revised fair copy and the 1820 printed text in close to sixty lines, roughly one out of every nine lines of the poem (plus a change in the poem's title and the addition, beginning with the first of Woodhouse's transcripts, of stanza numbers). Keats, in his revisions and choices when he went over the W^1 printer's copy, is responsible for the changes in half a dozen lines. Woodhouse and Taylor appear to be responsible for most of the rest (there are a few, showing up for the first time in the printed text, that cannot be specifically assigned to any of the principals who had a hand in the writing). The details of these changes have already been given in summary form in earlier work on Keats's texts.[5] On the present occasion, I am interested in the kinds of change that Keats's friends introduced, their likely motives for the changes, and the effect of the changes on our ideas concerning the development of Keats's poetic style.

2

None of Keats's helpers made (or tried to make) major changes in the plot, characterizations, theme, or narrative method of *Isabella*. In this they were very much like Keats himself, who also, in his characteristic two-manuscript, draft-and-revision method of composition in his narrative poems from *Endymion* on (at least until, toward the end of his career, he began revising *Hyperion* as *The Fall of Hyperion*), did not make significant changes in plot, character, or theme after the first draft. The important consideration here, however, is that the acknowledged "Keatsian" qualities of Keats's art—the qualities on which his reputation rests—have little to do with plot, character, and theme. As I have suggested elsewhere,[6] Keats arrived at a basic structure (a generic, all-purpose plot), as well as a repertory of basic characters, relationships, conflicts, and concerns, quite early in his progress (they are discoverable all through the poems of 1816 and 1817 and *Endymion*); and his markedly superior poems of 1819, beginning with *The Eve of St. Agnes* and continuing through *La Belle Dame sans Merci*, the five great odes, *Lamia*, and the Hyperion fragments, regularly make use of these standard materials. What is new and different about the so-called mature work manifests itself in Keats's *style*—and this, I wish to emphasize, is the principal matter that the reviewers faulted in *Endymion*, that Keats worked on in his revisions, and that his friends addressed in their suggestions and changes.

Reynolds was of course referring to style when he suggested (in the letter quoted above) that Keats look over the poem "with that eye to the *littlenesses* which the world are so fond of excepting to." And we have abundant evidence concerning Woodhouse's interest in Keats's style. In his interleaved copy of Keats's *Poems* (1817), which he acquired and began annotating probably in the spring or summer of 1818, Woodhouse used several of the added pages at the beginning and end to identify and illustrate the different kinds of metrical feet in Keats's poetry; some 165 markings above and opposite the lines of the poems point to metrical irregularities and odd pronunciations, and a number of the marginal comments concern scansion (for example, "syllable too much," "incomplete verse," "syllable omitted"). Many other notes in the interleaved *Poems* address clarity of expression—usually the point of Woodhouse's explanatory glosses, where he translates Keats's metaphors into literal-minded prose equivalents, and also of his citations of source and analogues. Still other markings attempt to correct or improve Keats's (or the 1817 printer's) grammar and punctuation.

Woodhouse's more numerous annotations in his interleaved *Endymion,* which he acquired in November 1818, again gloss individual words and phrases, explain mythological allusions, cite parallels of word and image in earlier writers, and fuss over scansion, pronunciation, and imperfect rhymes. Many hundreds of oddities of versification are indicated by marks above and beside the lines themselves, and a system of letter symbols in the margins—*P, N, F,* and *D*—calls attention to some pictorial and other stylistic features (Woodhouse explains his symbols at the end of the volume: *P* = "Picture," *N* = "Natural thoughts, or results easily expressed," *F* = "Dead nature endowed with passions feelings or Sentiment," *D* = "Short description"). The same preoccupations show up in Woodhouse's scholarly and critical annotations in his several collections of transcripts. Taken altogether, the markings testify to Woodhouse's main interests as a reader of Keats's poetry: clarity of expression (the literal meanings of words, the correctness of grammar and punctuation, the sources of literary, historical, and mythological allusions); the formal features of versification (rhymes, metrical "completeness"); and some of the pictorial aspects of poetry (description, imagery, figurative language). There are, in addition, biographical matters (datings, circumstances of composition, place of a work in Keats's career) and much valuable textual information (variants from both holograph and transcript sources, some of which are now known only through Woodhouse's record in his annotations). Notably absent is a concern with ideas, themes, or meaning in

Keats's poems; in the thousands of notes on *Endymion*, for example, there is no hint that Woodhouse was interested in an allegorical or a symbolic interpretation of the hero's quest, the heroine's elusiveness, or any of the individual events and episodes of the narrative.

Practically all of Woodhouse's suggestions and changes in the various texts of *Isabella* are further implementations of this stylistic interest. He worried over the meter in line 382, for example, where the holograph fair copy has "Three hours were they at this travel sore": not liking the required two-syllable pronunciation of "hours," Woodhouse penciled an alternative wording in Keats's manuscript— "Three hours beheld them . . ."—and then, repeating Keats's fair-copy wording, marked "hours" as a disyllable in the W^2 and W^1 transcripts ("hoürs"); Keats's alteration to the final form of the line in W^1 ("Three hours they labour'd . . .") was obviously a response to Woodhouse's marking.[7] Another change prompted by metrical considerations was the substitution of "steel" for "sliver" in line 393, which reads, in Keats's fair copy, "With duller sliver than the persean sword." Here Keats undoubtedly was thinking of "persean" (the adjective referring to Perseus, slayer of the Medusa) as a two-syllable word, but Woodhouse, who later corrected Keats's pronunciation of Greek names in *Lamia,* knew that the word was properly a trisyllable and marked it as such ("Perséan") in both the W^2 and W^1 transcripts. Keats's alteration to "With duller Steel . . ." above the line in W^1 neatly gets rid of the singsong effect of "duller sliver," but, probably more to the point, it allows "Perséan sword" to be read as the last four syllables of the line. Woodhouse also suggested a regularizing of the meter in line 430, "From the fast mouldering head there shut from view," penciling "And from the mouldering" on the facing verso page in Keats's fair copy (an amendment not of "numbers" but of the position of the stresses at the beginning of the line); in this instance Keats stuck with his original wording.

Like his fussing over Keats's rhymes in the W^2 transcript of the poem (for example, in 39–40, where Woodhouse marked and made a partial attempt to improve Keats's rhyming of the nouns "tears" and "cares," and 63–64, where he suggested "dwell" and "tell" for Keats's verbs "live" and "shrive"), Woodhouse's care for correct and smooth versification may seem a trivial matter to the present-day reader. It was clearly, however, a major concern to the hostile reviewers of *Endymion,* who used it as evidence of the poet's lower-class ignorance of the finer points of poetry. J. G. Lockhart makes a point of Keats's adoption of Leigh Hunt's "loose, nerveless versification, and

Cockney rhymes" (with, he adds, "defects . . . tenfold more conspicuous" than Hunt's) in his review in *Blackwood's,* and J. W. Croker
ridicules both what he considers perfunctory rhymes and Keats's bad
"taste in versification" (which he illustrates by contemptuous quotation of a dozen lines as "specimens of [Keats's] prosodial notions of
our English heroic metre") in his notice in the *Quarterly Review.*[8]

As part of this refining process, Woodhouse also corrected or
modernized Keats's grammar in his transcripts (for example, in 78
and 267, where he altered Keats's past-tense "Sung" to "Sang" and
the participle form "drank" to "drunk," and 334, where he corrected
Keats's "thou has" to "thou hast"), and he made a few small changes
for more pleasing sound effects (for example, "Thy hand . . . Thine
eyes" in 62–63, where Keats had written "Thine hand [in effect an *h*-
less "Thine 'and"] . . . Those eyes," and the alliterative "which
once," in place of Keats's "that once," in 276).

The bulk of Woodhouse's suggestions and changes pretty clearly
were directed toward improving the accuracy, decorousness, and
logic of expression—matters that the *Blackwood's* and *Quarterly* reviewers had faulted under the heading "diction"—and as such also
involved bringing the poet more into line with critical expectations.
Here, in the form of a brief list, are some representative examples (I
shall discuss two others in detail in the next section). In line 40, where
Keats had written "And at the worst" to describe a beneficial result of
Lorenzo's behavior, Woodhouse substituted "at the least" (which re-
tains Keats's intention in the line but avoids the contrary implications
of "worst" meaning "least good"). In line 62, Woodhouse worried
over Keats's archaic use of "fear" to mean "frighten"; he composed a
new version of lines 62–63 in pencil in Keats's fair copy ("Thine eyes
by gazing, nor sh^d thy hand fear / Unwelcome pressing . . .") and
called attention to the odd verb with a marginal gloss in the W^2
transcript ("i.e. alarm"), but here Keats left his original text unchanged.[9] In line 144, where Keats had illustrated the action of "see-
[ing] behind" with the image of "a hunted hare," Woodhouse substituted "the hunted hare" (an increase in scope of generalization very
much like the change that Keats himself made in his late copy of
Sonnet to Sleep, when he rewrote "a mole" as "the mole").

In line 261, Woodhouse's revision of Keats's "Month after
month" to "Time after time" simply makes better sense (Keats clearly
meant "repeatedly," "again and again," but his "Month after month"
wrongly suggests a tedious regularity of intervals). Woodhouse's
change in line 405, substituting "each fringed lash" for Keats's "each

single lash," is less logical: the revision avoids the original redundancy of "each single" but introduces a new kind of redundancy in "fringed lash" (since the lashes themselves constitute the fringe). In line 460, "Greatly they wonder'd what the thing might mean," where "thing" refers vaguely to Isabella's drooping behavior or the magical flourishing of her basil plant, Woodhouse suggested "what it all might mean" in Keats's fair copy and "what such grief might mean" in the W^2 transcript; in this instance, probably mindful of successful uses of "thing" in *Hamlet, Paradise Lost,* and Wordsworth's Intimations ode (among others), Keats retained the original wording.

In several places Woodhouse prompted revisions even though he did not himself invent the text that ultimately was printed. In his W^2 transcript, for example, he queried the fair-copy text of lines 151–52— "For venturing one word unseemly mean / In such a place on such a daring theme"; Keats's rewriting of these lines in the W^1 printer's copy is not much of an improvement ("For venturing syllables that ill beseem / The quiet glooms of such a piteous theme") but nevertheless has to be related to his friend's dissatisfaction with the vague impropriety of the original wording. In lines 199–200, again at the end of a stanza, Keats never completed the second line of the couplet in his fair copy, and Woodhouse left both lines blank in W^2 and W^1 (with penciled suggestions for a replacement in each of the transcripts); Keats created a new couplet for the printer in W^1, but probably used Woodhouse's penciling there as a help in recalling his earlier text of the lines. In the fair-copy text of line 315, Keats has Lorenzo's ghost lamenting the loss of "the heaven of a Kiss," which somewhat confusingly puts Lorenzo's new home (heaven) and his loss ("heaven") on the same plane; Woodhouse called attention to the problem with a penciled X opposite the line in the W^2 transcript, and it is not unreasonable to see Keats's revision in W^1 (to a more appropriately located "taste of earthly bliss") as a response to Woodhouse's questioning of the line.

3

Rather than continue this list for several more paragraphs, extending it to John Taylor's handful of similar changes in the W^1 printer's copy, I shall elaborate on two of Woodhouse's more significant contributions to the text of *Isabella.* The first occurs at the end of the seventh stanza, where for lines 55–56 Keats's fair copy has the following couplet spoken by Isabella and then a stanza of response by Lorenzo:

> "Lorenzo, I would clip my ringlet hair
> To make thee laugh again and debonair!"
>
> "Then should I be" said he "full deified;
>   And yet I would not have it, clip it not;
> For Lady I do love it where 'tis tied
>   About the Neck I dote on; and that spot
> That anxious dimple it doth take a pride
>   To play about—Aye Lady I have got
>   Its shadow in my heart and ev'ry sweet
>   Its Mistress owns there summed all complete."

From a conservative reader's point of view, there are plenty of problems concerning style, sense, and tone in these lines, and the *Endymion* reviewers, as Woodhouse knew, would have had a field day in making fun of them. The problems begin with Isabella's silly notion that she could please Lorenzo by cropping her hair, and continue with the nonparallelism of verb and adjective in "laugh . . . and debonair," the extravagance of Lorenzo's reaction (he would be "full deified"), the misleading suggestion that Isabella wears her hair tied around her neck, the potentially embarrassing physicality (and questionable location) of Isabella's "anxious dimple," the overly decorative personifications of both hair and dimple (the former "take[s] a pride" in its play, the latter is "anxious"), the ploddiness of the expression "have got," and the vagueness and obscurity of "shadow" and "ev'ry sweet" (and what it means to "sum" such things) at the end.

Some of these "problems" would be turned into virtues a century and a half later in Christopher Ricks's brilliant study *Keats and Embarrassment.* For Woodhouse at the time, however, they were further manifestations of what the *Edinburgh Magazine,* in a generally friendly notice of Keats's *Poems* (1817), had called "injudicious luxuriancies."[10] Woodhouse gave considerable attention to this passage of *Isabella,* and on several occasions. In Keats's fair copy, when he was making his shorthand transcript, he marked the eight lines of Lorenzo's reply with a vertical pencil line in the left margin, underscored "I have got" in the sixth line of the stanza, and, also in pencil, contrived a completely new text as a possible substitute for the ten lines, a passage intended to be spoken entirely by Isabella (it follows "[She] lisped tenderly" in 54) and full of both manly action and womanly emotion:

Lorenzo, in the twilight Morn was wont
To rouse the clamorous Kennel to the Hunt;

And then his cheek inherited the Ray
  Of the outpouring Sun; & ere the Horn
Could call the Hunters to the Chace away
  His voice more softly woke me: Many a Morn
From sweetest Dreams it drew me to a Day
  More sweet; but now Lorenzo holds in scorn
His Health; & all those by-gone Joys are Dreams
To me—to him, I mean—so chang'd he seems—

In the W^2 transcript, Woodhouse canceled Lorenzo's speech ("Then should I be . . . all complete") with a diagonal pencil stroke across the stanza and wrote six different fragmentary attempts at revision of lines 55–56:[11]

1. [Lorenzo,] on thy brow doth weigh a care
  Wh: Isabella w^d f

2. Lorenzo—   w^d I could chace
  The cloud of grief that weighs upon thy face

3. Lorenzo—some   weigh [?] a Care
  Lurk on thy brow wh: Isabel may share

4. Doth not
          Lorenzo sure some grief in
          Some grief Lorenzo harbors in thy breast

5.   wh: I wo^d fain—she co^d not say the rest
  I[sabella]   told the rest

6. Sure some deep woe
  Haply Lorenzo's Some grief dwells in Lorenzo's breast
  Which Isabel in sigh   the rest

In W^1, the transcript that was used as printer's copy, Woodhouse crossed out the stanza of Lorenzo's speech in both pencil and ink and then made three more attempts at lines 55–56 in pencil on the opposite verso:

1. Lorenzo! but her fluttering   fell,
  And left her blushing Cheek the rest to tell

2. Lorenzo! here she ceas'd, but in his Breast
  Her tone & look spoke silently the rest.

3. "Lorenzo" here she ceas'd her timid Quest
   But in her tone and look he read the rest

I quote Woodhouse's revisions thus fully not because they are superior poetry but simply because there are so many—nine or ten in all, depending on whether the W^2 items numbered 4 and 5 should be considered a single version or parts of two. Clearly Woodhouse strongly objected to Keats's original couplet about Isabella's clipping her hair, and his many attempts at remedy suggest that he felt a proprietary interest in the work.

We do not know how much of these scrawls Keats saw, even in the W^1 transcript. The 1820 text of the couplet is taken over from the last of Woodhouse's penciled versions in W^1; the publisher Taylor canceled the original couplet in the transcript and inserted Woodhouse's wording above the lines. Since Keats refers to his original text of lines 55–56 (specifically to the word "debonair") in a note that he made farther along in the W^1 transcript, when he was composing a new version of lines 199–200, it is possible that he first read the now-standard text of lines 55–56 in proofs of the volume. In any case, and regardless of whether or not Keats approved the changes before they were in print, Woodhouse is the one who got rid of ten potentially troublesome lines and contributed two more acceptable lines, the present 55–56, in their place. Miriam Allott wrongly assumes that Keats was the author of the various fragmentary attempts at revision (she takes them as evidence of his "dissatisfaction with the couplet"), and H. B. Forman praises the revision and shortening of the text as "among Keats's master-strokes of cunning craftsmanship."[12] The fact is, however, that the dissatisfaction and the masterstroke in this instance were Woodhouse's.

Most critics will agree that Woodhouse's alteration of these lines improved the poem. My second example is more aesthetically problematical. The present stanza 50, which begins with Isabella's severing of the dead Lorenzo's head, concludes in Keats's fair copy with a generalization about love attributed to "ancient Harps" and description of Isabella's kissing the head:

> The ancient Harps have said
> Love never dies, but lives immortal Lord:
> If ever any piece of Love was dead
> Pale Isabella kist it, and low moan'd
> 'Twas Love cold dead indeed, but not dethron'd. (396–400)

For this passage there is no long history of repeated attempts at revision, but in the W^1 transcript Woodhouse penciled on the opposite verso first a replacement for line 398 and then a second suggestion for lines 398–99, as follows:

> With fond caress, as if it were not dead
>
> The ghostly Features of her Lover dead
> Pale Isabella kissed & lowly moand

Taylor deleted the original line 398 in the transcript text and inserted the first of Woodhouse's suggestions above the line for the printer. The 1820 text has an entirely new line 398:

> If Love impersonate was ever dead,
> Pale Isabella kiss'd it, and low moan'd.
> 'Twas love; cold,—dead indeed, but not dethroned.   (398–400)

It seems fairly obvious that Woodhouse disliked Keats's emphasis on the deadness of Lorenzo's head and the bluntness of his language ("any piece of Love") in the original line 398; both of Woodhouse's revisions prettify the situation ("fond caress," "ghostly Features"), and the first, which Taylor wrote into the W^1 transcript text, even attempts to deny the fact of death ("as if it were not dead"). But the emphasis on deadness and the general descriptive roughness are consistent with the rest of the poem. Almost from its beginning, and with increasing frequency from the middle onward, Keats has been exploiting his source for the story of Isabella, the English translation of Boccaccio's *Decameron*. As narrator, he apologizes to Boccaccio for writing harshly and crudely about (and incidentally, in effect, for giving his own pre-Marxian Marxist interpretation of) "such a piteous theme" (145–52); makes a point of the contrast between the "old prose" of his source and his own "modern rhyme" (155–56); and introduces a series of gruesomely realistic descriptive details concerning Lorenzo's ghost (275–80), the physical effects of death (353–60, 475–76), the digging up of Lorenzo's body (367–68, 380–82), and the severing of the head with a dull knife (393–94). And in the stanza just preceding the lines about "ancient harps" and the immortality of love, he apologizes to the reader for the "wormy circumstance" of his story, a far cry from "the gentleness of [Boccaccio's] old Romance" (385–92).

The saying of the "ancient harps" in line 397—"Love never dies, but lives, immortal Lord"—is a reference to the heading of Boccaccio's story of Isabella in the English translation that Keats used: "The Fifth Novel. / Wherein is plainly proved, That Love cannot be rooted up, by any Humane Power or Providence; especially in such a Soul, where it hath been really apprehended." And the point of Keats's original line 398—"If ever any piece of Love was dead"—may be its ironic juxtaposition of the fanciful notion of immortality (according to the "ancient harps") and the reality of death (according to Keats's modern retelling of the tale).[13] Woodhouse either missed or dismissed the point, since both of his proposed changes in favor of "fond caress" and "ghostly Features" would have destroyed the juxtaposition. We do not know who was responsible for the new line that appeared in the printed text: "If Love impersonate was ever dead. . . ." It is closer in effect to the line that Keats wrote in the first place, but the vagueness of the phrase "Love impersonate" (literally, "Love embodied in a person") weakens the contrast.

In both of these illustrative examples, though it is clear that he thought he was acting to further Keats's best interests, Woodhouse made revisions independently—and perhaps divergently—from Keats's surmisable intentions. And it may be that in departing from these intentions, Woodhouse did in fact further Keats's best interests, if immediate success and critical acceptance are the measure. In the first instance, he brought conventional sanity, control, and a measure of dignity to curb Keats's extravagant dialogue and description; but it is always possible that the extravagance, rather than the sanity and control, was in fact what Keats wanted. The original passage does, after all, accord with several other passages of similar extravagance in the early stanzas of the poem (for example, 5–8, 11–12, 16, 23–24, 69–70) and can be thought of as part of the general courtly-love artificiality that the later gruesome reality purposely intrudes on and effectively demolishes. In the second instance, with a revision of an opposite tendency, Woodhouse tried to poeticize Keats's plainness, but at a point in the narrative where plainness, as I have suggested just above, is quite appropriate to the effect that Keats probably intended. In both cases, poetic extremes are normalized and Keats is made a more poetically accomplished author. While the rest of Woodhouse's fifty or so substantive changes in the poem may not be so interesting critically, they too are revisions, and arguably often improvements, of the stylistic practice of Keats's original fair-copy text. And in making them, Woodhouse both substantively and theoretically assumed a share of authorship in the text that was printed in 1820.

4

Isabella is not untypical of the way Keats's narrative poems were produced more generally, but each of the others published while he was alive has its own peculiar history of help (and sometimes well-intentioned interference) from Keats's friends. In the revised holograph manuscript of *Endymion,* which was printer's copy for the volume issued in April 1818, the publisher Taylor made significant revisions in both pencil and ink in the process of editing the work for the printer. The most interesting of his queries, underscorings, and changes, just like Woodhouse's in the various manuscript texts of *Isabella,* concern Keats's vaguenesses and infelicities in wording, faulty rhymes and meter, and, especially in book 1, several passages of physical and rhetorical extravagance. At 1.153–54, for example, where Keats's picture of a shepherd priest had included a couplet ending with "vase" and "stars"—"From his right hand there swung a milk white vase / Of mingled wine, outsparkling like the stars"— Taylor's main aim in revising was to get a less objectionable rhyme: "From his right hand there swung a vase milk white / Of mingled wine, outsparkling generous light." At 1.157–58, where Keats had written (in a description of the contents of the priest's basket) "Wild thyme, and valley lillies white as Leda's / Bosom, and choicest strips from mountain Cedars," Taylor's revision remedies another imperfect rhyme ("Leda's" with "Cedars") and at the same time eliminates the embarrassingly physical comparison of lilies with Leda's bosom (substituting, instead, Leda's swan!): "Wild thyme, and valley lillies whiter still / Than Leda's love and cresses from the Rill."

The physicality and potential double entendres of Keats's original passage at 1.440, describing Peona's comforting attentions to her brother Endymion, also attracted Taylor's pencil:

> She tied a little bucket to a Crook,
> Ran some swift paces to a dark wells side,
> And in a sighing time return'd, supplied
> With spar cold water; in which she did squeeze
> A snowy napkin, and upon her Knees
> Began to cherish her poor Brother's face;
> Damping refreshfully his forehead's space,
> His eyes, his lips: then in a cupped shell
> She brought him ruby wine; then let him smell,
> Time after time, a precious amulet,
> Which seldom took she from its cabinet.

So did the numerical extravagance of "thousand Shells . . . million whisperings . . . hundredth echo" in a passage that he marked and Keats then deleted at 1.494 and the overblown fervency of "maddest Kisses," "hot eyeballs . . . burnt and sear'd," and some other details of a passage that he marked and Keats deleted at 1.896. Whether Taylor's markings strengthened or weakened the poetry is less the issue here than that they manifestly altered its overall configuration; and it is to be noted that Keats often accepted the suggestions or revised further in response to them. He declared himself "extremely indebted" to Taylor's care for details and, when he saw the poem in print, thanked the publisher for his "kindness & anxiety": "the book pleased me much—it is very free from faults; and . . . I see in many places an improvement greatly to the purpose."[14]

The example of *The Eve of St. Agnes,* a year and a half later, involves a measure of conflict rather than harmony between Keats and his helpers. Keats drafted the poem in January and February 1819, set it aside for several months, and then revised it in a second manuscript in September. This revised manuscript is now lost, but its text, which we can reconstruct from extant transcripts by Woodhouse and George Keats, differs in fifty-seven lines (roughly one out of every six or seven lines of the poem) from the wording of the version that was printed in Keats's volume of 1820 and has a slightly different title ("Saint Agnes' Eve") and, more important, an additional stanza that Keats had written for the revision. Most of these differences are the work of Taylor and Woodhouse; it is highly likely that, once he had prepared the volume, Keats did not see the poem until it was set in type, and in any case, as Woodhouse remarked in a note opposite the beginning of the poem in his W^2 transcript, concerning variations in wording between the published text and the versions in Keats's draft and his revised manuscript, "K. left it to his Publishers to adopt which [readings] they pleased, & to revise the Whole."[15] And most of the differences again, like those in *Endymion* and *Isabella,* are primarily attributable to his friends' care for the effects of Keats's style.

Their most interesting alterations, however, came about in re-action to Keats's rewriting of the poem in the second manuscript, and in particular to his recasting of lines 314–22 to make the sexual consummation between his hero and heroine more explicit. Keats read his revised text to Woodhouse shortly after completing the new manuscript, and Woodhouse wrote in alarm to Taylor on 19 September:

You know if a thing has a decent side, I generally look no further—As the Poem was orig^y written, *we* innocent ones (ladies & myself) might very well have supposed that Porphyro, when acquainted with Madeline's love for him, & when "he arose, Etherial flush^d &c &c (turn to it) set himself at once to persuade her to go off with him, & succeeded & went over the "Dartmoor black" (now changed for some other place) to be married, in right honest chaste & sober wise. But, as it is now altered, as soon as M. has confessed her love, P. winds by degrees his arm round her, presses breast to breast, and acts all the acts of a bonâ fide husband, while she fancies she is only playing the part of a Wife in a dream. This alteration is of about 3 stanzas; and tho' there are no improper expressions but all is left to inference, and tho' profanely speaking, the Interest on the reader's imagination is greatly heightened, yet I do apprehend it will render the poem unfit for ladies, & indeed scarcely to be mentioned to them among the "things that are."—He says he does not want ladies to read his poetry: that he writes for men—& that if in the former poem there was an opening for doubt what took place, it was his fault for not writing clearly & comprehensibly—that he sh^d despise a man who would be such an eunuch in sentiment as to leave a maid, with that Character about her, in such a situation: & sho^d despise himself to write about it &c &c &c— and all this sort of Keats-like rhodomontade.

The revision in question, which actually is only nine lines long (obviously it *seemed* longer to Woodhouse when Keats read it to him), begins at the end of the present stanza 35, where Madeline recognizes Porphyro as he kneels by her bed and exclaims to him, "How chang'd thou art," asking him to resume the more spiritual voice and appearance that he had in her dream of him ("Give me that voice again, my Porphyro, / Those looks immortal, those complainings dear!"):

> See, while she speaks his arms encroaching slow,
> Have zoned her, heart to heart,—loud, loud the dark winds blow!
>
> For on the midnight came a tempest fell;
> More sooth, for that his quick rejoinder flows
> Into her burning ear: and still the spell
> Unbroken guards her in serene repose.
> With her wild dream he mingled, as a rose
> Marrieth its odour to a violet.
> Still, still she dreams, louder the frost wind blows. . . .

Another passage of questionable morality (and sales appeal) by Woodhouse's and Taylor's standard is a stanza that Keats had added in the revision after stanza 6. Woodhouse mentions this casually in his letter to Taylor, saying that Keats has "inserted an additional stanza early in the poem to make the *legend* more intelligible, and correspondent with what afterwards takes place, particularly with respect to the supper & the playing on the Lute." But the new lines greatly emphasize physical indulgence (food, music, "More pleasures . . . in a dizzy stream"), and the last line has ironic sexual implications in both "virgin morn" and "no weeping Magdalen":

> 'Twas said her future lord would there appear
> Offering, as sacrifice—all in the dream—
> Delicious food, even to her lips brought near,
> Viands, and wine, and fruit, and sugar'd cream,
> To touch her palate with the fine extreme
> Of relish: then soft music heard, and then
> More pleasures follow'd in a dizzy stream
> Palpable almost: then to wake again
> Warm in the virgin morn, no weeping Magdalen.

Taylor replied to Woodhouse's letter on 25 September with a stern ultimatum: Keats must clean up the poem or else find another publisher.

> This Folly of Keats is the most stupid piece of Folly I can conceive. . . . I don't know how the Meaning of the new Stanzas is wrapped up, but I will not be accessary . . . towards publishing any thing which can only be read by Men. . . . So far as he is unconsciously silly in this Proceeding I am sorry for him, but for the rest I cannot but confess to you that it excites in me the Strongest Sentiments of Disapprobation—Therefore my dear Rich^d if he will not so far concede to my Wishes as to leave the passage as it originally stood, I must be content to admire his Poems with some other Imprint, & in so doing I can reap as much Delight from the Perusal of them as if they were our own property, without having the disquieting Consideration attached to them of our approving, by the "Imprimatur," those Parts which are unfit for publication.

To this, as we know, Keats acceded, in effect, by letting the publishers, in the words of Woodhouse's W^2 note quoted above, "adopt which [readings] they pleased, & . . . revise the Whole."

The "publishers"—in this case Taylor and Woodhouse working collaboratively—restored the original, more innocent account of the lovers' sexual consummation, dropped the additional stanza that Keats had introduced after stanza 6, and made other significant changes rather freely (including the rewriting and softening of several oaths by Porphyro and Madeline's old nurse Angela). As a result, the printed text of 1820, which has been the standard ever since, is a composite version of readings from Keats's draft, readings from his revised manuscript, and new readings that do not appear in any manuscript; and Taylor and Woodhouse again became Keats's coauthors in the process of putting it all together.

With *Lamia,* which Keats wrote in July and August 1819, there are substantive differences between the extant holograph fair copy, which served as printer's copy, and the published text of 1820 in some fifty lines, and the fair-copy text is seven lines longer than the printed text. As we know from the extant proof-sheets, the bulk of the changes and excisions were made after the poem was first set in type, and again, as with *The Eve of St. Agnes,* they were mostly the work of Woodhouse and Taylor, although Keats had a hand also, and a number of the alterations appear to have been made by the three men working together. At least eight of the last-minute revisions in part 1 of the poem are the result of Woodhouse's explanations to Keats concerning the proper pronunciation of Greek names and adjectives—"Phœbean" (78), "Circean" (115), "Caducean" (133), "Cenchreas" (174, 225), "Peræan" (176)—and his correction of some three-syllable pronunciations of "Lamia" to two syllables (272, 371). Many of the rest affect meter, diction, and other primarily stylistic matters; for example, both Taylor and Woodhouse worried over Keats's use of "stark," describing Lamia, in the conclusion of Apollonius's climactic speech at 2.297–98, "Pray you Mark, / Corinthians! A Serpent, plain and stark!" (a problem that they ultimately solved by reducing four lines to two and omitting the last phrase altogether). The most significant change was made at an earlier stage of composition, when Keats in a letter of 5 September 1819 sent Taylor a fifty-nine-line extract from part 2, Taylor apparently responded coolly (he told Woodhouse on 25 September that he preferred *Isabella* to "what [Keats] copied out of Lamia in a late Letter"), and Keats, surely influenced by Taylor's reaction to the extract, dropped nearly a third of the passage (eighteen lines following 2.162) when he revised and rewrote part 2 in his fair copy.[16]

The only other long narrative poem published during Keats's lifetime is the fragmentary *Hyperion,* abandoned by the poet in or before April 1819 and printed in the volume of 1820 from a transcript (in the W^1 notebook) made by two of Woodhouse's law clerks working under Woodhouse's supervision. Their source was a transcript (in the W^2 notebook) that Woodhouse had made from the extant holograph now in the British Library, apparently Keats's only manuscript of the work. Successive recopyings, editorial changes, and printer's errors combined in the 1820 text to produce substantive differences from Keats's manuscript text in forty-three lines and the omission of nine other lines altogether. But Keats did not want the fragment published, and in this instance the individual details of textual change are of minor importance in comparison with the single large fact that Taylor and Woodhouse included the fragment in apparent violation of Keats's intentions concerning both the specific poem and the contents of his most important volume. According to the "Advertisement" that they printed on the first recto following the title page of the 1820 volume (a statement drafted by Woodhouse and then probably revised by Woodhouse and Taylor jointly), "If any apology be thought necessary for the appearance of the unfinished poem of HYPERION, the publishers beg to state that they alone are responsible, as it was printed at their particular request, and contrary to the wish of the author." As in everything else that they did for him, however, with or without his permission, clearly they were motivated by desire for Keats's success and good reputation. And the inclusion of *Hyperion* did have a satisfactory result, for it was the most highly regarded of his works at publication and for the rest of the nineteenth century.

5

The abundant documentary evidence concerning the revising, editing, and printing of Keats's nonposthumous poems gives us a rather attractive overall picture of Keats, Woodhouse, Taylor, and other friends (Reynolds and Charles Brown in particular) all pulling together to make the poems presentable to the public and to the reviewers. In the examples collected here, we have seen Woodhouse adjusting and polishing the style and sense of *Isabella,* Taylor doing the same in *Endymion,* and Woodhouse and Taylor together working to improve, according to their standards, the rhetoric and the associated moral tone of *The Eve of St. Agnes* and *Lamia.* All told, their changes and promptings affected the wording—and consequently our reading—of several hundred lines of Keats's best-known poetry. While the extent of Keats's approval of their contributions is not always clear, and it is certain that he sometimes decidedly did *not* approve (as with their editing of *The Eve of St. Agnes* and the printing of *Hyperion*), still one's general impression is that he welcomed their help, indeed regularly depended on it, and frequently believed that his poems were the better for it.

The practical usefulness of this kind of information ought to be obvious. (I shall consider the theoretical consequences in my final chapter.) For one thing, it illuminates some of the customary qualities of Keats's style and the way in which these qualities were viewed by his contemporaries. Virtually every recoverable suggestion or change by Woodhouse (and the same is true of those by Taylor) can be studied as a commentary on or criticism of a peculiarity of Keats's practice; indeed, one could write a Keatsian stylebook for 1818 and 1819 on the basis of the different kinds of help that his friends sought to provide.

The information is also useful as an aid in the recovery of Keats's probable intentions. Woodhouse's rewriting of the original line 398 of *Isabella,* concerning the deadness of Lorenzo's head in ironic juxtaposition with the "ancient harps' " maxim about the immortality of love, highlights Keats's likely purpose in the poem more generally in contrasting the naïveté of the "old prose" with his own tough-minded modern retelling of the story. Woodhouse, it is true, may not have recognized Keats's aim; but he may also have chosen to override it in the interest of another of Keats's aims—becoming a successful and respected poet. And Woodhouse's and Taylor's reactions to Keats's revisions in *The Eve of St. Agnes,* along with Keats's response and their subsequent treatment of the text, have proved extremely helpful as a basis for critical hypotheses concerning Keats's intention in that poem.

Above all, the information sharpens our understanding of how Keats's poems were historically produced, a matter of increased scrutiny in the present newly historicist critical scene. Before the middle 1970s, there were numerous mistakes in Keats scholarship about the relationship of one Keats text to another and about the significance of some oddity of text, as the statements by Allott and Forman quoted earlier in this chapter illustrate (the one seeing Woodhouse's revisions of *Isabella* 55–56 as evidence of Keats's "dissatisfaction," the other praising them as "among Keats's master-strokes of cunning craftsmanship").[17] And misinformation continues to circulate, as in Jerome

McGann's more recent discussion of *La Belle Dame sans Merci* and the sonnet *As Hermes once took to his feathers light* in his widely cited "Keats and the Historical Method in Literary Criticism."[18]

McGann's essay, presented as the first in a series intended to promote renewed interest in a sociohistorical method of literary study, undertakes to demonstrate the importance of "bibliographic" (that is, textual) history to critical interpretation, using *La Belle Dame* as a central example and providing standard facts about its composition, transmission of text, publication, and critical reception. As is well known, two principal texts of the ballad have come down to us—an earlier version in Keats's journal letter to his brother and sister-in-law, toward the end of April 1819 (nearly identical in wording with the extant transcripts by Woodhouse and Charles Brown), and a later version printed in Leigh Hunt's *Indicator* (10 May 1820). McGann, observing that Keats "did not choose to print the poem" in his 1820 volume and never printed the earlier version at all, argues that the later version, in the *Indicator*, should be considered "the text printed by Keats himself" and therefore the one that represents "Keats's last deliberate choices." Such a view invites a focus on the distinctive readings of the *Indicator* text, and McGann offers interesting interpretive suggestions concerning "wretched wight" in the opening line and "wild sad eyes— / So kiss'd to sleep" at the end of stanza 8.

When, however, McGann attacks not only the "impressionistic" scholars who have preferred Keats's earlier version but Charles Brown and R. M. Milnes as well (Brown's transcript was Milnes's source for the first printing of the earlier version in his *Life* of Keats in 1848), he makes a number of errors of historical fact and logic in the process. Ignoring the evidence of the earlier version in Keats's own hand (in the spring 1819 journal letter extant at Harvard), he attributes its distinctive textual features to changes by Brown and Milnes, and then rehearses the facts of Brown's "notorious" misogyny and Milnes's "enormous library of erotica and pornographic works" in order to explain *why* they changed Keats's text and to condemn the supposedly resulting "Brown/1848 text." McGann thinks that Keats closely supervised the *Indicator* printings of both *La Belle Dame* and *As Hermes once* (which appeared in the same periodical six weeks later), suggests that Keats "almost certainly" read proofs, and believes that the several unique readings of the periodical texts uniformly represent the poet's "purposeful change" rather than accident, interference, or other corruption.

But the historical scholarship is shaky in nearly every detail. Brown's transcript of *La Belle Dame* (like Milnes's text deriving from it) differs very little from the extant holograph, and on the basis of what we know of Keats's and Brown's close working relationship—as author and transcriber, respectively—there is good reason to believe that the transcripts of both poems would have been Keats's preferred texts, had he cared to have them printed. We have no information about Hunt's source for the *Indicator* versions, but our knowledge of Keats's general practices suggests that he had little to do with the printings, had little interest in and little control over the texts, and "almost certainly" did *not* read proofs. If we extrapolate from the known facts about Keats and his helpers in *Isabella* and the other narratives as set forth earlier in this chapter, then Keats, Brown, Milnes, and even Hunt and his printer become allies in a collaborative enterprise.[19]

Theoretically, McGann's approach here seems strangely inconsistent with his writing elsewhere. At the beginning of *A Critique of Modern Textual Criticism,* which he wrote after the Keats essay but before the republication of the essay in book form, McGann finds fault with textual theories (for example, those of Fredson Bowers and the MLA's Center for Scholarly Editions) that "so emphasize the autonomy of the isolated author as to distort our theoretical grasp of the 'mode of existence of a literary work of art' (a mode of existence which is fundamentally social rather than personal)." For this "Romantic conception of literary production" (he means the lowercase "romantic"—unrealistic, unreasonable, wrong), McGann valuably urges that we should substitute "a socialized concept of authorship and textual authority," a concept that involves complex relationships among authors, publishers, editors, readers, reviewers, and other "institutional affiliations" as well. In the middle of his *Critique,* he quotes with approval James Thorpe's statement that "the work of art is . . . always tending toward a collaborative status," and toward the end he considers cases in which textual "authority is dispersed among multiple authors" (citing a novel written jointly by John Ashbery and James Schuyler and *The Autobiography of Malcolm X*).[20] But in "Keats and the Historical Method," McGann seems unwilling to recognize that, regardless of what Keats would have preferred, and what role he played in their construction, the *Indicator* texts of *La Belle Dame* and *As Hermes once* are, no less than any of the competing versions, just two more examples of "socialized" literary productions, with at least some of their textual peculiarities the result of "collaborative status." This disparity between theory and practice is almost certainly owing to the return of the repressed mythic author, whom McGann wishes to exempt from the putative shortcomings of his work—in this case, unacceptable attitudes toward women.

3

Who Wrote
J. S. Mill's Autobiography?

In many cases multiple authorship begins, literally, at home. We are all familiar with the traditional prefatorial acknowledgment to an author's spouse, "without whom . . ." et cetera. The practice of spousal collaboration is so common (and the acknowledgments often so trite and perfunctory, if not patronizing) that it is difficult to focus on its consequences for authorial "authority" in a piece of writing. Indeed, when I published an earlier version of the present chapter in *Victorian Studies* (1983), an anonymous referee for the journal suggested that I "say a word or two about the implications in general . . . of the question of *normal* assistance of those mentioned in acknowledgments, copy-editors, later editors, etc." That very "normality" is exactly what I wish to emphasize here; its role in textual production can be quite significant.

A famous example is readily available in John Stuart Mill's *Autobiography,* which was first published in London by Longmans, Green, Reader, and Dyer on 17 October 1873, five months and ten days after the purported author's death in France at the age of sixty-six. No question was raised then, or for more than a century afterward, about the extent of Mill's authorship of the work. But if we define authorship as creation of the wording of a text, the *Autobiography* in its earliest printed form actually had no fewer than *seven* authors. I shall begin by explaining who these seven authors were. In recent years, textual scholarship has separated five of these from the rest, but there remain an irreducible two: John and Harriet Mill—joint authors of a much reprinted Victorian classic.

1

It should come as no surprise that the first of the seven authors was Mill himself, in the so-called Early Draft manuscript now in the library of the University of Illinois at Urbana-Champaign.[1] This version was written in the late months of 1853 and the early months of 1854 when Mill, then aged forty-seven, believing that both he and his wife were dying of tuberculosis, wished to set down (so that they "may not die with me")[2] some of his ideas for the "improvement of mankind" that had not yet got into print. As we have it, the manuscript that he produced consists of 169 leaves—139 leaves making up the earliest complete version of the *Autobiography* plus 30 leaves of rejected text retained together at the end of the draft. It represents a finished account, as Mill then would have given it to the public, of his life up to 1851, when he married Harriet Taylor.

Already in this manuscript we can see a second author at work. Harriet Mill read through the original version with pencil in hand, marking passages with queries, Xs, and vertical lines in the margins, deleting and sometimes revising Mill's initial wording, and occasionally commenting in the space that he routinely set aside for remarks and revisions at the left-hand side of each page.[3] Mill worked further on this version, making changes prompted by his wife's markings and generally accepting her revisions by writing over her pencil in ink, and then Harriet Mill read much of the work a second time, offering still more alterations and suggestions for him to consider. Her pencilings appear in 93 of the 169 leaves of the Early Draft, and affect three hundred passages of text ranging in length from single words to entire pages. In only a very few instances—I count just seventeen of the three hundred—did Mill not approve of or make some change in response to her markings.

Mill revised and recopied this first finished version and brought it up to date in the second extant manuscript, a 210-leaf holograph now in the Columbia University Library. He wrote the first 162 leaves of this manuscript in 1861, redoing the text of the Early Draft and adding three paragraphs mainly on the loss of his wife, who had died in 1858, and then wrote the final 48 leaves—the first and only draft of the remainder of the *Autobiography* as we now have it—in the winter of 1869/70. This second manuscript version is the latest authoritative text, the state in which Mill left the work when he died in May 1873. The rest of the authors did their authoring, as it were, posthumously.

Upon Mill's death, there was a concerted effort to get the *Autobiography* into print as speedily as possible. The Columbia manuscript was hastily transcribed by three writers working simultaneously—Mill's stepdaughter, Helen Taylor; his youngest sister, Mary Elizabeth Colman; and an unidentified French copyist—and the resulting transcript, now in the John Rylands Library, Manchester, is the press-copy from which the work was first printed. Helen Taylor penciled some changes in the Columbia manuscript (just as her mother had in the Early Draft) while she was copying it, and made a great many more alterations, omitted a paragraph, and reordered nine others in her sections of the Rylands transcript. The other two transcribers introduced further changes of wording and accidentals. All told, the transcript has more than 2650 variants, including several hundred "unauthorized" differences in wording, from the holograph that the transcribers were copying. Some of these departures were corrected in the process of setting and proofreading. But the printer inadvertently introduced still other changes; Helen Taylor made further alterations in proof-stage, omitting ten more passages amounting to 563 words; and another proofreader, Mill's friend and collaborator Alexander Bain, in the process of correcting mistakes made by the Rylands transcribers, appears responsible for yet more changes on top of all the rest. The path of textual "descent" is simple and straightforward:

Early Draft → Revised holograph → Transcript → First edition

(Illinois MS)   (Columbia MS)   (Rylands MS)   (1873)

But the right-hand half of the picture is cluttered with what theologically minded textual scholars call corruption.

In chronological order, then, the seven authors mentioned at the beginning of this chapter are J. S. Mill, the principal writer of both the Early Draft and Columbia manuscripts; Harriet Mill through her pencilings in the Early Draft; Helen Taylor in the changes she made in the Columbia manuscript, the Rylands transcript, and the proof-sheets of the first edition; Mary Colman and the unidentified French copyist, both of whom introduced suibstantive changes that survived into the first edition; the printer of the first edition (who may, of course, actually have been several compositors employed in setting the work); and Alexander Bain in the process of correcting the proofs.[4] The Rylands transcript, rediscovered and made available to scholars in 1959, is

indisputable evidence that Mill had no hand in the press-copy manuscript from which the first edition was printed, and editors since that
time have thus been able to restore Mill's intended text—that of the
Columbia manuscript—and in the process, by correcting or discarding
the changes introduced by the Rylands transcribers and the original
printer and proofreaders, eliminate five of the seven authors.[5] But it is
not possible, theoretically or practically, to reduce the number further.
We can for the most part recover Mill's original sentences in the Early
Draft manuscript, but these clearly do not constitute an intended text
of the *Autobiography;* they are merely first draft, the beginning stage
of the work. Subsequent to this stage, Mill and his wife revised
jointly—interactively and interdependently—and, while we can say in
quantitative terms that Mill's contribution to the final text was considerably greater than his wife's, still the two are inseparably involved in the
development of that text. Mill's *Autobiography,* in every form that we
know it, is a collaboration by two authors.

2

Harriet Mill's participation in the authorship of the *Autobiography*
ought to have some bearing on a question that has long occupied Mill
scholars—the extent of her influence on Mill's ideas and writings
generally. Mill himself, in passages of the *Autobiography* that she
read but did not mark or alter, describes her as "the most admirable
person I had ever known" (192, 193, 617)[6] and says she was more a
poet than Thomas Carlyle, more a thinker than himself, and at least
as great a promoter of freedom and progress as his father, James Mill,
had been (182, 183, 212, 213). He portrays her at length as both the
ideal human being and the ideal poet–philosopher (192–99, 617–23).
He credits her with substantial influence on his thinking and writing
in everything subsequent to *A System of Logic* (1843) and routinely
uses the term "joint production" to characterize her share in *Principles of Political Economy* (1848), *On Liberty* (1859), and other works
from the late 1840s on.[7]

These statements have aroused considerable skepticism over the
years and in the last three decades have been a subject of argument
among writers on Mill.[8] One problem has been and continues to be
the lack of corroborating evidence: there is nothing in anybody else's
letters, journals, reminiscences, reported conversations, or other
sources to support Mill's testimony. A second problem, of course, is

our unwillingness to see single authorship as a myth. And a third is a general reluctance to credit a woman with so much intellect. In any case, though we have Mill's own letters to his wife concerning their revisions for the second (1849) and fourth (1857) editions of the *Political Economy,* and though some inferences have been offered concerning her contributions to revisions for the third edition (1851) of the *Logic,* the only extensive *physical* evidence of her hand in writings attributed to him consists of her pencilings in the Early Draft of the *Autobiography.*[9] It is to the *Autobiography,* therefore, that we must turn to elucidate her role in his work.

Harriet Mill's markings and alterations, as I have mentioned, appear in ninety-three leaves of the manuscript and affect three hundred passages.[10] These may be categorized and described according to several different roles that she assumed as reader and reviser of Mill's initial text. First and foremost we may discern Harriet Mill the Copy-Editor. About 130 of her markings are classifiable as primarily editorial: she read carefully, with a sharp eye for infelicities in what Mill called "the minuter matters of composition" (254, 255)—faults of wordiness, unnecessary repetition, awkwardness, vagueness, ambiguity, inaccuracy, and the like.

Here are some typical examples from the early pages of the manuscript. At 6.4, where Mill initially described his father as "having at an early period, satisfied himself that he could not believe the doctrines" of the Scottish or any other church, Harriet Mill underscored (presumably as redundant or beside the point) "at an early period" and put an X in the margin, after which Mill deleted the four words and the comma. At 6.25, where he wrote that his father was "a man whom . . . nothing would have ever induced to write against his convictions," first she and then he deleted "ever," in this instance probably because "ever" and "never" are used three times elsewhere in the sentence (but probably also because she seems to have specially disliked such intensifiers—a dozen of her changes in the mansucript involve the removal of "ever" and "even"). In the same sentence, at 6.27, she improved the accuracy of Mill's wording by inserting "he thought" before "the circumstances" ("as much of his convictions as he thought the circumstances would in any way admit of"), and again Mill accepted her revision by writing over the words in ink. At the end of this sentence, 6.30, where he first wrote "performing it faithfully," she underscored the final adverb (a poor choice of word especially in the general context of James Mill's religious opinions), and Mill responded by substituting "adequately." At 8.31, where he began a sentence "But the things which were called lessons" and then revised the text to read "But the lessons so-called," she struck through "so-called" (which really makes no sense in the context— Mill himself had used "lesson" in the preceding sentence), and Mill canceled the words in ink. At 12.1, in a similar situation, where he wrote "I read few books of amusement properly so called," she this time underscored "properly" (probably questioning the logic of the word); in this instance, for the first time in the manuscript so far, Mill let his original text stand. At 12.11–12, he wrote a particularly round-about sentence: "In my eighth year I commenced learning Latin with a younger sister or rather I was required to learn Latin lessons and teach them to her, preparatory to their being repeated by her to my father." Harriet Mill underscored both "with a younger sister" and the first "her" and then, above the latter word, inserted "a younger sister"; she is responsible, therefore, for about half of the revision that produced the much simpler final reading of the Early Draft text: "In my eighth year I commenced learning Latin by means of teaching it to a younger sister, who afterwards repeated the lessons to my father." (The removal of the coercive "required to learn," however, seems to have been Mill's doing.)

These markings (they are the first seven by her in the manu-script) are representative of her critical scrutiny of rhetorical expres-sion throughout the work. A sizable number of her pencilings specifi-cally attend to matters of logic (Mill's own special province!), as when she deleted "though unavowed" at 46.18–20, where Mill had origi-nally written "The world would be astonished if it knew how great a proportion of its brightest ornaments . . . are complete though un-avowed sceptics in religion" (obviously she realized, earlier than he, that the skeptics would *have* to be "unavowed" if "The world would be astonished" to learn about them), and when she inserted "bills for the" at 158.15 to clarify the target of J. A. Roebuck's "vigorous opposition" ("bills for the puritanical observance of Sunday"). An-other sizable number of her pencilings reduce Mill's wordiness, as when she deleted fourteen words of his footnote at 94.35—originally, "It should be mentioned that my father was not the author of the continuation of this article in the second number of the review. That continuation was written by me"—to produce a much plainer ver-sion: "The continuation of this article, in the second number of the review, was written by me."

She attended to style even while revising for other than rhetori-cal reasons. In Mill's first sentence of the original "Part II" of the

Early Draft (617.9–11)—"My first introduction to the lady whose friendship has been the honour and blessing of my existence, and who after many years of confidential intimacy, deigned to be my wife, dates from as early as 1830"—she underscored "existence" and "many years of confidential intimacy," deleted "as early as" (and proposed "began in" as a replacement for "dates from"), and then in the left-hand half of the page rewrote the latter part of the sentence (as well as adding several other sentences that Mill then used almost verbatim in his revision at 192.4ff.). In redoing this sentence her main concerns appear to have been propriety and tone (to de-emphasize the earliness of the beginning of their relationship and neutralize the personal implications of "confidential intimacy" and "deigned"); the marking of "existence," however, whether for vagueness or extravagance, seems more purely a matter of style. Mill retained "honour and blessing of my existence" in his revised text of the Early Draft and expanded it to "honour and chief blessing . . ." in the Columbia manuscript (192, 193); but in most other places he deferred to her judgment, accepting her revisions as a matter of course.[11]

After Copy-Editor, Harriet Mill's next most prominent role, and unquestionably the most interesting, is that of Mother–Protector, in stereotypically maternal fashion shielding Mill from the harsh opinion of the world by correcting and improving the character he presents of himself. Along with a considerable degree of egotism, occasionally manifesting itself in snobbishness, he in general had an extraordinarily low opinion of his abilities, particularly in everyday practical matters; and in his original Early Draft text there are many passages of almost obsessive self-belittlement. Harriet Mill marked, revised, and deleted some sixty of these, large and small, effecting major changes especially in the tone and texture of details of the work.

Here is a reconstructed first version of the beginning of one of the longest passages that she marked in the manuscript:

Not, I am persuaded, by any inherent defect in my education, but certainly by some omission in it, I grew up with extraordinary inaptness and even incapacity in all the common affairs of every day life. I had hardly any use of my hands. I was far longer than children generally are before I could put on my clothes. I know not how many years passed before I could tie a knot. My articulation was long imperfect; one letter, r, I could not pronounce until I was nearly sixteen. I never could, nor can I now, do anything requiring the smallest manual dexterity, but all the common things which everybody does, I did not only in an ungainly and awkward but in a thoroughly ineffective and bungling manner like a person without the most ordinary share of understanding.[12] I was continually acquiring odd or disagreeable tricks which I very slowly and imperfectly got rid of. I was, besides, utterly inobservant: I was, as my father continually told me, like a person who had not the organs of sense: my eyes and ears seemed of no use to me, so little did I see or hear what was before me, and so little, even of what I did see or hear, did I observe and remember. My father was the extreme opposite in all these particulars. (608–9, from Early Draft rejected leaves R23–24)

Harriet Mill's pencilings in this passage include an exclamation mark beside "inherent defect" in the first sentence (which Mill changed to "necessity inherent"), the substitution of "great" for "extraordinary" and the deletion of "and even incapacity" in the same sentence, and then wholesale deletions and a revision at left to reduce the first six sentences to one: "Not, I am persuaded, by any necessity inherent in my education, but certainly by some omission in it, I grew up with great inaptness for everything requiring manual dexterity." She deleted "or disagreeable" in the next sentence ("I was continually . . . rid of"), changed "utterly" to "very" in the next sentence after that, and then struck through these, the rest of the sentences quoted above, and the next three *pages* of manuscript text as well. Mill wrote a condensed account of his deficiencies in a revision of these pages (rejected leaves R24²–25²), which Harriet Mill again read and marked disapprovingly. He next produced a still shorter version for insertion earlier in the work (611, rejected leaf R19/20). She read this too, made a few revisions, but this time did not mark the whole for deletion. It was, nevertheless, set aside, and there is nothing from any of these attempts in the final text of the Early Draft manuscript. After her death, Mill reintroduced the topic in the Columbia manuscript, in the long final paragraph of chapter 1 (37–39); but the text there is much changed in wording, emphasis, and tone from the one that Harriet Mill first read and marked.

　　She revised or deleted a good many shorter passages of similar self-deprecation—for example, Mill's ignorance of modern history (16.4–5, changed by her to lack of interest); his "various deficiencies" while living in France with the family of Sir Samuel Bentham (58.8–9); his inexperience in society (62.15–16); his "useless, ineffectual way" of first studying Condillac's philosophy and his inability to understand it "until it was explained to me" by James Mill (64.9–11); his lack of qualifications, lack of originality, and other weaknesses in his first contribution to the *Westminster Review* (96.29—Harriet Mill's numerous alterations are detailed at 98 n.); his uncritical attitude toward people of "any kind of superiority" (182.11—possibly deemed objectionable as a reflection on his attitude toward her) and then more specifically his slowness in forming "a definitive judgment" of Carlyle (182.20–27—she did not, however, mark or alter the end of the paragraph, where Mill describes her as "the superior of us both . . . whose own mind and nature included all [Carlyle's] and infinitely more").

A number of her other pencilings are more subtle in effect. She altered limiting details—for instance, "as much as three" (60.35, changed to "several"), "The northern half of" (86.2), "as far as Pæstum" (86.5), to make his sojourn with J. B. Say appear longer than it was and his travels in France and Italy more extensive—and, by cutting out some details concerning George Grote and John Austin (the facts that they visited his father while he himself, being younger, went to them), elevated an inferior relationship into the more nearly equal idea of "association" (74.15). In one of the rejected leaves, there are three such changes by her in part of a sentence recounting his early acquaintance with David Ricardo (614.10–12): where Mill wrote that Ricardo "sometimes had me to breakfast," she changed "sometimes had" to "often invited," thus increasing both the frequency of their meetings and the warmth of Ricardo's hospitality; and she turned Mill's description of being examined by Ricardo into a mutual discussion of "questions of political economy" (in Mill's revised text of the Early Draft, 54.19–20, these show up as "sometimes invited" and "converse on the subject").

In her enhancement of Mill's public character, she also marked or deleted some passages that are unpleasantly egotistical in tone or tendency. In an early version of 32.26–27, for instance, where Mill says that he is rather below than above average in natural gifts, she canceled the accompanying clause "as all are aware who have intimately or closely observed me." In preliminary and intermediate versions of 54.11–15 (see 613.27–28 and n.), she queried and marked his overemphatic denial that he was in any way influenced by his father's regular associates. At 60.33, where he discusses the rarity in England of friendly feeling and behavior, she marked a sneering reference to "a multitude incapable of making suitable response." At 164.2, she questioned (and no doubt caused the omission of) his statement that "In this part of my life . . . I had a really active mind." Numerous other extravagances are similarly queried, reduced, or struck out, though probably in most cases primarily for stylistic reasons (for example, the grandiose servant–master metaphor at 242.33 to describe the relationship of the *Political Economy* to "a larger and higher philosophy").

The third of her roles that I would single out is Harriet Mill the Victorian. Mill's plain style and wide-eyed confessional mode produced some forty passages where, as her pencilings seem clearly to indicate, she considered the language objectionably physical or the details overly personal. Thus she deleted the humorously ambiguous phrase "particularly in the modern form of it" loosely connected to "physical relation" between the sexes (108.36), reduced "confidential intimacy, entirely apart from sensuality" to the less suggestive "confidential intimacy only" (236.16), changed "sensual tie; or . . . sensuality" to "sensual relations; or . . . the feelings alluded to" (236.21–22), and deleted mention of Mill's "vibrating in unison" with, and being "excitable" by, "the beautiful and elevated" (623.26–28). Among what might be deemed private details, she consistently edited out those having to do with money and financial affairs. They include James Mill's "narrow income . . . and his unwillingness to invite any persons to his house whom he could not . . . make as comfortable as they were at home" (613.29–32); his "personal obligations" to Jeremy Bentham and the manner in which he paid rent for the house that Bentham sublet to the Mills (56.3–5); general mention of "uneasiness about the means of subsistence" (84.20); several references to "the pecuniary means" of establishing the *Westminster Review* and details concerning its financial support (92.12–16, 92.27–28, 102.21, and *Early Draft,* pp. 89–90); and Mill's statement that "Money, indeed, having no expensive tastes, I only wished for as a means of independence and of promoting public objects" (112.1).

She was of course concerned with propriety in the passages describing her own life, especially with respect to her first marriage and her long friendship with and then marriage to Mill. Here are a few examples from the original "Part II" of the Early Draft. At 618.31–35, she changed Mill's "Married at an early age" to "Married at a very early age" (to put her first marriage farther back in time and perhaps also to reduce her own responsibility for entering into it); softened Mill's rather harsh characterization of her husband, John Taylor—originally, "of liberal opinions but of no intellectual or artistic tastes, nowise a companion for her"—to read "of liberal opinions and good education, but not of the intellectual or artistic tastes which would have made him a companion for her"; and enlarged the degree of her former feeling for Taylor by changing "true esteem and affection" to "true esteem and the strongest affection." For Mill's original description of the beginning of his own relationship with her, written up as an event of romantic destiny ("I have always been convinced that sooner or later, and rather sooner than later, we should have found each other out"), she substituted three sentences of down-to-earth circumstantial detail: her first husband's grandfather had lived next door to Mill's family, Mill as a boy had been invited to play in the old man's garden, the old man was very kind to children, and so on (compare 617.11–15 with 192.6–11). At 619.5, she slowed down the progress of their becoming "at all intimate" by changing "years" to "many years," and at 623.19 she rewrote "my friendship with her" to read "our acquaintance." In the Early Draft rejected leaf RII.20, where Mill bluntly repudiated "the ordinances of society" concerning their private conduct before marriage ("though we did not consider the ordinances of society on a subject so entirely personal, in the smallest degree binding on us in conscience, we disdained . . . "), she revised and expanded, with an eye toward Taylor's and her own reputations, to produce "though we did not consider the ordinances of society binding on a subject so entirely personal, we did feel bound that our conduct should be such as in no degree to bring discredit on her husband nor therefore on herself and we disdained . . . " (wording that Mill took over verbatim in his revision at 236.16–19, merely adding a comma and a semicolon).

For a variety of reasons, she marked and altered a great many other passages about herself besides those having to do with her marriages. Some of them describe her intellectual preeminence (for example, several sentences about "the predominating influence of my wife's intellect and character" and Mill's being "wholly her pupil" in the canceled text rewritten at 234.4ff.—see also her numerous markings of similar statements at 620–23); probably she eliminated these in the general process (described above) of building up Mill's self-image. Other changes are of an opposite tendency, as when she deleted a phrase restricting her artistic ability to "any department in which she had had the requisite mechanical instruction" (619.30–31) and cut out a well-meant but, as she realized, unflattering comparison between her visionary character and "those who are reputed the most dreamy enthusiasts" (620.4–5). All revisions of this sort are recorded in the notes of *Early Draft* and CW, 1 (with a special concentration in the rejected leaves of the original "Part II," *Early Draft,* pp. 191–200, and CW, 1:617–24). The rewriting is so extensive that she has fair claim, in some of these passages at least, to be considered the main author.

The fourth role that I would call attention to is a very minor one, Harriet Mill the Wicked Sister- and Daughter-in-Law. Mill's sisters and mother were thought not to approve of his friendship with and especially his marriage to her, and she in effect returned the compliment by cutting out several references to them—Mill's sisters at 12.23–24 and 36.2–5 and his mother at 36.9, 56.16 (in the canceled footnote in R36 on the "mode of life at Ford Abbey"), 610.17–18, and 612.21–27, the only four places where she was mentioned in the original text. Mill's references to his mother are generally disparaging—she "only knew how to pass her life in drudging," she "worked from morning till night for her children," he "never had the slightest regard" for her remonstrances—and it is possible that his wife's deletions in these instances were a kindness rather than a slight. The fact remains, however, that Mill's mother does not appear in the final text of either the Early Draft or the Columbia manuscript; he is, as more than one reader has observed, the most famous person in nineteenth-century England to have been produced by only one parent (see 4 and 5, in both versions the first sentence of the second paragraph). For that sole parent, on the other hand—James Mill, who died before John and Harriet were married—she here and there made the same kind of subtle status-improving alteration that she did elsewhere for her husband. In Early Draft rejected leaves R34–35, for example, where Mill described his father as going out to other people's houses, her revision has him simply seeing them, without any specification of place or who was receiving whom (614.3–5); Mill's account of the "greater closeness of my father's connexion with [Bentham]" is changed to "close intimacy which subsisted between [Bentham] and my father" (54.27–28); Bentham's making "an intimate companion" of James Mill is altered to "they became very intimate companions" (54.31–32); and Mill and his father's accompanying Bentham is turned into the three of them—all equals now—making an excursion (54.36). Interestingly, Harriet Mill's changes of this sort enforce a vision of a largely masculine world.

Granted that her markings and revisions improved Mill's style, enhanced his self-portrait, and observed the proprieties, the question remains whether her work on the Early Draft manuscript contributed to, or altered, Mill's *ideas*. The short answer is: not much. It is of course difficult to consider ideas separately from their contexts. In the rejected leaf R113 (specifically the first version of 182.19–20), for example, where Mill is discussing the influence of Carlyle on his own philosophy, she changed Mill's "never approached much nearer" to "never approached nearer" and "intimacy" to "acquaintance." Her revisions altered the account of both the philosophical and the personal relationships between the two men; but pretty clearly her interest here was primarily in the personal, and it would seem a mistake to connect them with Mill's thinking. Some twenty of her other changes do, however, seem assignable solely or mainly to the realm of ideas.

There are, first of all, her handful of comments—on knaves and fools, the "voice of Society," severity and authority in education, the burdensomeness of social life—recorded in the notes at CW, 1:50, 238, 612, and 623; at least some of these influenced Mill's thought and expression in the *Autobiography,* and they are probably representative of many more, perhaps a score, that have since been erased or otherwise become illegible in the manuscript. Among recoverable changes by her in the text, several have the effect of turning Mill's individual experience into general truth, as when, at 12.20–22, she altered the past-tense verbs in "The teaching . . . was very inefficient as teaching, and . . . the relation between teacher and taught . . . was a most unfavourable moral discipline" to present tense (to produce a sentence about all such teaching rather than just Mill's).

Other markings change the meaning and emphasis of religious and political statements. In a cluster of revisions of the paragraph beginning at 40.7, she prompted Mill's qualification of "religious belief"—"in the ordinary meaning of the term"—by altering his original "any religious belief" (in rejected leaf R25) to "any of what is called religious belief"; changed past-tense verbs—"were the difficulties . . . there were the same" (40.14–15)—to present; and rewrote "could say nothing against Christianity but what could be triumphantly retorted . . ." (40.20–21) to read "can say little against Christianity but what can be retorted. . . ." Her substitutions at 46.32–33—"which" for Mill's original "whose approbation" and "ideal of good" for his "ideal God"—could be considered stylistic clarifications but probably were motivated primarily by the desire to dehumanize his "ideally perfect Being." As to political ideas, she marked Mill's initial description of himself and Roebuck as "radicals and democrats," prompting the omission of the latter term in the revision at 154.3–4 (see *Early Draft,* p. 127 n.), and dissociated herself from his political progress by rewriting "We were now less democrats than before" to read "We were now less democrats than I had been" (238.13). Her markings of some original statements concerning the *Political Economy* resulted in revision and deletions at 240.11 and 18. But there is very little else of this sort. Mill's works from the late 1840s on may indeed have been, as he wrote in a canceled passage of the Early Draft, "largely and in their most important features the direct product of her own mind," but her actual markings in this manuscript seem not to have much to do with his thought.[13] They are more aptly characterized by his description of an earlier period of their relationship, when his writings were "revised by her, and freed by her judgment from much that was faulty, as well as enriched by her suggestions" (234 n.), a description that he worked into his revised text of the *Autobiography* where he speaks of her help "in the minuter matters of composition, in which respect my writings, both great and small, have largely benefited by her accurate and clear-sighted criticism" (255).

3

While Harriet Mill cannot, on the evidence at hand, be said to have been a principal originator or shaper of the ideas in the *Autobiography*, the examples in the preceding section ought to have made clear that she was a significant contributor to the style, tone, texture, characterizations, and even representation (and inclusion or exclusion) of events. The facts of collaboration do not, in this case, present any serious textual problems. A "genetic text" could be constructed to show the progress of composition in the Early Draft, sentence by sentence, and to single out John's and Harriet's separate contributions, but in general we can now acknowledge the joint intentions of the two authors and accept the results as embodied in both the final text of the Early Draft (the earlier authoritative version of the work) and the final text of the Columbia manuscript (the later authoritative version).

In matters of interpretation, however, since John Mill alone is usually the focus of interest, one must proceed with caution. Any examination of Mill's self-assessment in the *Autobiography*—of his character there, his personality, what kind of man he was—may be based as much on his wife's revision as on his own original description. There is a genuine tension underlying the work between his own idea of himself (and what he wished to tell the world about himself) and Harriet Mill's idea of how he should appear instead. The initial tone—overall and in many specific details—was one of anguish; the tendency of Harriet Mill's revisions was to substitute aloofness and reserve.[14]

Students of Mill's style in the *Autobiography* will of course be studying John's style as partly revised by Harriet. She is responsible for the omission of literally hundreds of details of the original text that Mill wrote down, and not just in sizable passages like those on the Mill family's relationship with Bentham and the "mode of life at Ford Abbey" (54–55 n., 56–57 n.), the Mills' cottage at Dorking (84–85 n.), and the characterizations of himself and her in the rejected leaves (608–24), but in various isolated places all through the work. The revised text that they jointly produced, aesthetically considered, is more graceful and straightforward than the original but also barer, starker. There are fewer people, places, facts, and events in their revised version. And in fine points of explication, where the exact wording may be important, one again must be wary. At 46.22, for example, in commenting on religious skeptics' "apprehension lest by speaking out . . . they should do harm instead of good," Mill seems to give as "my opinion" the notion that such apprehension is "most mistaken." Actually the manuscript of the Early Draft shows that he originally wrote just the single word "mistaken" and that it was Harriet Mill who led the way in intensifying his opinion to the degree of "most mistaken."

All of the above are naturally matters that would figure in any biographical investigation. Consider, as one more example, this rich sentence describing Bentham's Ford Abbey:

> The middle age architecture, the baronial hall and the spacious and lofty rooms of this fine old place, so unlike the mean and cramped externals of English middle class life, gave the feeling of a larger and freer existence, and were to me a sort of poetic culture, aided also by the character of the grounds in which the Abbey stood; which were riant and secluded, umbrageous, and full of the sound of falling waters. (56.11–16)

The biographer (perhaps taking a hint from CW, 1:xi and n.) might justifiably quote the last dozen words to exemplify Mill's unusual ability to recall specific sights and sounds nearly four decades after he experienced them. In the manuscript, however, Mill wrote that the

grounds, "though not picturesque, were riant and secluded, and full
of the sound of falling waters," and it was his wife who, despite the
fact that she never saw the place, deleted "though not picturesque"
and added "umbrageous." For the sake of precision, it is worth knowing that the description, like much else in the *Autobiography*, is the
"joint production" of John Mill's own recollected experience and
Harriet Mill's imaginative literary artistry.

In general, biographers and critics have not been sufficiently
circumspect, and misstatements concerning the writing and revision
of the work abound in the scholarly literature. Michael St. John
Packe, for instance, quoting a passage from the rejected leaves of the
Early Draft in which Mill says he lacked "a really warm hearted
mother" and in consequence "grew up in the absence of love and in
the presence of fear" (612.21–28), comments that Mill "eventually . . . thought better of it, and in the *Autobiography* as published
there was no mention of his mother at all"—a statement that was true
according to the evidence available when Packe wrote his biography
but subsequently has become erroneous (we now know that it was
Harriet Mill who deleted the passage). In a study of James Mill's
theories of education, W. H. Burston quotes longer excerpts from the
same leaves of the draft—"a section of the original manuscript . . .
which John Stuart Mill subsequently cut out, and refused to have
published"—and then, undertaking to "assess this evidence with
care," asserts: "the fact that . . . Mill declined to publish it means
more probably that he felt that it was unfair, or incorrect as a record
of his childhood experiences." Peter Glassman's psychoanalytic study
mistakenly uses Harriet Mill's revisions as evidence for John Mill's
inverted Oedipus complex and the idea that he "figuratively dis-
created," even "murder[ed] his mother in the *Autobiography*," a kind
of "metaphorical assassination." And in a recent critical work on
Victorian prose, Jonathan Loesberg dismisses Harriet Mill's contributions to the *Autobiography* as "minor stylistic emendations."[15]

I have to confess here that I too, in my 1960s writings on the
Mills, underestimated Harriet's contributions. And even in the late
1970s, neither of the editors of the *Autobiography* in the University of
Toronto Press's Collected Works (John Robson and myself) was sharp
enough to notice that our photographer, in making the facsimile of
folio R24r that we included opposite the first page of text in the
appendix of rejected leaves (608), virtually eliminated Harriet's revisions from the picture by purposely using a high-contrast film to block
out what he considered superfluous pencilings!

4

To return briefly to the question posed at the beginning of section 2, I wish to suggest that the physical evidence of Harriet Mill's hand in the *Autobiography* may be a quite reasonable basis for surmises about the way she entered into the composition of *On Liberty* and other of John Mill's works for which we lack surviving drafts and have only, in their place, Mill's testimony about the nature and extent of her contribution.

On Liberty, in particular, has been a battleground for scholars, partly no doubt because of its status as the most enduring nonautobiographical work in the Mill canon but also because of Mill's public statements about his wife's share in the authorship, beginning with the dedication that appeared in the first edition in 1859: "To the beloved and deplored memory of her who was the inspirer, and in part the author, of all that is best in my writings. . . . Like all that I have written for many years, it [*On Liberty*] belongs as much to her as to me."[16] According to Mill's account in the *Autobiography* (in a passage written after his wife's death),

> The *Liberty* was more directly and literally our joint production than anything else which bears my name, for there was not a sentence of it that was not several times gone through by us together, turned over in many ways, and carefully weeded of any faults, either in thought or expression, that we detected in it. It is in consequence of this that, although it never underwent her final revision, it far surpasses, as a mere specimen of composition, anything which has proceeded from me either before or since. With regard to the thoughts, it is difficult to identify any particular part or element as being more hers than all the rest. The whole mode of thinking of which the book was the expression, was emphatically hers. But I also was so thoroughly imbued with it that the same thoughts naturally occurred to us both. That I was thus penetrated with it, however, I owe in a great degree to her. (CW, 1:257–59)

Scholars debating the credibility of these statements have tended to focus exclusively on the *ideas* of the work: either the ideas are a noticeable departure from John's earlier thinking (in which case Harriet must have played a major role in the composition) or they are the same that he held long before he first met Harriet (in which case she cannot be shown to have been an influence).[17] Neither position seems logical, and both ignore Mill's own emphasis on

writing—"expression . . . revision . . . specimen of composition"—
in the first two sentences of the passage just quoted from the *Autobiography*. Regardless of the professional interests of philosophers and
political scientists, it is the rhetoric of *On Liberty* that has kept it
alive and in print. Extrapolating from her criticisms and revisions of
Mill's prose in the Early Draft of the *Autobiography*, I think it is
highly likely that Harriet Mill made a significant contribution to that
successful rhetoric.

Such extrapolation is at best no more than speculation. But we
do have one additional piece of evidence in the example of *The
Subjection of Women* (1869), which Mill says in the *Autobiography*
"was written at my daughter's suggestion"—that is, the suggestion of
his wife's daughter, Helen Taylor—and "was enriched with some
important ideas of my daughter's, and passages of her writing" (CW,
1:265). A letter from Helen Taylor to Lady Amberley, dated 11 September 1869, just four months after *The Subjection of Women* was
published, gives a detailed picture of how she and her stepfather
worked together, by way of offering to "suggest improvements" in an
article that her correspondent has just written:

> Mr Mill tells me I alter other people's writings particularly well and
> should make a good editor from my power of seeing what they mean to
> say and bringing out their meaning with as few modifications of their
> own words as possible. I have a great deal of practice in doing this,
> beginning with Mr Mill's writings which I go over five or six times,
> putting in words here, stops there; scratching through whole paragraphs; asking him to write whole new pages in particular places where
> I think the meaning is not clear; condensing, enlarging, polishing &c.
> In short I take very much greater liberties with his things than with
> anyone else's, because there is no *amour propre* to be hurt in his case
> or mine, and I have confidence in him to reject my alterations if he
> does not really think them improvements.[18]

Some forty-five years earlier, when he was eighteen, Mill had
undertaken to organize, condense, rewrite, and fill gaps in the five-volume work published as Jeremy Bentham's *Rationale of Judicial
Evidence* (1827), a task that he says "gave a great start to my powers
of composition": "So long a course of this admirable writing had a
considerable effect upon my own" (CW, 1:119). Both before that
year-long occupation and several times later, Mill was a silent collaborator in his father's publications, and he undoubtedly entered into the

revision of articles published under his editorial supervision in the *London and Westminster Review*. He had, then, beginning at an early age, plenty of experience as collaborator in other people's writing, and there is little reason to think that he would not have routinely used the same method when he (instead of Bentham or his father or the article-writers) was the nominal author. The conclusion of all this is a strong likelihood that *On Liberty* and other works may indeed be the "joint productions" that Mill repeatedly called them.

4

Multiple "Consciousnesses" in Wordsworth's Prelude

Wordsworth could serve as an instance of several kinds of multiple authorship. In the first place, there is his widespread and profound influence on his contemporaries and on subsequent writers. Both Keats and Mill (who are close at hand in preceding chapters) knew Wordsworth personally and were greatly affected by his example and his writings—in subject matter, themes, attitudes, and basic structures of thinking in the case of Keats, and no less than a major change of philosophy in the case of Mill. Keats's *Isabella,* to consider only the earliest of the narratives in the 1820 volume, is a Wordsworthian lyrical ballad two decades after its time, complete with deranged heroine, excited narrator, direct address to the reader, balladic refrain, and, for a main interest, depiction of "the primary laws of our nature" (as Wordsworth described his own "principal object" in the preface to *Lyrical Ballads*) "chiefly, as far as regards the manner in which we associate ideas in a state of excitement." In his *Autobiography* Mill credits Wordsworth with restoring his sanity following the momentous "crisis in my mental history" and with awakening him to the importance of feelings, which became (as he says in a passage leading up to an account of his first serious reading of Wordsworth) "one of the cardinal points in my ethical and philosophical creed."[1] It is not farfetched—indeed, with the term "intertextuality" it is becoming theoretically commonplace—to see major influence as a type of collaboration in the works that are affected by it, and examples of such influence are not only abundant all through the history of literature but, according to some theorists, inescapable.

Then there is Wordsworth's role as actual collaborator in *Lyrical Ballads* of 1798, the most famous coauthored book in English literature. We have always known, of course, that this project had two authors. Coleridge contributed the opening poem, *The Rime of the*

69

Ancient Mariner, which has proved to be the most enduring piece in the Coleridge canon, and three other shorter poems including *The Nightingale,* whose subtitle, "A Conversation Poem," has been taken over to describe the genre of his principal achievement in blank verse, the so-called Conversation poems. Wordsworth contributed the closing piece, *Tintern Abbey,* one of the most admired poems in *his* canon, and eighteen other works that include frequently studied and anthologized items like *Simon Lee, We Are Seven, Expostulation and Reply, The Tables Turned, The Thorn, The Idiot Boy,* and—the piece that was first in popularity with Wordsworth's contemporaries— *Goody Blake and Harry Gill.* But as Neil Fraistat has most recently reminded us in his study of the unity of its contents, *Lyrical Ballads* was originally published without any author's name attached to it, and the several references to "the author" (singular), "his expressions," "his personal observation," "his friends," and "the author's own person" in the prefatory "Advertisement" clearly implied, and were taken to indicate, single authorship.[2] In the three subsequent editions, in 1800, 1802, and 1805, when an author's name was given, the title page in each case specified "By W. Wordsworth." Near the beginning of the preface in the 1800–1805 editions Wordsworth did mention "the assistance of a Friend, who furnished me with the Poems of the ANCIENT MARINER, the FOSTER-MOTHER'S TALE, the NIGHTINGALE, the DUNGEON, and the Poem entitled LOVE" (this last item added in 1800), but Coleridge's name never appeared in the work. Nearly two decades passed before *The Ancient Mariner* was published as Coleridge's own work, in the *Sibylline Leaves* volume of 1817.

The biographical evidence surrounding the publication of *Lyrical Ballads* supports the hypothesis that both Wordsworth and Coleridge were in agreement on the single-author anonymity of the first edition and the suppression of Coleridge's identity beginning with the second. So intricately connected and interinvolved were the contributions of the two writers that their relationship has been convincingly likened to biological symbiosis and lyrical dialogue.[3] Coleridge wrote *The Ancient Mariner,* true, but both men developed the story, with Wordsworth (as he much later recalled in a note dictated to Isabella Fenwick) providing first the general idea of the commission of "some crime," to be followed by "spectral persecution . . . and [the Mariner's] own wanderings," and then the more specific detail of killing an albatross, as well as several images and complete lines.[4] And Wordsworth's preface of 1800 and later editions, his most elaborate and influential statement of critical theory, grew out of mutual conversations and was begun (at least according to one of the partners) on the basis of notes written by Coleridge. "Wordsworth's Preface is half a child of my own Brain," Coleridge told Robert Southey in a letter of 29 July 1802; it "arose out of Conversations, so frequent, that with few exceptions we could scarcely either of us perhaps positively say, which first started any particular Thought."[5] At the very least, then, we have in *Lyrical Ballads* a multiply authored book, a multiply authored *Rime of the Ancient Mariner,* and, beginning in 1800, a multiply authored preface of enduring critical importance.

Wordsworth of course had other "helpers" besides Coleridge. He asked the young chemist Humphry Davy, who was a friend of Coleridge, to correct manuscripts and proofs for the second edition of *Lyrical Ballads*—"You would greatly oblige me by looking over the enclosed poems and correcting any thing you find amiss in the punctuation a business at which I am ashamed to say I am no adept"—and Davy saw the work through the press in Bristol.[6] Thomas De Quincey did even more for Wordsworth's *The Convention of Cintra* in 1809. He not only dealt with the press, corrected punctuation, and read the proofs, but carried on research for the poet, wrote notes, revised the original prose, and read the work through to get rid of libelous passages. Wordsworth's letters in the spring of 1809 testify to the extent of De Quincey's assistance—for example, "All your alterations are amendments"; "If you deem it advisable to add any remarks in the Appendix . . . pray take the trouble of doing so"; "I am well satisfied with the manner in which you have filled up the imperfect sentence"; "I am quite satisfied with your note upon Moore, which is very well done"; "I am much pleased with all the passages which you had altered"—and the letters also, most ungratefully, complain about delays caused by De Quincey's fussiness over details.[7] Nineteen years later, to give just one more example, an admirer named Barron Field sent Wordsworth, in two letters of April 1828, a series of detailed suggestions for substantive revision of his texts of 1827, many of which the poet incorporated into later collected editions.[8] And it is well known that all through his career Wordsworth was surrounded by willing amanuenses—his sister, his wife, his sister-in-law Sara Hutchinson, his daughter Dora, and other relatives, friends, neighbors— taking dictation, copying, and recopying (and no doubt spelling and punctuating in the process) whatever work was at hand.

Penultimately (in this brief survey) there is Wordsworth's interaction with his sources and influences—the same kind of interaction described in the opening paragraph of this chapter but in the reverse direction, with Wordsworth as recipient rather than donor of the benefit. Like every other artist, major or otherwise, Wordsworth had to build in large part with the materials available to him, and where these materials are literary, and especially where they are distinctively present and distinctively drawn on in a work, they can be (and in some logical schemes must be) considered an element in the authorship of the work. His best-known sources range all over the literary map, from Milton, the single greatest influence on Wordsworth's career overall—especially evident in allusions, quotations, echoes, and imitative figures and phrasings in the blank verse intended for *The Recluse* (as, most obviously, in Wordsworth's "Prospectus" in *Home at Grasmere* 754–860)—on down to a sentence in Thomas Wilkinson's manuscript of *Tours to the British Mountains* ("Passed a female who was reaping alone: she sung in Erse as she bended over her sickle; the sweetest human voice I ever heard: her strains were tenderly melancholy, and felt delicious, long after they were heard no more"), out of which Wordsworth fashioned the much anthologized *The Solitary Reaper*. One of the most interesting and important cases of source becoming part author involves Dorothy Wordsworth's journals—specifically the Alfoxden Journal of 1798 and the Grasmere Journals of 1800 and 1802—on which some critics think Wordsworth based all or parts of *Beggars, Resolution and Independence, Alice Fell, I wandered lonely as a cloud,* and at least half a dozen other poems and passages. In *The Sparrow's Nest* Wordsworth records heartfelt indebtedness to his sister: "She gave me eyes, she gave me ears"—but he should have added that she gave him recollections, words, phrases, and images as well. Christopher Morley's *Dorothy* is a sardonic comment on the situation:

> William danced with the daffodils, and took the word from her:
> Then he rested, and had his nap leaning against her shoulder—
> Only the very wise would guess whose poems they really were.[9]

All these manifestations of multiple authorship could be developed at length. But the type that I want to introduce here is still another variety—the author revising himself. Wordsworth wrote his poems over and over in a process that with some works went on for decades before publication (for example, *Peter Bell, Guilt and Sorrow,* and *The Prelude,* first published twenty-one, forty-eight, and forty-five years, respectively, after they were initially completed) and with others continued for decades *after* first publication (for example,

some of the pieces of *Lyrical Ballads* that Wordsworth kept altering
for the next forty years). Frequently the interval between original
composition and significant revision involved not only temporal but
psychological distance, and in such cases the revising poet may be
thought of—should be thought of—as having a separate identity
from the poet who composed in the first place.[10] Wordsworth was
keenly aware of temporal and psychological separations, as a condition not so much of poetry-writing as of life more generally—for
example, in these lines from the opening paragraph of *The Prelude,*
book 2:

> . . . so wide appears
> The vacancy between me and those days,
> Which yet have such self-presence in my mind,
> That, musing on them, often do I seem
> Two consciousnesses, conscious of myself
> And of some other Being   (28–33)[11]

and he made such "vacancies" a moving cause of worry or celebration
in some of his best-known poems (*Tintern Abbey, Nutting,* the Intimations ode, and short lyrics like *To a Butterfly* ["Stay near me"], *To the
Cuckoo,* and *My heart leaps up*).

   I wish to investigate some problems connected with Wordsworth
as reader and reviser of his own work—a situation in which the
"multiple," in its simplest form, consists of a younger Wordsworth
who composed the first or early text of a work and an older Wordsworth who revised it into a later version.[12] *The Prelude* offers the
richest single example, because of its lengthy history and the abundance of extant materials, and so I shall turn to it first, briefly rehears-
ing the routine facts of composition and publication and then considering some of the consequences of the way in which twentieth-century
scholars have discovered and promoted other versions preliminary to
the one that we think Wordsworth wanted us to read. Academic
argument over *The Prelude*—beginning innocently enough with such
questions as, How many *Prelude*s are there? Which one is the "real"
Prelude?—has inadvertently led us into a textual and critical predica-
ment that threatens the survival of the later Wordsworth. A kind of
textual primitivism is taking hold—grounded in the beliefs that there
is only one text for each poem and that each poem corresponds to a
single author—that in effect is burying, possibly forever, some of the
poet's most admired writing.

1

Wordsworth began drafting the work that ultimately became his masterpiece at Goslar, Germany, during the autumn and winter of 1798/ 99, resumed composition in England the following autumn, and by the end of 1799 had produced a two-part fragmentary work of 978 lines.[13] Much of the rest of what we now think of as *The Prelude* was first drafted in 1804 and 1805. Wordsworth seems in the early months of 1804 to have carried the 1799 project forward with a five-book scheme in mind, and then, in mid-March, to have abruptly set that aside in favor of a much grander plan. After little more than a year of amazing productivity, he completed a poem of thirteen books—close to 8500 lines—in May 1805. He then, intermittently during the next thirty-four years, revised and retouched it, section by section and line by line, altering in one way or another nearly half of those 8500 lines. The latest revisions of any consequence date from 1839, by which time the original book 10 had been divided into two. The poem was first published, in the fourteen-book version, in July 1850, three months after the poet's death.

For seventy-five years the printed text of 1850 was the only version known outside the Wordsworth family. Then in 1926, in one of the landmark editing feats of this century—slapdash in detail, as it has turned out, but of the utmost importance as a stimulus to appreciation and understanding of Wordsworth's achievement—Ernest de Selincourt made public the thirteen-book version of 1805, taken from MSS. A and B (in the hands of the poet's sister and wife), in an edition giving the texts of 1805 and 1850 on facing pages. De Selincourt's edition, revised by Helen Darbishire in 1959, with corrections and additions to both the text and the apparatuses and notes, was the much admired standard for scholarly and critical use until a spate of new editions appeared in the 1970s. Stephen Gill revised de Selincourt's text of the 1805 version (which had been separately issued by Oxford University Press) in 1970, and J. C. Maxwell produced *The Prelude: A Parallel Text,* again with facing texts of 1805 and 1850, for Penguin Books in 1971. The so-called two-part *Prelude* of 1798–99, constructed on the basis of MSS. V and U (again in the hands of Dorothy Wordsworth and Mary Hutchinson), was published three times between 1974 and 1979—first in a text prepared by Jonathan Wordsworth and Stephen Gill for M. H. Abrams's *Norton Anthology of English Literature,* 3rd ed. (1974), then in the Cornell

Wordsworth volume devoted solely to the 1798–99 work edited by Stephen Parrish (1977), and finally in the Norton Critical Edition of *The Prelude, 1799, 1805, 1850,* edited by Jonathan Wordsworth, Abrams, and Gill (1979).[14] A five-book version of early 1804 has been constructed and championed by Jonathan Wordsworth.[15] W. J. B. Owen's magisterial reediting of the fourteen-book text, this time from the latest authoritative manuscript rather than the printed text of 1850, has recently been issued in the Cornell Wordsworth series (1985). And a major reediting of the thirteen-book text and related mansucripts by Mark Reed, currently in press, will add two more large *Prelude* volumes to the Cornell series.

It is a moot question how many of the distinctive versions of *The Prelude,* if any, Wordsworth himself considered finished. Scholars nowadays tend to recognize three, four, or five stages but do not agree on their completeness and (in general) are careful to guard against excessive claims. The earliest stage, the two-part work of 1798–99, begins in the middle of a line with two pronouns lacking antecedents: "Was it for this . . . ?" It gives us draft versions of some of the most memorable passages of the later texts—boat-stealing, ice-skating, the drowned man of Esthwaite, spots of time, "Blest the infant Babe," and so on—but without connecting one with another structurally or thematically. The work is probably best viewed (and probably was so regarded by Wordsworth) as an assemblage of materials for a serious poem to come. It is unquestionably of interest, and deserves the attention it has received, but the fact that it exists in fair copies is not enough to persuade even its several editors that it was ever thought of as a finished poem.

The second of the stages, the five-book version of early 1804, has only a hypothetical existence based on Wordsworth's remark in a letter to Francis Wrangham of late January or early February 1804: "At present I am engaged in a Poem on my own earlier life which will take five parts or books to complete, three of which are nearly finished."[16] Jonathan Wordsworth has elaborately reconstructed the supposed contents of the five books—or what *would* have been the five books, had Wordsworth carried out the project—and praised the result as "in many ways the most impressive of the *Preludes,* bringing together in a densely packed, unique, and formally satisfying unit the great poetry of Wordsworth's original inspiration at Goslar in 1798, and the new magnificent sequences of early 1804." But the work in this stage, as Jonathan Wordsworth himself admits, "does not survive as a whole in fair copy and cannot be printed, as can *1799* and *1805*"[17]—a condition that seriously stands in the way of its being "impressive" and "satisfying."

The third stage can be printed and read, and has been available in successively more accurate texts ever since 1926—the thirteen-book *Prelude* of 1805. This is the earliest version that Mark Reed thinks Wordsworth considered a complete poem,[18] and I am inclined to agree, at least provisionally. The fourth stage is a novelty, known thus far mainly to the audiences of some papers at recent MLA conventions. This, roughly dated circa 1819, is an intermediate version of the poem between 1805 and the "final" text of the late 1830s. Though not fair-copied (and therefore perhaps having a foot in the hypothetical category of the earlier five-book poem), it exists as a distinctive level of revision all through the thirteen books, a revision that, according to its discoverer, Mark Reed, produces a more lofty and formalized rhetoric than in any of the other stages earlier or later. The details of this intermediate stage will appear in Reed's forthcoming Cornell edition of *The Thirteen-Book "Prelude."* The fifth stage is of course the version we have had longest—the last that Wordsworth had a hand in, the one that, by means of an intermediary fair copy and the agency of the poet's widow (who gave the poem its title), his nephew Christopher Wordsworth, and several helpers at the press, was posthumously published in 1850.

Of all these versions, the most reckonable, and clearly the ones having the best claim to be considered complete poems, are the thirteen-book text of 1805 and the fourteen-book text of the final manuscripts and 1850 (the versions of the facing-page editions of the last sixty years). The earlier has plenty of historical value as the text that Wordsworth read aloud to Coleridge, recently returned from Malta, on a succession of evenings in December 1806 and January 1807; Wordsworth did not publish it because at the time, and for many years afterward, he continued to have hopes of writing the magnum opus (*The Recluse*) for which *The Prelude* was supposed to be an introduction. The 1850 text has the legitimacy traditionally accorded to the latest authoritative version. Wordsworth himself anticipated textual scholars of the first half of the twentieth century in this principle: "you know," he reminded Alexander Dyce in a letter of mid-April 1830, "what importance I attach to following strictly the last Copy of the text of an Author."[19] Latest also has an attractive practical advantage: "first," "earliest," and especially "earliest complete" are elusive entities, frequently difficult or even impossible to establish, but we can almost always determine what is latest with a high degree of certainty.

The fact remains, however, that, apart from a handful of short excerpts, Wordsworth never published any version of *The Prelude* (a remarkable fact of literary history in itself), and we are left with two principal texts that are separated by thirty-four years and differ from each other in thousands of substantive and accidental details. This plurality of texts has made a great many scholars and critics uncomfortable, suggesting that multiple authorship is undesirable even when all the authors have the same name. Almost from the first publication of the 1805 text, in the 1920s, there has been controversy over which of the *Prelude*s, left-hand or right-hand sides of the facing pages, is superior—whether poetically, aesthetically, biographically, psychoanalytically, or even, for some readers, politically, religiously, or philosophically. And in the last decade the controversy has begun to have unfortunate consequences. In accord with the unacknowledged assumptions that one author produces one text, and that the one text must necessarily be the best text, the argument leads to a suppression of the history of Wordsworth's literary production.

2

When de Selincourt published the 1805 version, he was by no means producing merely a variant text and apparatus of antiquarian interest. For several reasons (and surely the normal human desire to aggrandize one's achievements was among them) he presented the 1805 version as a better, more authentic, more vital creation than the received text of 1850. Critical opinion from Victorian times had thoroughly established the notion of two Wordsworths—the youthful, radical, freethinking, and highly innovative genius of the *Lyrical Ballads* and *Poems, in Two Volumes,* and the pitiful old man (old, in this view, practically before he was forty) who had declined into flat versification, boring subjects (railroads, capital punishment!), and, what was much worse, political conservatism and religious orthodoxy. This latter Wordsworth is the figure depicted by the thirty-one-year-old Robert Browning as "The Lost Leader," a traitor who "alone sinks to the rear and the slaves." It was natural that the new version of *The Prelude,* in a manuscript text written during the great decade of creativity and dated almost half a century earlier than the text of the first

printed edition, would be looked at eagerly for revelations concerning the political and philosophical ideas of the younger Wordsworth.
De Selincourt played up this interest in his introduction, where,
after a thirty-page account of the manuscripts and the known facts
concerning composition, he entered into comparison of the early
and late texts, first "in point of style" (with sections on "later improvements" and "later deterioration") and then as to "changes of
idea." The section on later stylistic improvements begins innocently
enough—"No one would doubt that the 1850 version is a better
composition than the A [1805] text"—and goes on to praise the
stronger phrasings, the more closely knit texture, the greater precision of diction (in short, the craftsmanship) of 1850. The section on
later deterioration, seemingly offered in order to strike a judicious
balance, counters with examples of abstract language, "pompous
phrase-making," loss of the earlier text's "delicate simplicity."
Shortly thereafter, rather out of the blue, comes a separate section
headed "The ideal text of 'The Prelude' ":

> The ideal text of *The Prelude* . . . would follow no single manuscript. It
> would retain from the earliest version such familiar details as have any
> autobiographical significance. Of purely stylistic changes from that
> text, it would accept those only which Wordsworth might have made
> (and some he would certainly have made), had he prepared the poem
> for the press in his greatest period, changes designed to remove crudi-
> ties of expression, and to develop or clarify his original meaning: but it
> would reject those later excrescences of a manner less pure, at times
> even meretricious, which are out of key with the spirit in which the
> poem was first conceived and executed. Most firmly would it reject all
> modifications of his original thought and attitude to his theme.

The main point of this statement, and especially the last sentence, becomes clear with the final three sections that follow it, in
which de Selincourt depicts only deterioration—changes of idea concerning the poet's life at Cambridge, resulting in "criticisms directed
by a man of seventy winters against his own past"; changes in his
attitude to the French Revolution, showing "clear signs of his growing
conservatism"; and, in the longest section of all, changes in his "Philosophy of life and religion": Wordsworth "felt it incumbent on him
to remove from *The Prelude* all that might be interpreted as giving
support to . . . heresy"; these "most to be regretted" alterations are
"foreign to [the work's] original spirit," and they "cover up the traces

of his early pantheism," "disguise his former faith," and "have no rightful place in the poem."[20]

The London *Times Literary Supplement* reviewer felt that de Selincourt "makes . . . too much of what Wordsworth alters, and too little of what he keeps," and refused to approve the editor's notion of an ideal text. Leslie N. Broughton, in the *Journal of English and Germanic Philology,* likewise judged that de Selincourt was too severe on Wordsworth's religious changes:

> After all what concerns us most is the Wordsworth of the years prior to the writing of the poem, and of him at best we can have only an approximation. As for the rest, whether we have the Wordsworth of 1804 or 1820 matters little; he may be a man of thirty-four or of sixty-nine trying to recall his youth.

Generally, however, the reviewers accepted, echoed, and even enlarged on de Selincourt's strictures, beginning with de Selincourt's own student Helen Darbishire, who, writing in *Nineteenth Century and After,* commented that "the changes most to be deplored in [Wordsworth's] later text are those which overlay or obscure that naïve immediate expression [of the inner workings of his mind]. They generally mar the poetry; they always disguise the truth." G. C. Moore Smith, in *Modern Language Review,* remarking on the "very different spirit [in 1805] from the poem as revised for publication when the poet was an old man" and "the many changes which were for the worse," gave "hearty assent" to de Selincourt's suggestion for an ideal text. Wordsworth's biographer George M. Harper, in the *Saturday Review of Literature,* similarly approved of the ideal text, describing 1850 as "an incongruous mixture of [Wordsworth's] early convictions with the conservative views of his old age." Henry King, in a piece in the *Adelphi* entitled "Wordsworth's Decline," had "no hesitation in declaring that I vastly prefer the original version": "for the most part the revisions are a depressing record of growing timidity and impotence"; the poem "is a fascinating study in poetic degeneration" and "makes a unique, but alas! a terribly depressing record, of the decline of a great poet."[21]

This preponderant opinion among the reviewers in 1926 and 1927 is the one that, in both modest statements and high flights of rhetoric, has prevailed ever since. Here, for example, is a statement from a standard literary history of the 1930s: "Of all these troubled years the *Prelude* tells the engrossing story; but it should be read in its first impassioned form, written close to the events, though unpublished till 1926, not in the version to which Wordsworth reduced it in old age when he was no longer a great poet."[22] Edith C. Batho, in *The Later Wordsworth* (1933), and Mary E. Burton, in *The One Wordsworth* (1942), the latter work devoted specifically to a defense of the *Prelude* revisions, argued for unity and continuity in Wordsworth's career—one Wordsworth rather than two—and R. D. Havens's comprehensive study of *The Prelude* published in 1941 aimed throughout at explication of the 1850 text;[23] but these stand out as exceptions. Biographers and critics in large numbers resorted to the 1805 version for its supposed greater truthfulness, and the earlier text became the standard for routine scholarly quotation and reference.

In the last decade or so there has been, especially in short and medium-size journal articles, a great deal of highly sophisticated analysis and interpretation based on comparison of earlier and later texts, most often 1805 against 1850 but also 1798–99 (and sometimes 1804) against 1805—and not infrequently earlier texts against both 1805 and 1850.[24] This is much to the good, and the general trend of the studies has been that, while Wordsworth may have had different purposes during different periods of his work on the poem, he seems to have known what he was doing all along. But comparative *evaluations* of early and late versions still mechanically favor the earlier, and where de Selincourt had tried to balance the two texts' stylistic differences, later critics, wishing to align quality of style with quality of ideas, have declared 1805 preferable not only as biography, politics, and philosophy, but also as poetry. We see this in remarks like Richard Schell's acknowledgment ("of course") that 1805 "is generally superior biographically and aesthetically to the 1850 version of the poem" and Jonathan Arac's ironic reference to "the piously revised text of 1850."[25] An extreme statement of the same tendency is Philip Hobsbaum's, in an essay entitled "The Essential Wordsworth": "The promulgation of the 1850 text is a matter for keen regret." Using verbs like "maltreat," "fade out," and "blur" to describe Wordsworth's revisions, Hobsbaum finds 1805 so conspicuously better in artistic and narrative technique that he thinks the Victorian novelists, if they had been able to read the earlier version, would have written long poems instead of novels: "It is . . . not too much to suggest that, had *The Prelude* been published when it was written, in 1805, these successors [George Eliot and other novelists] would not have used prose as the medium for their fictions."[26]

Hobsbaum has no standing as a Wordsworth critic, but another extremist who on occasion employs the same extravagance of rhetoric has considerable reputation: Jonathan Wordsworth. The first sentence of the preface to *The Music of Humanity* (1969) sets forth a theme, and implies a program, of much of Jonathan Wordsworth's scholarship of the last two decades: "On the whole poets are known by the best versions of their works: Wordsworth is almost exclusively known by the worst."[27] In separate essays, then prominently in the Norton Critical Edition of *The Prelude* (in which he was senior editor responsible for, among other parts, the earlier texts and the sections on "Composition and Texts"), and most recently in *William Wordsworth: The Borders of Vision* (1982), he has passionately advocated early texts of *The Prelude*—1805 over 1850, 1804 over 1805, 1798–99 over 1804—and of other poems as well, beginning, of course, with *The Ruined Cottage.* Here, as part of a comparison of the 1805 and 1850 texts of the ascent of Snowdon in the final book of *The Prelude,* is a typical example of his opinion of Wordsworth as reviser:

> Wordsworth does not merely destroy one of his greatest pieces of poetry [in his later alterations], he weakens precisely those aspects which had made it the fitting climax to his poem. To watch him in full retreat is to be reminded of the grandeur of the claims that he no longer dares to make. It is difficult to know whether it is the episode itself, or the gloss, that suffers most in revision. From the moment when the light first falls upon the turf, only half a dozen isolated lines have not been changed for the worse.

The 1850 revision, we are advised, has "nebulous, safe, apologetic lines," "a cosier moon . . . seen in conventional terms," and elements that are "intrusive and distracting," "irrelevant," and representative of "dwindling," "self-abasing," and "fudging."[28]

Surely this is strange language to apply to one of the most admired episodes in *The Prelude* of 1850 (as it is in that of 1805). Such judgments are not totally irresponsible, however. Jonathan Wordsworth is the principal discoverer and best expositor of some of the early texts he is promoting, and his gusto is understandable. And when he organizes and chairs a Wordsworth Summer Conference debate (in Grasmere, August 1984) on the "relative merits" of 1805 and 1850, dividing up the proponents into "teams," the result is mainly good fun—an entertaining activity to span the time between hiking excursions and evenings in the pub.[29] But certain aspects of his influence are more worrisome, extending into the Cornell Wordsworth (of which he has been an advisory editor from the beginning) and the state of the poet's texts more generally.

3

The Cornell Wordsworth, with fourteen of its projected twenty volumes now in print, beginning with *The Salisbury Plain Poems,* edited by Stephen Gill (1975), is a work of immense practical usefulness for the study of Wordsworth and one of the most significant editing projects in Romantic literature in this century. Concerned to present full and accurate texts of early versions of Wordsworth's poems, rather than the hitherto customary later or "final" texts, the new series is conspicuous for several praiseworthy features: its spaciousness of treatment (several hundred pages may be given to the materials underlying a poem of only a few hundred lines), generosity of detail (frequently there are *three* separate printings—in photographs of the manuscript, exact transcription, and reading text—of a single version of a poem), and ingenuity of presentation (the editors use several sizes and styles of type, several kinds of bracket, deletion linings, superimposition shadings, and some other devices). Throughout it embodies a concept of "no-fault" editing: the scholarly procedures are clearly explained, all necessary information concerning a text is given in one place or another in the appropriate volume, and special circumstances are plainly noted wherever they occur. One may disagree with a choice of reading text or with a decision to emend (or not to emend), but the alternatives are nearly always available in the apparatuses; one may disagree with some detail in the transcription of Wordsworth's or a copyist's handwriting, but the photographs are there for all to see. The series is universally admired as a model of painstaking editorial work, and the press has done a superb job with the design and production of the volumes. Nevertheless, the Cornell Wordsworth, in its condemnation of "the worst" of Wordsworth[30] and its understandable eagerness to discover, promulgate, and extol early versions to take the place of later ones, is in the process of doing away with the later Wordsworth once and for all. I shall briefly sketch what I see as four problems associated with the project, beginning with two that seem less consequential than the ones that follow.

First, there is the elusiveness of the "earliest complete state" of a work, the expressed goal of some part or another of more than half the Cornell volumes so far published. The difficulty of determining what is "earliest" in combination with what is "complete" may show up in isolated details of a text—single lines, phrases, even words—and also in whole versions. Here is an example from the volume entitled *"The Ruined Cottage" and "The Pedlar,"* expertly edited by James Butler (1979). In the middle of his introduction (p. 15) Butler quotes the following passage from the Alfoxden Notebook:

> Why is it we feel
> So little for each other but for this
> That we with nature have no sympathy
> Or with such idle objects as have no power to hold
> Articulate language.

Butler says in a footnote that he is quoting "the unrevised base text" of the passage, but the photograph and facing transcription of the notebook's leaf 20v (pp. 120–21) show some deletion and revision in the next-to-last line:

>   things
> Or with such ~~idle objects~~ as have no
>   power to hold

Almost surely Wordsworth deleted "idle objects" and inserted "things" *before* continuing with the rest of the line, "as have no power to hold" (the final three words are runover, not interlineation). The "earliest complete" version of the line is the pentameter "Or with such things as have no power to hold," and the longer line quoted as "unrevised base text"—thirteen or fourteen syllables that fit no known metrical pattern—is a scholarly construct that had no existence as a unit in anybody's mind before the late 1970s.

The fact is that, wherever deletions, interlineations, and many other kinds of alteration occur, inevitably there are questions of sequence and chronology, and until one arrives at the *final* text of a version the possible combinations of revised and unrevised readings (not to mention the complication of several successive alterations in a single passage or even a single line) are, with a work of substantial length, virtually endless. Both *The Ruined Cottage* and *The Pedlar* are poems of substantial length. In earlier and later manuscript texts of both works, there are additions and alterations—Wordsworth filling gaps left by a copyist, revisions over erasures (with the erased text sometimes recoverable, sometimes not), "occasional minor corrections of meter, grammar, and internal inconsistencies" (p. 37). I am confident that Butler has done the best possible job of choosing among original and later readings in devising his texts; but the results are editorial constructs, simply approximations to the ideal, and the "earliest completeness" of so complicated a network of particulars has to remain a matter of speculation.

A question may also be raised (but not definitively answered) concerning the completeness of these poems as a whole. *The Ruined Cottage* exists in two distinctly different texts dating from 1798 and 1799, was revised further as part of *The Pedlar* in several more versions between 1802 and 1804, and ultimately was incorporated into book 1 of *The Excursion* and first published in 1814. These prepublication forms are currently considered "lost poems" or "new poems" in the Wordsworth canon, and the MS. D text of *The Ruined Cottage* in particular, first published by Jonathan Wordsworth in *The Music of Humanity* (1969), has widespread circulation among the Wordsworth selections in *The Norton Anthology of English Literature*. It is doubtful, however, whether the poet himself considered any version complete before the printed text of 1814. As Stephen Gill has recently pointed out in a thoughtful essay on Wordsworth's texts generally, the MS. D *Ruined Cottage* is complete mainly because scholars have declared it to be so: "Only those prepared to study all of the evidence in Butler's edition can be expected to realize that the text most readily available is . . . an editorial creation."[31] Very likely the same will apply to other so-called lost poems being discovered by the Cornell editors.

The second problem has to do with the focus or scope of annotation in some of the Cornell volumes, and is of consequence only as one more manifestation of bias favoring early texts over later. Whether inadvertently or as a matter of principle, there is, in facing-texts situations, a tendency to regard the earlier version (on the left) as the main text at hand and the later (on the right) as a variant having inferior status. My example here will be *The Borderers,* edited by Robert Osborn (1982), in which the last sentence of the editorial introduction to the parallel reading texts explains, "Beneath the early version are critical and interpretive notes, most of which apply equally to the late version" (p. 69). This is reasonable procedure as far as it goes, but it means that passages of revised text where there is no corresponding early text on the left-hand side necessarily go unannotated.

Thus "some natural tears" in the late version line 762 (echoing the same phrase in *Paradise Lost* 12.645), "not a nerve would tremble" in 779 (echoing *Macbeth* 3.4.101–2), and "fallen, / Like the old Roman, on their own sword's point" in 2310–11 (cf. *Macbeth* 5.8.1–2), each of which gets a note in de Selincourt's Oxford English Texts *Poetical Works,* are presented without commentary in the Cornell volume. (They are not especially striking parallels, but nevertheless are exactly the kind of citation that Osborn provides in hundreds of notes to the early version.) In two notes on page 104, to early version 1.3.5–23, Osborn refers to the "eighteenth-century tradition of mad maidens" and cites Cowper's "Crazed Kate" in *The Task* and parts of Wordsworth's *A Ballad* and *Dirge.* A more useful reference, especially relevant to 15, 18, and 22—"no one ever heard . . . in rain or storm . . . they say"—would have been Wordsworth's *The Thorn;* and the phrase "an Infant's grave" on the facing right-hand page, in late version line 393, suggests that the poet himself was aware of the echo. I think Osborn would have included such a reference (*The Thorn* has "many a time and oft were heard," "In rain, in tempest," "They say," "Some say," "an infant's grave" in 159, 79, 122, 205, 214, 55, 61), had he devoted more serious critical attention to his later text of the play.

The third problem, to my mind much more serious than either of the preceding, is the virtual exclusion of Wordsworth's final texts from the Cornell Wordsworth, as though Wordsworth at the end was not an author at all. The volume containing *Peter Bell,* edited by John E. Jordan (1985), is a handy example. Its parallel reading texts are an editorial composite of two manuscripts of 1799 on the left-hand pages (principally MS. 2, with passages from MS. 3 where the former is defective) and the text of the first edition of 1819 on the right-hand pages. As in most of the other volumes in the series, a complete collation of variants from lifetime (and, where appropriate, posthumous) printings allows readers to reconstruct—in their minds or on paper—any of the subsequent authoritative versions, including of course the last, with a high degree of accuracy. Nevertheless, these later versions are available here *only* via the apparatus readings, and this means that for all practical purposes they have dropped out of sight and, given the likely influence that the Cornell Wordsworth will exert in the future, out of the Wordsworth canon entirely.

Wordsworth's composition of *Peter Bell,* in five distinct manuscript versions and a succession of printed texts thereafter, by no means ended with the publication of the poem in 1819. He made changes for the version printed in his *Miscellaneous Poems* in 1820, further changes for each of the three versions in his *Poetical Works* of

1827, 1832, and 1836, and still more for his *Poems* in 1845. Between the first edition of 1819 and the final lifetime printing in the *Poetical Works* of 1849–50, he altered the poem substantively in close to two hundred lines (roughly one-sixth of the total). From his point of view, of course, these later changes, just like those in the successive manuscripts earlier, were improvements, and it is fairly easy to find examples that seem to justify the process.

The ass's "loud and piteous bray" in the first edition (505) is replaced by "long and clamorous bray" in the final text (465), and this revision enabled Wordsworth to strengthen another descriptive phrase three stanzas later, rewriting "long dry see-saw of his horrible bray" (520) as "hard dry see-saw . . ." (480). The following in the first edition (in which "He" refers to the ass) is purely narrative business:

> That Peter on his back should mount
> He shows a wish, well as he can,
> "I'll go, I'll go, whate'er betide—
> "He to his home my way will guide,
> "The cottage of the drowned man."   (636–40)

The final version of the same stanza, more straightforward in narration, adds thematic implications in the last two lines:

> But no—that Peter on his back
> Must mount, he shows well as he can:
> Thought Peter then, come weal or woe,
> I'll do what he would have me do,
> In pity to this poor drowned man.   (591–95)

For this passage describing Peter's thoughts in the first edition—

> And once again those darting pains,
> As meteors shoot through heaven's wide plains,
> Pass through his bosom—and repass!   (783–85)

—the corresponding final text has more emotion ("ghastly" in place of "darting"), is more consistently located (within Peter rather than shooting through heaven), and is more substantial rhetorically ("and repass" in the earlier text seems merely to fill out the line):

> And once again those ghastly pains,
> Shoot to and fro through heart and reins,
> And through his brain like lightning pass.   (733–35)

"Renounced his folly" at the end of the final text (1133) seems much more in keeping with the idea of Peter's conversion than the first edition's "repressed his folly" (1183). And so on.

I am not especially interested in arguing that the final text of *Peter Bell* is rhetorically, narratively, or thematically better than earlier printed versions (and in any case I am probably incapable of objective judgment in the matter simply because I have been reading and teaching the final text for several decades). But I am concerned to emphasize that the latest readable text of *Peter Bell* in the Cornell edition is the *first,* not the last, printed version, and that Wordsworth's subsequent revisions, in bits and pieces in the Cornell apparatus, can be reconstituted only fragmentarily—a substitution here, another there—in a process inconvenient even to the trained textual scholar and, realistically considered, out of the question for the student and general reader. (In the Cornell edition, to arrive at the final text of 733–35, which I have just quoted from my Riverside *Selected Poems and Prefaces,* one must combine line 783 of the 1819 text with the apparatus variant "ghastly," a revision that first shows up in the printing of 1836; add the variant lines to 784–85 that Wordsworth inscribed in his personal copy of *Poetical Works* of 1832; and then insert into *those* lines two further readings first appearing in 1836.)

Parrish, describing Wordsworth as a poet who strove "tirelessly for perfection of his art," says that the Cornell series will "make it possible . . . to follow the maturation of his poetic genius, and to honor his lifelong concern about his poems."[32] For readers using the Cornell *Peter Bell,* the poet's maturation may seem to come to an abrupt stop with the text of 1819; the rest of his lifelong concern is relegated to the apparatus. The same is true of Wordsworth's mature revisions in several other volumes (for example, *An Evening Walk* and *Descriptive Sketches,* where the latest reading texts are those of 1836; *Benjamin the Waggoner,* in which the latest text is, as with *Peter Bell,* the first edition of 1819; and the volume containing *Poems, in Two Volumes,* for which the latest texts are those of 1807). In all these volumes the apparatuses are remarkably full and precise. But the apparatuses are not (nor are they intended to be) the equivalent of the poetic texts themselves.

The fourth and largest problem, a product and extension of everything I have so far discussed in this section, is the general effect that the Cornell emphasis on early texts may have on the study and understanding of Wordsworth in the next several decades. I shall use some examples from Jared Curtis's edition of *"Poems, in Two Volumes," and*

Other Poems (1983), which like all the others is an exemplary piece of scholarly editing. Let us imagine a student in the library seeking a respectable text of, say, *I wandered lonely as a cloud*. Let us further imagine the student standing in front of the twenty or so grayish-green volumes of the Cornell Wordsworth, clearly the handsomest, most substantial, most scholarly edition in sight, and somehow (by luck or by means of a general index in the final volume) managing to locate the poem in Curtis's volume, on pages 207–8. In this version the poem is eighteen lines long (not twenty-four, as formerly in the standard texts), has "dancing" instead of "golden" daffodils in 4, has "Ten thousand dancing" instead of "Fluttering and dancing" in 6, has a "laughing" instead of a "jocund" company in the fourth line of the second stanza (what standardly used to be the third), and has lost the following stanza that formerly constituted 7–12:

> Continuous as the stars that shine
> And twinkle on the milky way,
> They stretched in never-ending line
> Along the margin of a bay:
> Ten thousand saw I at a glance,
> Tossing their heads in sprightly dance.

Reading the shorter, plainer text in the Cornell volume, the student may well wonder how the poem came to be so famous. It is an attractive piece, certainly, but somehow not so vivid and imaginative as one had thought it would be.

It is mainly the inadvertent *standardizing* of these early texts that worries me.[33] This same hypothetical student, looking elsewhere in Curtis's volume, will unwittingly miss other lines and images that were formerly (back in the 1970s!) a familiar part of Wordsworth's best-known work—for example, "Beside a pool bare to the eye of heaven" in a couplet of *Resolution and Independence,* lines 53–54 (a later revision in place of 1807's "When up and down my fancy thus was driven"); "life's pilgrimage" in the same poem, line 67 (replacing 1807's "their pilgrimage," referring to the leechgatherer's "feet and head"); "Proteus rising from the sea" in the penultimate line of *The world is too much with us* ("coming from the sea" in 1807); "I listened, motionless and still" in *The Solitary Reaper* 29 ("I listen'd till I had my fill" in 1807); the cuckoo's "twofold shout . . . At once far off, and near" in the second stanza of *To the Cuckoo* ("restless shout . . . About, and all about!" in 1807); "fond illusion of my heart" in *Elegiac Stanzas* 29 ("fond delusion" in 1807). The long title of the Intimations ode—*Ode: Intimations of Immortality from Recollections of Early Childhood* (simply "Ode" in 1807)—and the epigraph from *My heart leaps up* are other later additions by Wordsworth that are absent from the texts (though of course present in the apparatus) in Curtis's volume.

My notion of the imminent standardization of early texts is less hypothetical than the student I have just described.[34] There is already in print, well established in the new Oxford Authors series, a 750-page *William Wordsworth* edited by Stephen Gill (1984), in which, to quote the editor's preface, "for the first time a selection of Wordsworth's work is offered in which the poems are ordered according to the date of their composition, and presented in texts which give as nearly as possible their earliest completed state." Here we have the early readings that I just cited from *Poems, in Two Volumes,* plus (along with much else) early versions of *Lyrical Ballads,* a manuscript text of *Peter Bell* (which, in lacking the Prologue stanzas that banish "dragon's wing, the magic ring" and extol the "nobler marvels [of] the mind . . . in life's daily prospect," is even barer than the first printed text), a manuscript text of *The Ruined Cottage* (again MS. D, which came *after* the "earliest"), and of course the 1805 *Prelude.* In his 1983 essay on Wordsworth's texts, Gill argues that the effect of the traditional procedure (for example, in the de Selincourt–Darbishire Oxford English Texts edition) of printing Wordsworth's final versions, while recording earlier readings in apparatus and notes, "is to *efface* a poem's earlier existence," and he thinks that a chronological order employing final texts "*completely destroys* the usefulness of the chronological arrangement."[35] But surely Gill's own procedure in the Oxford Authors *William Wordsworth* even more effectively (because there is no apparatus) effaces the later texts, not to mention the historical fact of Wordsworth's ongoing self-revision. The new chronological presentation reveals a poet who neither declined nor improved but was all along less brilliant than we had remembered.

It is possible to see the beginnings of the present situation in de Selincourt's publication of the early *Prelude* sixty years ago and to trace its development in scholars' increasing interest in what, from a skeptical point of view, sometimes seems to have become novelty for novelty's sake. Meanwhile, the once standard texts are on the verge of becoming rare books. *Whitaker's Books in Print* for 1989 lists only the fourth and fifth volumes of the de Selincourt–Darbishire

Oxford English Texts *Poetical Works* as still available. Perhaps one day someone will be making yet another startling discovery—the later Wordsworth!

4

The shifting attitudes toward Wordsworth's texts in this century are not exactly a credit to Wordsworth scholarship. Initially the critics were interested mainly in the poet's ideas, and their motives were political in a broad sense: Wordsworth's later conservatism in politics and religion was to be rejected (as de Selincourt's introduction to *The Prelude* in 1926 made clear), and the late text of *The Prelude,* when an alternative became available in the 1805 version, was to be scorned as an embodiment of contemptible, even dangerous, beliefs. Scholars for a long time seem not to have noticed that by 1805 Wordsworth had already arrived at practically all his "later" ideas. Expressions of the hated piety of old age (as in Arac's phrase quoted earlier, "the piously revised text of 1850") actually occur in Wordsworth's earliest surviving correspondence—for example, this sentence of September 1790, when he was twenty: "Among the more awful scenes of the Alps, I had not a thought of man, or a single created being; my whole soul was turned to him who produced the terrible majesty before me"[36]— and they are especially frequent in letters referring to John Wordsworth's death in February 1805, just when the poet was completing the thirteen-book *Prelude.* The notion that the 1805 version must be more reliable than the later texts as a record of Wordsworth's politics (etc.) of the 1790s is not logically valid, and the known biographical facts go against it.

The gradual equation of imagined bad politics (etc.) with bad poetry is similarly untenable. The following, from the ascent of Snowdon in the 1850 text, book 14, is a familiar battleground:

> —It was a close, warm, breezeless summer night,
> Wan, dull, and glaring, with a dripping fog
> Low-hung and thick, that covered all the sky.
> But, undiscouraged, we began to climb
> The mountain-side. The mist soon girt us round,   15
> And, after ordinary Travellers' talk
> With our Conductor, pensively we sank
> Each into commerce with his private thoughts:

Thus did we breast the ascent, and by myself
Was nothing either seen or heard that checked   20
Those musings or diverted, save that once
The Shepherd's Lurcher, who, among the crags,
Had to his joy unearthed a Hedgehog, teased
His coiled-up Prey with barkings turbulent.
This small adventure, for even such it seemed   25
In that wild place, and at the dead of night,
Being over and forgotten, on we wound
In silence as before. With forehead bent
Earthward, as if in opposition set
Against an enemy, I panted up   30
With eager pace, and no less eager thoughts.
Thus might we wear a midnight hour away,
Ascending at loose distance each from each,
And I, as chanced, the foremost of the Band:
When at my feet the ground appeared to brighten,   35
And with a step or two seemed brighter still;
Nor was time given to ask, or learn, the cause;
For instantly a light upon the turf
Fell like a flash; and lo! as I looked up,
The Moon hung naked in a firmament   40
Of azure without cloud, and at my feet
Rested a silent sea of hoary mist.
A hundred hills their dusky backs upheaved
All over this still Ocean; and beyond,
Far, far beyond, the solid vapours stretched,   45
In Headlands, tongues, and promontory shapes,
Into the main Atlantic, that appeared
To dwindle, and give up his majesty,
Usurped upon far as the sight could reach.
Not so the ethereal Vault; encroachment none   50
Was there, nor loss; only the inferior stars
Had disappeared, or shed a fainter light
In the clear presence of the full-orbed Moon;
Who, from her sovereign elevation, gazed
Upon the billowy ocean, as it lay   55
All meek and silent, save that through a rift
Not distant from the shore whereon we stood,
A fixed, abysmal, gloomy breathing-place,
Mounted the roar of waters—torrents—streams
Innumerable, roaring with one voice!   60
Heard over earth and sea, and in that hour,
For so it seemed, felt by the starry heavens.

Only twenty of these fifty-two lines are substantively identical with the corresponding text in 1805; that is to say, Wordsworth changed the wording, in some places revising entire sentences, in more than three-fifths of the lines. The handful of single-word revisions may seem indifferent: 1805 has "mist" for "fog" in 12, "silently" for "pensively" in 17, "stood" for "hung" in 40 (though this change probably should be considered related to a larger revision in 50ff.), and "its majesty" for "his majesty" in 48 (an alteration that, had it been in the opposite direction, from "his" to "its," no doubt would have been displayed by critics as one more instance of Wordsworth's "covering up" his earlier animism). At the next level up, the revisions of phrases may seem mainly to illustrate de Selincourt's characterization (in his introduction of 1926) of later stylistic improvements: "Weak phrases are strengthened, and the whole texture is more closely knit."[37] The 1805 version of the first of the quoted lines—"It was a Summer's night, a close warm night"—could be considered somewhat repetitious; in revision Wordsworth got rid of the extra "night," thereby making room for an additional adjective: "breezeless." Further examples of the same process may be seen in 32 (1805: "perhaps an hour"; 1850: "a midnight hour"), 45 (1805: "the vapours shot themselves"; 1850: "the solid vapours stretched"), and 47 (1805: "Into the Sea, the real Sea"; 1850: "Into the main Atlantic").

The 1805 equivalent of 14–15 has a detail that Wordsworth later deleted: "having faith / In our tried Pilot" (which, had it been added rather than omitted in the later text, might have been censured as further evidence of the aging poet's orthodoxy). The 1805 description of the dog and the hedgehog (corresponding to 1850's 22–24)—

> The Shepherd's Cur did to his own great joy
> Unearth a Hedgehog in the mountain crags
> Round which he made a barking turbulent

—might be deemed agreeably plainer than the elaborate (indeed, nearly mock-epic) passage of 1850. The 1805 version of 40–42 is also plainer:

> The Moon stood naked in the Heavens, at height
> Immense above my head, and on the shore
> I found myself of a huge sea of mist,
> Which, meek and silent, rested at my feet.

But in this instance the later poeticizing (and condensing) might be thought to result in a more impressive picture ("firmament," "azure," "without cloud," and "hoary" have no counterpart in the 1805 version, while 1805's "meek and silent" appears further on in the 1850 text, at line 56).

The most interesting (and, in the scholarly literature, the most controversial) difference has to do with the last thirteen lines of the passage (50–62). The corresponding text of 1805 consists of two sentences:

> Meanwhile, the Moon look'd down upon this shew
> In single glory, and we stood, the mist
> Touching our very feet; and from the shore
> At distance not the third part of a mile
> Was a blue chasm; a fracture in the vapour,
> A deep and gloomy breathing-place through which
> Mounted the roar of waters, torrents, streams
> Innumerable, roaring with one voice.
> The universal spectacle throughout
> Was shaped for admiration and delight,
> Grand in itself alone, but in that breach
> Through which the homeless voice of waters rose,
> That dark deep thoroughfare had Nature lodg'd
> The Soul, the Imagination of the whole.

The 1805 text emphasizes the chasm ("rift" in 1850) and the roar of the waters emanating from it, symbolic of "The Soul, the Imagination of the whole." In the 1850 text, the focus has shifted from the ground to the sky, and it is the moon, unencroached upon and sovereign, that becomes emblem of the imagination. It is an open question, in these revisions, whether Wordsworth was clarifying his original idea (and emblematization) of imagination or was consciously expressing a different idea by means of the difference of emphasis among the details of the scene. There are many concepts and images of imagination in *The Prelude,* not all of them compatible with one another, and we can never know for sure (perhaps Wordsworth himself did not know) whether the 1805 and 1850 versions of the passage should be considered as constituting one more or two.

I should think both passages, early and late, would qualify as beautiful and moving descriptions introducing Wordsworth's powerful conclusion to the poem. Yet the Norton Critical Edition's footnote to the 1850 lines is niggling in the extreme:

> None of the other great passages of *The Prelude*—indeed of Words-
> worth's poetry as a whole—suffered in revision as did the Ascent of
> Snowdon. From the earliest reworkings (*1850*, 50–53, e.g., belong to
> 1816/19) to the final concession to orthodoxy in 61–62 (1839 or later),
> alterations are consistently for the worse.

Lines 61–62 are no more a "concession to orthodoxy" than the earlier
images of earth–sky reciprocity (ennobling interchange!) in the opening paragraph of *Tintern Abbey* and the final lines of Coleridge's
Frost at Midnight. With this note in the Norton edition, as with all
such statements based on "the worst of Wordsworth," we are in the
realm of aesthetic politics, about which "team" is going to be right.

What suffers in revision, what is better or worse—even, in such a
matter, what constitutes consistency ("consistently for the worse")—
can hardly be demonstrated, much less proved. What *is* demonstrable
is that Wordsworth did revise his poems—*The Prelude* and all the
others. One can, in the manner of the disapproving tradition beginning
with de Selincourt, call his revising "obsessive" and "compulsive"; one
can also, taking a different view (and tone), see a great deal to admire
in Wordsworth's craftsmanly improvements. But regardless of our evaluations, we do have at hand the historical reality of a major poet, one
of the greatest in English, writing and repeatedly revising his poems.

The textual primitivists—the long line from de Selincourt to
Hobsbaum and Jonathan Wordsworth—have reacted to this history
in the worst possible way. They hate revisions, considering anything
later than the "earliest complete state" a deterioration.[38] The author
they apotheosize, evidently, is an abstraction from his own history,
providing no clue to the actual circumstances of literary production.
Granting that the best and worst of Wordsworth are only preferences,
it would be far more responsible to acknowledge the legitimacy and
interest, intrinsic or in connection with other texts, of *all* the versions
of *The Prelude* and the rest of the poems in the canon. Recent textual
theory—in the writings of James Thorpe and Hans Zeller, for
example[39]—favors this more catholic view, and it has the additional
support of common sense: Wordsworth did, after all, write the 1805
version *and* the 1850; the 1798 *Peter Bell* and the rest of the versions,
including those of the printed texts of 1819, 1820, 1827, 1832, 1836,
and 1845; *The Ruined Cottage, The Pedlar,* and *The Excursion*—and
each of these versions (and of course others that I have not mentioned) embodies some degree of the poet's intention and authority.
It is possible to argue that some versions carry more authority than

others; it is not, I think, possible to argue that authority resides only in a single version, and that the rest of the texts in a series, whether early or late, should be banished to some limbo of poor relationship. Least of all is it possible to bestow authority on a text merely because the critic prefers it over all other versions—especially if it is a text with only a hypothetical existence.

The most interesting recent critical work on Wordsworth's texts and revisions argues or assumes this broader notion of literary authority. Raymond Carney, reviewing the first four volumes of the Cornell Wordsworth in 1981, ponders "the extent to which the concept of a final text is itself a critical fiction" and answers with major statements concerning writing and revision as a continual process. For example:

> It is the concept of the well-made text that needs jettisoning. We need to begin to talk about writing as a process with a significance in and of itself, composition as an activity of consciousness and not merely as a means of producing ultimate meanings. Can we begin to understand manuscripts and revisions not as imperfect or approximate versions of some unrealized final event, but as events unto themselves with their own self-satisfying logic and rationale?

Robert Young, replying to Baker's "Prelude and Prejudice" in 1982, defends the equally legitimate claim to authority of each of the three versions of *The Prelude* in the Norton Critical Edition. Clifford Siskin, in a 1983 study of "literary change," uses Wordsworth as a principal example of the "complementary relationship between revision and spontaneity": "What Wordsworth did was to innovate upon the idea of change, and thereby to valorize the formal procedure of revision, by positing a new relationship between parts and wholes. . . . In Wordsworth, process and product fuse as parts and wholes enter a mutually interactive relationship." And Susan Wolfson, in a 1984 essay comparing the 1799, 1805, and 1850 versions of the drowned man of Esthwaite, begins with the statement that "recent critical studies in a variety of fields have encouraged us to revise our understanding of what constitutes an authoritative version of a work and to regard textual variants and the dynamics of revision as significant events in the shape of a career." Her essay is the most elaborate study to date of revision as a continual process of self-reading, self-reconstructing, and *The Prelude* as a poem constituted by all its texts at once,[40] just as Wordsworth as an author is constituted by all the poems, and versions of poems, that he wrote.

5

Creative Plagiarism: The Case of Coleridge

Although nobody can even imagine the first work of literature ever written, it seems safe to say—and, wherever texts exist, it is demonstrable—that every subsequent work to some extent draws on and derives from other works that precede it. This is a solidly established fact of literary history, so much so that scholarly or critical consideration of a work apart from the vast array of underlying sources and influences is virtually impossible. Wordsworth, generally viewed as one of the most original writers in English, cannot properly be understood without knowledge of Milton and a host of earlier and later predecessors, and a similar network of relationships is more or less taken for granted with every other writer worth our attention.[1] All extant works are composites of previously existing materials *plus* what Wordsworth, attempting to define "genius" in his "Essay, Supplementary to the Preface" (1815), described as "the introduction of a new element into the intellectual universe: or . . . the application of powers to objects on which they had not before been exercised, or the employment of them in such a manner as to produce effects hitherto unknown."[2] As I have already suggested near the beginning of the preceding chapter, when these "previously existing materials" are literary, and especially when they are conspicuously present as a contribution to the intellectual, stylistic, dramatic, or narrative complexity of a work that draws on them, it is not unreasonable, at least in theory, to identify them as components of the authorship of the work.

In this contrived but quite practical sense, every work is necessarily the product of multiple authorship. Recent theoretical discussions where "intertextuality" substitutes for "source and influence" make this inevitably joint aspect of literary production even clearer. But obviously some situations of intertextuality or authorship-via-sources are more interesting than others, and possibly the most interesting of all is the case of Coleridge, who has frequently been the focus in source studies for several reasons. One of these is Coleridge's own authorship—at least in part—of the shortest, most cryptic, and most famous definition of creative imagination in modern times, those tantalizing sentences near the end of chapter 13 of *Biographia Literaria* describing the activity of the "secondary Imagination": "It dissolves, diffuses, dissipates, in order to re-create; or where this process is rendered impossible, yet still at all events it struggles to idealize and to unify. It is essentially *vital,* even as all objects (*as* objects) are essentially fixed and dead."[3] For several decades, beginning in the late 1920s with the publication of John Livingston Lowes's tremendously influential exploration of Coleridge's sources for *The Rime of the Ancient Mariner,*[4] this passage was read as a summary account of the transforming interaction between individual literary genius and the inert repository of source materials and, even thus obscure, was routinely offered as a basic theory to justify the activity of source study.

Another reason for Coleridge's prominence in source studies is his acute awareness of, and frequent reference to, questions of origins and originality—and the practical and moral problems of derivativeness and plagiarism—in both his own and other writers' creations. His earliest poem still widely read, *The Eolian Harp,* ponders and dramatizes the sources of our ideas of life, joy, unity, and even divinity in the world; his best later poems (*This Lime-Tree Bower My Prison, The Ancient Mariner, Frost at Midnight*) continue the investigation of the mind's, or imagination's, ability to connect with those sources; and his latest poem still widely read, *Dejection: An Ode,* laments the loss of contact through suspension of the speaker's "shaping spirit of Imagination."[5] In none of these poems is the speaker referring to literary sources, but the repeated concern with epistemological problems— how we get our information, ideas, and images, how we relate to any part of the otherness surrounding us—has an immediate relevance. For Coleridge and Wordsworth alike (see, for example, *The Prelude* 5.586–607), books were not represented as categorically different from nature as sources of information, ideas, and images; readers interact imaginatively with "the great Nature that exists in works / Of mighty Poets" (Wordsworth's phrase) in the same way that perceiving minds interact creatively with "living Nature" itself.

Coleridge refers to his own supposed literary sources in several works—for example, in the *Waste Land*–like scholarly gloss to *The*

Ancient Mariner line 132, identifying "the Spirit that plagued us so" as "one of the invisible inhabitants of this planet, neither departed souls nor angels; concerning whom the learned Jew, Josephus, and the Platonic Constantinopolitan, Michael Psellus, may be consulted," and in the explanation, with quotation, of his reading of Purchas's *Pilgrimage* in the prefatory account of the composition of *Kubla Khan.* Coleridge's public and private prose fairly bristles with references to sources, influences, borrowings, and plagiarisms. A famous letter of December 1811, for instance, discusses this last category for several pages, beginning with the affirmation that he has "ever held parallelisms adduced in proof of plagiarism or even of intentional imitation, in the utmost contempt" and then going on to distinguish between "two Kinds of Heads in the world of Literature. The one I would call, SPRINGS: the other TANKS." The ostensible subject of the letter is Sir Walter Scott's imitation, in *The Lay of the Last Minstrel* (1805), of the distinctive metrical scheme of Coleridge's then-unpublished *Christabel,* which Scott had heard recited from a manuscript text in 1803.[6] Coleridge used the images of spring ("rill") and tank again in the preface to *Christabel* when he finally published the unfinished work in 1816:

> The dates [of composition of the two parts, said to be 1797 and 1800] are mentioned for the exclusive purpose of precluding charges of plagiarism or servile imitation from myself. For there is amongst us a set of critics, who seem to hold, that every possible thought and image is traditional; who have no notion that there are such things as fountains in the world, small as well as great; and who would therefore charitably derive every rill they behold flowing, from a perforation made in some other man's tank.

And then there is the perennial matter of Coleridge's own plagiarisms and the still unsettled question of whether he was ultimately, in his own words just quoted, spring or tank (or some more complicated mechanism mediating between the two) in his philosophical and critical writings. It has been known at least since the 1830s that, here and there in his works, especially in his lectures and in *Biographia Literaria,* he appropriated without acknowledgment—in a word, stole—sizable passages from F. W. J. von Schelling, A. W. von Schlegel, J. G. E. Maass, Immanuel Kant, J. G. Fichte, and other German philosophers. His reliance on these writers, or at least his use of them, is extensive; it includes both large ideas and minute particulars of illustrative example and phrasing (sometimes translated verbatim) and frequently occurs in or near passages in which he emphasizes his own originality or attacks the derivativeness of other writers and thinkers. His admirers have had a difficult time especially with the moral aspects of this strange practice; here is a situation in which sources and influences not only underlie but seem to *become* the works on which they exert their effect, and Coleridge's sole authorship of some of the ideas and writings for which he is most renowned is repeatedly overshadowed by questions concerning both his originality and his honesty. His plagiarisms constitute a unique form of multiple authorship in English literature; no other author as eminent as Coleridge seems to have written in this way.[7] But calling them unique, as the Coleridgeans themselves are well aware, does not make them disappear.

1

The distinctive character of the plagiarisms may be highlighted by some preliminary instances of Coleridge's use of sources in a more conventional (and generally more acceptable) manner. There are of course thousands of examples readily available, ranging from pointed allusions that Coleridge expected his readers to recognize immediately—as in the near quotation of Samson's "my genial spirits droop" (*Samson Agonistes* 594) at the beginning of the third stanza of *Dejection: An Ode* ("My genial spirits fail," 39) and the elaborate reference to Wordsworth's *Lucy Gray* at the end of the seventh stanza of the same poem:

> . . . the tender lay,—
> 'Tis of a little child
> Upon a lonesome wild,
> Not far from home, but she hath lost her way:
> And now moans low in bitter grief and fear,
> And now screams loud, and hopes to make her mother hear
>
> (120–25)

—to a type of echo or "borrowing" that may have been completely unconscious on both sides of the author–reader transaction, as in the connection between "I would build that dome in air" in *Kubla Khan* (46) and Michelangelo's reported boast that in the design of St. Peter's, in Rome, he would build or raise the dome of the Pantheon "in the air."[8] Quite apart from whatever light may (or may not) be thrown on the process of poetic composition or the historical assemblage of reading matter, the principal value of relating such passages to their sources lies in the additional meanings that the passages thereby take on: the desperate plight (likenable to the doomed Samson's) of the speaker in *Dejection;* his sentimental depiction of loneliness, grief, and fear (the situation of the lost child in *Lucy Gray*) along with a tinge of envy (Coleridge's own, in contemplating the much more successful career of Wordsworth); the bolstered context of artistic creativity (by reference to one of Michelangelo's most admired achievements) in *Kubla Khan.*

For an extended example, consider the opening paragraph of the finest of Coleridge's "Conversation poems," *Frost at Midnight,* written in February 1798:

> The Frost performs its secret ministry,
> Unhelped by any wind. The owlet's cry
> Came loud—and hark, again! loud as before.
> The inmates of my cottage, all at rest,
> Have left me to that solitude, which suits   5
> Abstruser musings: save that at my side
> My cradled infant slumbers peacefully.
> 'Tis calm indeed! so calm, that it disturbs
> And vexes meditation with its strange
> And extreme silentness. Sea, hill, and wood,   10
> This populous village! Sea, and hill, and wood,
> With all the numberless goings-on of life,
> Inaudible as dreams! the thin blue flame
> Lies on my low-burnt fire, and quivers not;
> Only that film, which fluttered on the grate,   15
> Still flutters there, the sole unquiet thing.
> Methinks, its motion in this hush of nature
> Gives it dim sympathies with me who live,
> Making it a companionable form,
> Whose puny flaps and freaks the idling Spirit   20
> By its own moods interprets, every where
> Echo or mirror seeking of itself,
> And makes a toy of Thought.[9]

The second of the poem's four paragraphs (23–43), taking off from the reference to the "film" of soot in lines 15–16 and the superstition (which Coleridge explained in a note in the first two printings) that such a phenomenon portends the arrival of an absent relative or friend, relates incidents from the speaker's childhood days at school (and also recollections from times still earlier, before he had left his "sweet birthplace"). The third paragraph (44–64), addressed to the "cradled infant" of 6–7 (in an autobiographical scheme Coleridge's first son, Hartley, then aged seventeen months), contrasts the speaker's confined upbringing—"I was reared / In the great city, pent 'mid cloisters dim, / And saw nought lovely but the sky and stars"—with the greater freedom and richer experience that he imagines his son will enjoy "wander-[ing] like a breeze / By lakes and sandy shores, beneath the crags / Of ancient mountain." The final lines (65–74) use general blessing of the son ("Therefore all seasons shall be sweet to thee") as a means of returning to the descriptive details of the beginning ("secret ministry of frost . . . silent icicles, / Quietly shining to the quiet Moon").

Frost at Midnight is one of those "greater Romantic lyrics" susceptible of many different interpretations.[10] There are, among other features, at least four levels of time in the poem (the present, two or more pasts, and an indefinite future); social and family motifs; a great many images of nature; a pointed contrast of urban and rural situations; a general concern with education ("school," "stern preceptor," the son's "learn[ing] far other lore," God as "Great universal Teacher"); and steady attention to mental processes (meditation, dreaming, gazing, thinking, seeing, hearing). Like Wordsworth's *Tintern Abbey,* which followed five months later, imitating its form, structure, and style, Coleridge's poem seeks both to celebrate nature (with implicit and explicit representation of the human mind's successful contact with the external world) and, at the same time, to express dissatisfaction with some aspect of the speaker's present situation. Just as with Wordsworth's ruminative lyric, these conflicting tendencies in *Frost at Midnight* frustrate attempts at a unified reading.

Let me suggest, to make my point concerning one of Coleridge's sources in the poem, that the basic contrast in *Frost at Midnight* is the difference between the speaker's recollected upbringing in the city and his son's prospective upbringing in nature and, correspondingly, that the structure is a series of movements from confinement (the speaker indoors, in the schoolroom, in the city) to an opening-out (the son's growing up among lakes and mountains); from the mind's fancying ("idling Spirit," "toy of Thought," childhood dreams and superstition) to reciprocal contact with nature; from "Echo or mirror" solipsism (20–22) to an apprehension of "God . . . in all, and all things in himself" (60–62).[11] Such a view of the poem depends in large part on one's interpretation of the opening paragraph—the twenty-three lines quoted above—and more specifically on the idea that Coleridge is *deprecating* the mental activity that he depicts in lines 20–23 (and, in the contrast, valorizing the creative interaction with nature that he foresees for his son in 58–64). Critics are divided concerning Coleridge's tone and intention in the passage, and it is here that I think knowledge of a source can be of considerable help. The source that I have in mind is the following from Cowper's *The Task*, book 4 ("The Winter Evening"), first published in 1785:

> Me oft has fancy, ludicrous and wild,
> Sooth'd with a waking dream of houses, tow'rs,
> Trees, churches, and strange visages, express'd
> In the red cinders, while with poring eye
> I gaz'd, myself creating what I saw.   290
> Nor less amus'd have I quiescent watch'd
> The sooty films that play upon the bars,
> Pendulous, and foreboding, in the view
> Of superstition, prophesying still,
> Though still deceiv'd, some stranger's near approach.   295
> 'Tis thus the understanding takes repose
> In indolent vacuity of thought,
> And sleeps and is refresh'd. Meanwhile the face
> Conceals the mood lethargic with a mask
> Of deep deliberation, as the man   300
> Were task'd to his full strength, absorb'd and lost.
> Thus oft, reclin'd at ease, I lose an hour
> At ev'ning, till at length the freezing blast,
> That sweeps the bolted shutter, summons home
> The recollected pow'rs; and, snapping short   305
> The glassy threads, with which the fancy weaves
> Her brittle toys, restores me to myself.
> How calm is my recess; and how the frost,
> Raging abroad, and the rough wind, endear
> The silence and the warmth enjoy'd within![12]   310

Similarities between Cowper's and Coleridge's passages are immediately obvious. Cowper's speaker is indoors on a frosty evening gazing at a fire, fancifully creating visions of a town and the townspeople, and indulging himself in the same superstition concerning the film of soot and a "stranger's near approach" (Coleridge calls the film "that fluttering *stranger*" in line 26). There is a "freezing blast" outside (cf. Coleridge's "trances of the blast" in line 71), and "the frost, /

Raging abroad" at the end of Cowper's lines contrasts with the "calmness" of the speaker's "recess," "The silence and the warmth . . . within." Most pertinent, of course, are Cowper's mildly self-mocking descriptions of his speaker's mental processes: "fancy, ludicrous and wild," "waking dream," "myself creating what I saw," "indolent vacuity of thought," and fancy's "glassy threads" and "brittle toys"— virtually all of which may be seen to have some counterpart in Coleridge's own descriptions. It is certain that Coleridge knew Cowper's lines: Cowper was, at the time, England's most distinguished and most popular living poet, and William Hazlitt tells that Coleridge "spoke of Cowper as the best modern poet" within just a few months of the composition of *Frost at Midnight*.[13] There is no question that the passage was a major source for Coleridge's poem.

None of this can be taken to prove that Coleridge's speaker is adopting the Cowper speaker's belittling view of his mental processes (indeed Humphry House, in pointing out the connection with Cowper's lines, argues just the opposite). But Coleridge's documented familiarity with Cowper's work makes it impossible that he could have written the opening paragraph of *Frost at Midnight* without awareness of what Cowper had done in a similar context only a few years earlier. The consequence, stated in simplest terms, is that Coleridge had to be either (1) consciously taking over and reproducing the Cowper speaker's attitude or (2) consciously departing from it. While each of the alternatives can in some degree be defended, I think it would be easier to argue the former. Knowledge of Cowper's lines has the effect of emphasizing the points of similarity in Coleridge's poem and in particular of calling special attention to the tone and implications of Coleridge's "puny flaps and freaks," "idling Spirit," "Echo or mirror seeking of itself," and "toy of Thought" in lines 20–23. Cowper's lines thus offer (or, if the offer is not needed, help circumstantially confirm) a critical hypothesis about Coleridge's poem: maybe Coleridge's speaker is not entirely happy with his mental processes; maybe he wishes he had had richer experiences with nature; maybe the sleeping infant, his son, will do better; and so on. Such an interpretive line can be thought up and pursued without knowledge of the Cowper passage, but it comes more readily, and in general "works" more satisfactorily, when the two texts are brought together.

The connection of Coleridge's lines with Cowper's is a standard instance of the relationship of text to source, as is my use here of the precursor text as an aid to interpretation. Within the terms of this study, Cowper is evidently one of the authors of *Frost at Midnight*.

2

Why, then, should Coleridge's plagiarisms in his prose—the stealthy borrowings that have given the Coleridgeans so much trouble—be quite another matter? These plagiarisms involve the wholesale incorporation of other writers' ideas and words, and even the scholarly trappings of illustrative citation and documentation. A paragraph on the mutual truths of philosophical systems in chapter 12 of *Biographia Literaria,* to use an example featured prominently in recent reviews of the comprehensively annotated new edition by James Engell and W. J. Bate, formerly was read as the product of Coleridge's wide reading and deep thinking; more recently was shown (by Thomas McFarland) to be a combination of three different passages from Leibniz, two of which Coleridge represents in English and the third in French; and now is revealed (in Engell's detailed notes) to be made up of verbatim translations from a single source in German, F. H. Jacobi's *Über die Lehre des Spinoza* (1789 edition), where two of the Leibniz passages are given in German and the third (just as in *Biographia Literaria*) is left in French.[14]

This may be an extreme instance, because of the complicatedness of Coleridge's lifting one German writer's quotations from another German writer's original works in French, but the disguised appropriations more generally in *Biographia Literaria* are numerous and substantial. Engell's appendix A, "Unacknowledged Uses of German Works in Chapters 5–9, 12–13" (2:251–54), divides the borrowings into four categories: direct translation, close paraphrase, loose paraphrase, and "Material Summarised (but reworded)." Coleridge's indebtedness in the four categories adds up to 34 percent of the text in chapter 8 and perhaps as much as 40 percent in chapter 12; the combined total for the seven chapters surveyed in the appendix is close to 25 percent—and, as Norman Fruman points out, the individual and total proportions would be considerably increased if one set aside "anecdotes, quotations, digressive footnotes, and all other matter which is irrelevant to the question of Coleridge's originality."[15]

Coleridge's greatest indebtedness of this sort is to Schelling, whose *System des transscendentalen Idealismus* (1800) and *Abhandlungen zur Erläuterung des Idealismus der Wissenschaftslehre* (in a text of 1809) are drawn on heavily in chapters 8, 9, 12, and 13 of *Biographia Literaria.* Other sources cited frequently in Engell's introduction and notes, but rarely acknowledged in Coleridge's text, include Maass's *Versuch über die Einbildungskraft* (revised edition of

1797) and several works by Kant and Fichte. McFarland has identified a source (containing "repeatedly the exact words used by Coleridge") for the famous descriptions of primary imagination, secondary imagination, and fancy at the end of chapter 13: J. N.
Tetens's *Philosophische Versuche über die menschliche Natur und ihre Entwick-
lung* (1777). Fruman and earlier scholars have found a great many
plagiarized sources for other works—for example, W. G. Tennemann
for Coleridge's philosophical lectures of 1818–19, Schelling and Hein-
rich Steffens for the writings on science and the posthumously published *Theory of Life,* and Schlegel in abundance for some of the best-
known Shakespeare criticism (including much of the wording for
"Coleridge's" distinction between organic and mechanical form).[16]
Engell, contemplating the borrowings in *Biographia Literaria,* suggests that we "are not dealing—or at least not dealing primarily—
with orderly blocks of verbatim translation, but something more like
a chemical compound" (1:cxx). Whether chemical compound or
piecemeal mechanical compilation, however, it is a compositional
procedure that brings disgrace and disciplinary action when students
are caught doing it in college courses.

Thomas De Quincey, a onetime friend and a notable plagiarist
and opium-eater in his own right, was the first (publicly) to charge
Coleridge with plagiarism, in the opening installment of an essay in
Tait's Edinburgh Magazine, September 1834, two months after Coleridge's death. His aim, he says mildly enough at the beginning of the
two pages that he gives to the matter, is "to forestal . . . other discov-
erers who would make a more unfriendly use of the discovery," but
his subsequent description of Coleridge's "real and palpable plagiarism" takes on a Heepish tone—"what was my astonishment, to find
that the entire essay [chapter 12 of *Biographia Literaria*] from the first
word to the last, is a *verbatim* translation from Schelling, with no
attempt in a single instance to appropriate the paper, by developing
the arguments or by diversifying the illustrations!"—and concludes as
serious accusation: "this was a barefaced plagiarism, which could in
prudence have been risked only by relying too much upon the slight
knowledge of German literature in this country."[17]

Five and a half years later, in the lead article of the March 1840
issue of *Blackwood's,* entitled "The Plagiarisms of S. T. Coleridge,"
J. F. Ferrier, a philosopher soon to become professor of civil history
at Edinburgh, devoted thirteen closely printed pages (and considerable vehemence) to Coleridge's unacknowledged borrowings from
Schelling and Maass. In 1846 the philosopher Sir William Hamilton,

citing the essay by "my friend Professor Ferrier," added further details of Coleridge's "blundering plagiarism, from Maass" in his edition of Thomas Reid.[18] The principal defender of Coleridge in the nineteenth century was his daughter, Sara, who in editing *Biographia Literaria* for a new edition of 1847 confronted Ferrier directly, giving the first forty-four pages of her introduction to a point-by-point refutation (under the heading "Mr. Coleridge's Obligations to Schelling, and the Unfair View of the Subject Presented in Blackwood's Magazine") and then, in her annotations to Coleridge's text, providing copious citations of Schelling, Maass, and others in translation.[19] Like some later would-be rescuers of Coleridge, she combines forceful rhetoric with open display of the borrowings to good effect.

In the first six decades of the twentieth century, the most notable assailants were René Wellek and Joseph Warren Beach. Wellek's contempt for Coleridge as an original thinker initially appears in chapter 3 ("Samuel Taylor Coleridge and Kant") of the 1931 study *Immanuel Kant in England* (for example, "Coleridge has little insight into the incompatiblity of different trends of thought. . . . It is not the fact that several central passages in Coleridge are borrowed or paraphrased or influenced by other thinkers; it is rather the circumstance that these adaptations of other thought are heterogeneous, incoherent and even contradictory which makes the study of Coleridge's philosophy so futile") and pervades several subsequent writings—for instance, Wellek's survey of scholarship in "Coleridge's Philosophy and Criticism" in the first three editions of the MLA-sponsored *English Romantic Poets: A Review of Research,* beginning in 1950, and his Coleridge chapter in the second volume of *A History of Modern Criticism* in 1955 (which, while expatiating on the derivativeness, looseness, and inconsistency of his thinking, does finally acknowledge Coleridge's "importance for the transmission of German literary ideas to the English-speaking world . . . especially today when the German romantics have almost disappeared from the horizon").[20]

Beach's contribution, a 1942 *ELH* article entitled "Coleridge's Borrowings from the German," is a powerful account—rather in the manner of Ferrier, but with considerably more evidence—of appropriations mainly from Schelling, Steffens, and Schlegel. Beach is especially disdainful of the passage in *Biographia Literaria* (toward the end of chapter 9) in which Coleridge defends himself in advance against "ungenerous concealment or intentional plagiarism" on the grounds that he regards "truth as a divine ventriloquist: I care not from whose mouth the sounds are supposed to proceed, if only the words are audible and intelligible." "What a curious mixture," exclaims Beach, "of cunning, false humility, self-congratulation, and general confusion of mind! It is thus that Coleridge salves his conscience once for all, and at the same time prepares an eternal alibi."[21] Wellek and Beach made strong cases; the notable defenders at this time were, in effect, the numerous writers on Coleridge's philosophy and criticism who responded not by refuting but simply by ignoring them. In retrospect there seems to have been a clear division between scholars who could read German and those who could not; Wellek and Beach were in the former group, and Coleridge's faithful supporters in the latter.

Then in 1969 and 1971 appeared three works of a much more sophisticated (and some would say sophistical) character—McFarland's *Coleridge and the Pantheist Tradition,* published in July 1969; G. N. G. Orsini's *Coleridge and German Idealism,* published in August 1969; and Fruman's *Coleridge, the Damaged Archangel,* published in December 1971. The greater sophistication of McFarland and Orsini lies in their strong belief, even while acknowledging (and even increasing) the extent of the borrowings, that Coleridge was an original thinker. Orsini in his preface pokes fun at "purely literary scholars" who "still poohpooh Coleridge's indebtedness to Schelling and shrug away his derivations from Kant. Ideas which Coleridge obtained indubitably from the Germans are still extolled as his original creations"—and then, in the very next paragraph, announces his "firm conviction, ever since the year 1923 when I first read the *Biographia Literaria,* that Coleridge *is* a genius, and I believe that a genius can be creative even when he is borrowing." In his first Schelling chapter, maintaining that Coleridge's use of "Schelling's arguments and ideas in . . . [*Biographia Literaria*] practically without acknowledgment, does not support the charge of plagiarism," Orsini writes,

> This is not a matter of plagiarism, but a case of assimilation, carried out in a peculiar manner due to Coleridge's special conditions. To put it in the simplest terms, Coleridge was a peculiar genius. . . . He borrowed, but he usually borrowed creatively, incorporating other men's views with his own views as bricks in a wall, and reaching ultimate conclusions which were essentially his own. . . . The fact that Coleridge incorporated so much of Schelling in his own book, either by translation or

adaptation, simply means that, at that time, he accepted Schelling's arguments and adopted his philosophy.[22]

McFarland would disagree with this last statement but nevertheless takes the same general line concerning Coleridge's originality and the depth and breadth of his learning. He argues that since originality is not a principal value in philosophy, as it is in literature and art, "the concept of 'plagiarism' cannot stand the stress of historical examination" (p. 45); Coleridge's thinking differs from, and rises above, the ideas in his unacknowledged sources, and his philosophy is best considered as a "reticulation," a "mosaic," or an organic compound of given materials. Coleridge's various deceitful practices—lies, misdirections, failures to acknowledge, and the like—should be viewed as psychological curiosities *apart from* the integrity of his philosophy.

Some of this is ingenious, to be sure. McFarland's excursus note 1, on Coleridge's debt to Schlegel (pp. 256–61), is typical of his method in the book more generally and also in his various subsequent writings on Coleridge's originality. The basic question addressed in the note is whether Coleridge derived his concept of "organic form" from Schlegel's dramatic lectures. McFarland begins with detailed display, principally from earlier scholarship by Raysor and Orsini, of Coleridge's word-for-word translations of Schlegel. He then faults both Raysor and Orsini for not being severe enough on Coleridge (Raysor, he says, gives the wrong impression that Coleridge did something more than merely translate; Orsini regarded the relationship as "literary influence," not plagiarism). Just when McFarland seems about to pronounce sentence on Coleridge, however, there is an abrupt introduction of mitigating explanations: Coleridge did not need Schlegel; he knew about organic form already; Schlegel did not invent the idea— "Organic form, in short, was every intellectual's possession." McFarland documents this statement at length and concludes, "These citations alone invalidate any belief that A. W. Schlegel originated the idea or introduced Coleridge to it." What McFarland does not return to, or ever really explain, is the troublesome matter that he started with—Coleridge's unacknowledged word-for-word translations of Schlegel.

Orsini's and McFarland's studies are among the standard works on Coleridge; Fruman's *Coleridge, the Damaged Archangel*, however, is something more than just that. An energetically written work, with seemingly scandalous revelations concerning Coleridge on nearly every page, it was widely reviewed in the United States—usually with intense expressions of either acclaim or outrage in both the popular and scholarly press—and when it was issued in London by George Allen and Unwin in 1972, the two hundredth anniversary of Coleridge's birth, it was (to the dismay of many who were celebrating the occasion) "the chief publishing event to mark the bicentenary in England."[23]

The sophistication of Fruman, who announces that he completed the final chapter of his study in June 1969 and has "not taken note of any of the books and articles on Coleridge that have appeared since then" (p. ix)—including, as hostile reviewers pointed out, the two recent books by McFarland and Orsini most relevant to his own subject—lies in the combination of devastating exposure, moral indignation, and (especially in the psychoanalytical inquiry into the causes of Coleridge's strange behavior) considerable compassion for the man. As more than one reviewer noticed, Fruman's prolonged investigation, with its massive documentation (the notes alone amount to 140 pages of very small print), has the effect of making Coleridge both more real and more human than he is usually portrayed: "this Coleridge [writes one] is more immediate and more alive for us than either the dreary monologist of nineteenth-century tradition or the masterful poet and man of ideas . . . of twentieth-century tradition. And I suspect that the Coleridge Fruman fleshed in for us is closer to the man the Wordsworths loved and lamented."[24]

Fruman's work was, to speak broadly, admired by the amateurs and general critics who wrote about it, and also by scholars in fields other than Romanticism or with other specialties besides Coleridge. Thomas Lask, for example, in a *New York Times* review that was reprinted in Washington and Paris newspapers, called it "one of the most exciting [books] I have read in years," comparing it with Dewey's *Art as Experience,* Dover Wilson's *What Happens in "Hamlet,"* and Bernard Knox's *Oedipus at Thebes:*

> No book I think will do more to indicate the dimensions of the "problem of Coleridge" than Mr. Fruman's. In the process he will make every reader rethink his conclusions as to the nature and meaning of the Romantic movement, the nationalism of literature, the trustworthiness of literary evidence, the relation of language to the ideas and sensibility of an age. . . . The book has one unpredictable effect. It brings the man very close.

Cyril Connolly in the London *Sunday Times* praised it as a "long, close-textured, deeply researched and powerful study. . . . Professor Fruman's exposition of the borrowings from Schelling, Schlegel, Tennemann and Kant seems to me incontrovertible," while for Anthony West in the *New Statesman* it was "a splendid example of American scholarship at its very best. . . . It's as exciting a book as John Livingston Lowes's *The Road to Xanadu* was in its day, and a good deal more penetrating." Other admiring reviewers include Paul West, the novelist (in *Book World*); Hugh Kenner, the Pound and Eliot critic (in the *Los Angeles Times Book Review*); Robert E. Spiller, the historian of American literature (in the Philadelphia *Sunday Bulletin*); and anonymous writers in the *Economist* ("We put down the massive study with a feeling of intense sympathy for a man whose great intellectual powers were so often perverted by his appalling emotional insecurity. . . . [The book] is far from being a work of destruction, and will not break the spell that Coleridge the man and poet exercises over twentieth-century readers") and the London *Times Literary Supplement* ("a work of considerable importance which present and future Coleridgeans cannot afford to ignore," "a wealth of carefully reasoned proof," "brilliant demonstration"). Christopher Ricks and Geoffrey Hartman gave it mixed reviews, mostly expatiating on some general implications that Fruman should have followed up concerning art as forgery and imposture, but also, since they were writing in the *Saturday Review* and the *New York Times Book Review,* gave it additional prominence for the notice of general readers. George Steiner wrote a long and thoughtful piece about it in the *New Yorker.*[25]

In contrast, the reception by the professional Coleridgeans (and the professional Coleridge-on-Shakespeareans) was almost uniformly negative. L. C. Knights in the *New York Review of Books* faulted Fruman for numerous wrong and misleading emphases. Owen Barfield in the *Nation,* calling the book an "eddy" of "quite startling hatred" and an "abyss of incomprehension," declared that Fruman's charges were simply unanswerable. Roy Park wrote in the first of two reviews, in the *Listener,* that Fruman "smashes through the oeuvre with the delicacy of an enraged bull-elephant, leaving little if anything standing," and in a second, in the *British Journal of Aesthetics,* that, apart from serving as a "source-book of what might be termed the anti-Coleridge lobby . . . the book is of little interest to students of Coleridge's poetry, criticism, philosophy or aesthetics." Richard H. Fogle in the *Virginia Quarterly Review* took a sarcastic tone: "Mr. Fruman, despite his profound respect and deep personal affection, steadily maintains that [Coleridge] was a fraud, a sham, a plagiarist, and a liar—qualities which he presumably finds endearing." J. B. Beer in the *Review of English Studies* mainly focused on Fruman's lack of "the sensitivity and discrimination that are the hallmark of humane criticism": "Coleridge's is a mind distinguished particularly by its processes—and to these processes Mr. Fruman seems totally unresponsive." Elinor Shaffer in the *Southern Humanities Review* went straight to the point:

> this is a bad book: crass, sensational, unoriginal, using texts and secondary material in a biased and unfair manner, ignorant of the very sources it charges Coleridge with having plundered, loaded with psychological innuendo which the author sees fit to equate with moral indictment—a Know-nothing of a book, whose animus is not merely against Coleridge but against all ideas.

R. A. Foakes in *Essays in Criticism* protested the enthusiastic praise with which Basil Cottle had reviewed the book in the same journal a year earlier—"It is depressing to find that your reviewer . . . swallowed Fruman's book with relish"—and, while allowing that Fruman "has built up a massive indictment, the details of which are so many and so apparently convincing that his case is superficially overwhelming," pointed out a number of Fruman's mistakes, shortsightednesses, and prejudices connected with those details. Finally (in this selected survey) Thomas McFarland in a thirty-five-page review essay in the *Yale Review,* describing the work as "a dismayingly inadequate book: amateurish in its handling of ideas, uncontrolled in its tone, derivative in the research on which its conclusions are based, and tendentious to a degree almost not to be credited," charged Fruman with "selectivities that verge on suppression," "vital omissions," "distortions," "forcings of evidence," deficiencies in cultural sophistication, contradictions of statement and detail and procedure, unworthy motivation, and failure to cite McFarland's own work, among other shortcomings.[26]

Now it might be supposed, since these were Coleridge experts who were assailing it so vigorously, that *Coleridge, the Damaged Archangel* was, as Shaffer said and the others more than implied, a bad book, and that the nonspecialists who praised it so highly simply did not know their Coleridge. But the Coleridgeans had personal and career interests at stake. Knights had recently written on Coleridge's notions of idea and symbol, and another critic had placed Knights himself in the Coleridgean tradition of Shakespeare critics, a tradition now publicly tainted with plagiarism. Barfield had just produced the modestly titled *What Coleridge Thought* (1971), a large book that says hardly a word about what Coleridge stole. Park had recently published several articles on Coleridge's philosophy and aesthetics. Fogle was the author of *The Idea of Coleridge's Criticism* (1962). Beer was known at the time for *Coleridge the Visionary* (1959) and a number of essays. Shaffer had several years earlier completed a Ph.D. dissertation entitled "Studies in Coleridge's Aesthetics" and more recently (1969–70) had published a handful of articles based on it. Foakes had just edited *Coleridge on Shakespeare: The Text of the Lectures of 1811–12* (1971) and had agreed to edit the lectures on literature for the Collected Coleridge.[27] McFarland's involvement with Coleridge and his sources, begun in *Coleridge and the Pantheist Tradition,* was a continuing occupation that would lead to several other significant publications, including *Originality and Imagination* (1985).

For all these reviewers (except McFarland, who made his discoveries independently and took a different interpretive line), the very subject matter of their professional concerns, the unitary author Coleridge, was being called into question. The philosophical and critical prose hitherto attributed solely to Coleridge had suddenly—and all the more embarrassingly because of the public attention Fruman was receiving—become an untrustworthy composite authorship consisting of Coleridge and his unacknowledged German sources. The Coleridgeans who had written mainly on the poetry—Max Schulz, for example, author of *The Poetic Voices of Coleridge* (1963), who reviewed Fruman favorably in *Modern Philology*[28]—were very little affected, because the poetry that anyone cared about was never threatened; Coleridge really does seem to have been the principal author of his best poems. But the scholars of Coleridge's prose appeared to have a serious problem. It is no wonder that they responded with bluster, sputter, and rage.

Their first solution was to adopt McFarland's mosaic metaphor and disregard or reject Fruman's *pastiche,* because the mosaic implied an author in the traditional or mythic sense. One critic, in a routine scholarly discussion of Coleridge's ideas, observes: "I am not going to concern myself with just what [Coleridge's] sources were—how far, for instance, he plagiarised from Schelling and the German *Naturphilosophen.* I think Professor McFarland has dealt perfectly with this question."[29] Another calls "McFarland's profound book . . . convincing in its conclusion that Coleridge was capable of developing independent positions and even using the verbal counters of other systems to think in a mosaic pattern."[30] Fruman's name does not figure prominently, and in many instances does not appear at all, in the scholarship of the later 1970s and early 1980s, including the volumes from those years in the Collected Coleridge. For about a decade, the preponderance of writers on Coleridge, just as in the days of Wellek and Beach, solved the problem, at least among themselves, by ignoring the charges and redefining the evidence.[31]

McFarland, as I have already suggested, has made notable contributions to the discussion. His central idea in *Coleridge and the Pantheist Tradition,* that "we are faced not with plagiarism, but with nothing less than a mode of composition—composition by mosaic organization rather than by painting on an empty canvas" (p. 27), has a certain attractiveness, even though subsequent research (as in the matter of Coleridge's chunkish use of Jacobi mentioned at the beginning of this section) has shown some of the tesserae to be rather larger than familiarity with mosaic art might lead one to expect. In *Originality and Imagination* McFarland comes closer to exploding the unitary-author theory by his proposal to add plagiarism "as an ugly duckling seventh" to the six types of "revisionary ratio" that Harold Bloom had devised to account for writers' responses to their literary precursors.[32]

Other interesting strategies to accommodate the issue of plagiarism within frameworks that depend on the myth of single authorship include theories advanced by Laurence Lockridge and Jerome Christensen. Lockridge, in *Coleridge the Moralist* (1977), resorts to an analogue based on drama or melodrama, the "phantom plagiarist," a self-defeating persona that Coleridge created in *Biographia Literaria* and other works as a "representative image" of intellectual fraud and ethical collapse—a device that enabled him to hide his real (interior) self and at the same time dramatize and confess his wrongdoing.[33] Christensen, in a 1977 *PMLA* essay revised in *Coleridge's Blessed Machine of Language* (1981), chooses an analogue from textual editing, the "marginal discourse." Taking a hint from an entry in one of Coleridge's early notebooks—"My nature requires another Nature for its support, & reposes only in another from the necessary Indigence of its Being"—Christensen outlines a method in which the plagiarized sources in effect serve as texts for Coleridge's explanatory annotations: "What Coleridge practices is not mosaic composition but marginal exegesis, not philosophy but commentary."[34] Occasionally, of course, the extent of the verbatim appropriations may seem to make the "marginal" commentary rather insignificant, or even nonexistent, but in general the suggestion has possibilities (and fits in agreeably, in classroom discussions, with Coleridge's editorializing commentary in the real marginal glosses that he added to the text of *The Ancient Mariner* beginning in 1817).

Then there are the purely biographical explanations, not so much to defend Coleridge from the charge of plagiarism as to provide an extenuating context of human weakness and difficult circumstances. The most prominent recent example appears in part 1 of the editors' introduction to the new *Biographia Literaria,* where, after remarking that the philosophical chapters "were finished in about a month," Bate continues:

> The fact has a direct bearing . . . above all, on the famous "plagiarisms". This is not to excuse the plagiarisms. But a distinction can be kept in mind between "excuse" and a mere explanation of circumstances that could seduce or frighten Coleridge into acts against which the cushions of leisure, financial security, calmer (or firmer) temperaments, or even sheer moralism would preserve others. In connection with the "plagiarisms" the reader should bear in mind the chronology of the work, the circumstances, the pressures to get it done rapidly, the self-doubts, the exhaustion.[35]

As Bate makes clear, the chronology supporting this view is in part based on a 1977 article in *Studies in Bibliography* by D. M. Fogel, a piece that Fruman, in his review of the Engell–Bate edition, charges with serious flaws in logic and interpretation of evidence ("There is *no* compelling reason," Fruman says, "to suppose that Chapters 12 and 13 [the philosophical chapters] were written last, and good reasons to think they were not").[36] Still it is easy to imagine that Coleridge's financial anxieties, self-doubts, and fatigue transcended the minuter details of 1815 chronology; there has to be a measure of general truth in Bate's explanation.

Fruman himself, attempting in various chapters of *Coleridge, the Damaged Archangel* to account for Coleridge's bizarre and self-destructive behavior, provides a great deal of biographical information and psychoanalytic speculation concerning the circumstances of *Biographia Literaria* and other writings, and his cumulative portrayal of Coleridge's life—surely one of the most miserable that we know in such detail—constitutes an extended apology for the plagiarisms and other misdeeds that he is exposing. And there is plenty of admiration for Coleridge the artist in Fruman's work. It is sometimes forgotten, in the reaction against his attacks on earlier scholars, how much light Fruman sheds on Coleridge's genius as a reader, appropriator, manipulator, obscurantist—not the same qualities for which he has been most highly praised and prized for much of the past century, but reckonable categories of achievement in their own right.

Whatever view one takes—composer of mosaics, designer of bricks in a wall, creator of chemical compounds, phantom plagiarist, marginal commentator, struggler against crushing circumstances, entrepreneurial genius—no one has yet been willing to designate Coleridge as purely a "tank" in relation to the sources that he raided. And indeed it is indisputable that Coleridge's writings have had a life, attractiveness, and consequent fame and influence that far surpass the works to which they are indebted. Fruman rightly claims (and his book overall demonstrates) that, even when the borrowings are fully exposed, Coleridge remains a "giant":

> No man of his time had so exalted a vision of the shape of humanistic studies. He was a great pioneer in introducing German thought to England. If in his surreptitiousness he often muddied the current, he also bequeathed to us the classic language in which many a particular formulation is remembered. It is difficult to think of a single important idea from the early nineteenth century in which Coleridge was somehow not involved. It is impossible to study any area of English thought in the Romantic period which does not somehow either proceed from, or very quickly get round to him. He stands in the mainstream of English literary history like a colossus, often obstructing the view, often diverting the currents nearby from their true course, but indispensably *there*.[37]

3

At present (the late 1980s) Coleridge's plagiarisms are very much out in the open. The editors of the new *Biographia Literaria* address "the vexed problem of plagiarism" on the first page of their preface, and in their annotations make a heroic attempt to give in full the German passages that Coleridge translated or paraphrased, along with copious reference to other sources that he appropriated more casually. "We present the facts, without the rhetoric of either defence or accusation," Engell writes in the introductory section on "The German Borrowings and the Issue of Plagiarism"; when he goes on to speak of Coleridge's weaving his material "into a larger context of his own, where 'the organic Whole' is greater than the sum of its parts" and subsequently describes Coleridge's method of composition as "fascinating and complex," his text as "an amazing trail left by his active mind," and his reading as "a perpetual stream of mind, more active than passive . . . a transfusive process" (1:cxviii, cxxix, cxxxi), one may suspect that some "rhetoric of . . . defence" has in fact crept in. But the emphasis throughout the edition is on Coleridge's use of his sources, and the plagiarisms are highlighted rather than obscured or suppressed in the scholarly apparatus.

Fruman, after a period of exile (as it were), now occupies a secure place among the leading American scholars of Romantic literature. He is among the contributors to *Coleridge's Imagination: Essays in Memory of Pete Laver,* edited by Richard Gravil, Lucy Newlyn, and Nicholas Roe (1985), a collection in which several other writers refer freely to Fruman and McFarland with roughly the same frequency and a uniform neutrality of tone.[38] Fruman is also a significant presence on several pages of Max Schulz's survey of Coleridge scholarship in the latest edition of the MLA-sponsored *The English Romantic Poets: A Review of Research and Criticism* (1985), and he was given nearly unlimited space for an authoritative review of the Engell–Bate *Biographia Literaria* in *Studies in Romanticism.*

As a result of Fruman's work, and with the examples of later 1970s critics like Lockridge and Christensen and the continuing attention given to the subject by McFarland, the plagiarisms are more frequently discussed, and more matter-of-factly taken into account, in the recent studies of Coleridge's prose. Yet the urge to see Coleridge's authorial stamp continues to propel the interpretations, and the word "plagiarism" is ultimately avoided or rejected. Here are some representative ways in which the plagiarisms are handled, or not handled, in a selection of books of the 1980s (I have already mentioned Christensen's 1981 *Coleridge's Blessed Machine of Language* in the preceding section).

Rosemary Ashton's *The German Idea* (1980), a study of Coleridge, Carlyle, G. H. Lewes, and George Eliot in their roles as introducers of German thought to the British, brings up the plagiarisms, along with references to De Quincey, Fruman, McFarland, and others, in the first paragraph of her Coleridge chapter. Ashton is not interested in "the minutiae of direct and indirect borrowings of 'ideas' or of verbal nuances": "the question of influence, foreign or not, on any writer must remain indeterminable," she says, and then quotes Shelley's famous statement that "all the best writers of any particular

age" show "a certain similarity . . . from the spirit of that age acting
on all"—without, however, bothering to explain how the spirit of the
age could sometimes, in the case of Coleridge, produce those certain
similarities in exactly the same (translated) words. Her thoroughgo-
ing survey of Coleridge's interactions with the Germans suggests a
new explanation—the British reviewers' hostility toward German literature in the first decade of the nineteenth century—for Coleridge's
suppression of the identity of some of his sources.[39]

In *Sources, Processes and Methods in Coleridge's "Biographia
Literaria"* (1980), Kathleen Wheeler discusses the plagiarisms briefly
in chapter 2 ("Philosophical Sources") and at greater length in chapter 5 ("Metaphor: Process and Method in *Biographia* [Volume] I").
Attempting to go beyond the mosaic method of McFarland and the
marginal method of Christensen, Wheeler pursues the interesting
idea (made clearer in the notes, where, rather in the manner of
Coleridge himself, she tells the reader what she is doing in the text)
that the unacknowledged quotations and borrowings are primarily
used symbolically, as "either metaphorical or as functioning as 'reader
recipes' . . . not for the sake of content or dogma, but for their role in
[Coleridge's] method of producing metaphoric situations." Paul Hamilton, in *Coleridge's Poetics* (1983), is another critic who takes the
plagiarisms not only in stride but into his interpretive scheme, reading
Biographia Literaria in terms of Coleridge's ideas of "desynonymy."
"Owing to the closed quality Coleridge attributed to his native philosophical tradition," Hamilton writes,

> he was always trying to incorporate within his own philosophy other
> forms of thought which would allow him a more flexible and open-
> ended definition of experience. These forms, however, sometimes ob-
> stinately retained their original shape and resisted assimilation. Instead
> of expanding the range of his thought from within, they often imposed
> on it from without, producing ragged contradictions and lumpish, half-
> digested plagiarisms. The unacknowledged quotation of Schelling in
> *Biographia* is the most obvious example.[40]

A more traditional (and reactionary) attitude may be seen in the
comprehensive and detailed work on Coleridge's scientific thinking
by Trevor H. Levere, *Poetry Realized in Nature: Samuel Taylor Coleridge and Early Nineteenth-Century Science* (1981). Levere, who is a
historian of science, had access to Engell's introduction and annotations to *Biographia Literaria* before the new edition was published

but seemingly refuses to take seriously their implications for his subject (and appears unaware of Fruman's work of ten years earlier containing a chapter on "*Theory of Life* and Coleridge's Writings on Science," which quotes Beach and other scholars to the effect that every one of Coleridge's scientific ideas in *Theory of Life* came from either Steffens or Schelling). Levere asserts, in his own introduction, that

> [Coleridge's] use of German sources in the years immediately following the composition of the *Biographia Literaria* is as significant in metascience as in other interdependent regions of his thought; here as elsewhere, Coleridge used his sources in ways that demonstrate understanding of the issues they confronted, moving frequently and perceptively beyond them. He used the facts of science, drawn from impeccable researches and reliable compendia, together with the ideas of philosophers, in working toward his own system.

Levere appends a note to this last sentence: "It is not appropriate to discuss here exaggerated charges of plagiarism. . . ."[41]

Catherine M. Wallace, in *The Design of "Biographia Literaria"* (1983), similarly brushes aside the problem with confident references to general and particular authority: "The plagiarisms from Schelling have been evaluated in general by Thomas McFarland, and in painstaking detail by Elinor Stoneman Shaffer, both of whom conclude that the literal appearance of plagiarism is misleading. In the light of recent scholarship, this traditionally *prima facie* evidence loses its impressive appearance." A note to the first of these sentences cites McFarland's *Coleridge and the Pantheist Tradition* and two works by Elinor Shaffer (her 1966 Columbia dissertation and a 1970 *Comparative Literature Studies* article extracted from it), but, just as in Levere's work, the "recent scholarship" does not include Fruman. Wallace's chapter 5, concentrating on the philosophical chapters 12 and 13 of *Biographia Literaria,* again cites McFarland and Shaffer, adds a reference to Orsini's *Coleridge and German Idealism* (the "most detailed and reliable analysis that judges C[oleridge] derivative"), and adopts the line, mainly Shaffer's, that the lengthy borrowings from Schelling do not constitute plagiarisms because Coleridge *disagreed* with the ideas that he borrowed (in Shaffer's words, in one of Wallace's quotations from her dissertation, "The fact that [Coleridge] often adopted whole phrases and passages literally is deceptive; the spirit, if not the letter, has been altered").[42]

A. J. Harding, in a study of Coleridge's religious ideas, *Coleridge and the Inspired Word* (1985), seems to waver on the issue. In chapter 2, "Beyond Nature: *Naturphilosophie* and Imagination," he describes the essay "On Poesy or Art" as "the fullest example we have of Coleridge's version of the organicist argument" and then adds: "As might be expected, it draws heavily on Schelling . . . but it is not a mere translation. Coleridge imitated not Schelling's results merely, but the very processes of his thought." Half a page later, however, we hear, concerning the question of a distinction between nature and the human soul, of "Coleridge's answer, or rather Schelling's." Subsequently Harding says that Coleridge "found [a] . . . basis" for certain of his ideas in the works of J. N. Tetens, and he uses the phrases "Schellingian prolegomenon," "Schellingian chapter," and "Schellingism" to characterize chapter 12 of *Biographia Literaria.*[43]

Raimonda Modiano, in *Coleridge and the Concept of Nature* (1985), a work closely related to the subject of Levere's book and Harding's chapter just mentioned, has lengthy discussions of Coleridge's reading of Kant, Schelling, Steffens, and other Germans and the relationship of his thinking to theirs, but not a hint concerning the unacknowledged verbatim borrowings. Her sole reference to the plagiarisms is tucked away in a note documenting the statement that "Orsini once marvelled at the extent to which Coleridge became converted to the doctrines of German transcendentalists, Kant and Schelling in particular": "See Orsini, *Coleridge and German Idealism,* pp. 219–20: 'The fact that Coleridge incorporated so much of Schelling in his own book, [*Biographia Literaria*] either by translation or adaptation, simply means that, at that time, he accepted Schelling's arguments and adopted his philosophy.' "[44]

As may be seen even in this skimming survey, some of the recent books on Coleridge's prose refer to the plagiarisms more openly than others; but all are alike in explicitly or implicitly assuming that Coleridge alone must be the author if these works are to be discussed. His conscious intentions must inform and control these works in order for their art and ideas to be subjects for understanding, explanation, and interpretation in terms of authorial design. Obviously, then, there is still considerable reluctance to confront the fact that other writers wrote words, sentences, and even whole pages of Coleridge's famous works. The answer to the question posed earlier in this chapter—why Coleridge's plagiarisms in his prose should constitute a unique problem—is that the myth of single authorship itself is at stake here. The plagiarized segments cannot be rejected, as might emendations or contributions by other hands, because they are clearly constitutive of the very fabric of the text. Yet failing to acknowledge these debts, Coleridge fails to free his work from them, so to speak—fails to author them. Thus the plagiarized texts have no author, or, if they have one, the author is not Coleridge. This being so, the plagiarisms will necessarily continue to be a problem for any critic attempting to evaluate or interpret the prose in which they occur.

6

Pound's Waste Land

One of the more tantalizing of the unsolvable questions in literary history is the precise nature of the collaboration between Wordsworth and Coleridge—the actual processes of their interaction, the proportionate shares of responsibility—in the celebrated work of the late 1790s that so radically affected the subsequent course of English poetry. The two men met in 1795, were neighbors and constant companions in Somersetshire in 1797 and 1798, and traveled together (in Germany and Scotland) and saw each other (in the Lake District) frequently thereafter. We have an enormous accumulation of contemporary and retrospective biographical detail in letters, journals, notebooks, and records of conversations. Some of that material would seem to speak to their collaboration—Wordsworth's urgent requests for Coleridge's help with *The Recluse,* for example, and a great many statements by both men concerning the composition of *The Ancient Mariner.*

In fact, however, we have no solid documentary evidence for any aspect of their practical working relationship (in the examples given, Wordsworth never received Coleridge's ideas for *The Recluse—*Coleridge says that he sent them from Malta but that his letter was destroyed by Gibraltar authorities when the English acquaintance to whom he had consigned it died of plague[1]—and the details for *The Ancient Mariner,* which in any case are inconsistent with one another, are sketchy). As a consequence, even the most assured critical statement on the subject is only a hypothesis, and the opinions vary widely for many different reasons, not excluding the individual critic's imaginative identification with one or the other of the principals and the consequent projection of the critic's own personality into the interpretation. At one extreme of generalization, there is H. W. Garrod's frequently quoted remark that "Coleridge may fairly be thought of as the guardian angel of Wordsworth's poetical genius. Perhaps, indeed, Coleridge's greatest work is Wordsworth—and, like all his other work, Coleridge left it unfinished." As an example of the other extreme, there is Norman Fruman's depiction of Coleridge's almost pathological dependence on the older poet: "whereas Wordsworth was perfectly capable of writing superbly in complete isolation, Coleridge seems scarcely to have been able to write independently at all, after separating from Wordsworth." Squarely in the middle are the descriptions by Thomas McFarland and Paul Magnuson, already mentioned in the introductory section of Chapter 4, of the Coleridge–Wordsworth intellectual relationship as a symbiosis or lyrical dialogue.[2] Nobody knows for sure what really went on.

It ought to be of more than passing interest, in this connection, to consider a similarly epoch-making literary collaboration between two important writers 120 years later—that of Ezra Pound and T. S. Eliot in the creation of *The Waste Land*. In this case we do have documentary evidence—Eliot's manuscripts with Pound's alterations and marginal criticisms, which have been in the Berg Collection of the New York Public Library since 1958 and were made widely available nearly two decades ago in a facsimile edition by Eliot's widow[3]—and we can thus strengthen our speculations with some detailed factual information. Both individually and as a pair, Pound and Eliot were very different persons from what we know of Wordsworth and Coleridge, to be sure. But still it is possible that our better-evidenced knowledge of the later relationship can throw light on certain aspects of the earlier. In any case, *The Waste Land* stands as a notable instance of multiple authorship of a major poem that is constantly attributed to one author alone.

1

The abundance of superficial and circumstantial similarities between Eliot and Coleridge is quite striking. They were born well outside the cultural centers in which they eventually became prominent. Each was the youngest child in a large family of middle-aged parents and dominant siblings. They were precociously intelligent, dreamy and bookish at school, developing strong philosophical and metaphysical bents that entered into practically all their intellectual activities, whatever the ostensible subject at hand. As young men they tried supporting themselves on income from periodical essays, book reviews, and public lectures; and both, beset by serious financial problems, were to an extent rescued by patrons. They made disastrous marriages and agonizingly separated from their wives a decade or more afterward. They suffered various gruesome illnesses and physical afflictions all their lives. They drank too much. To add a few of the more bizarre coincidences (coincidences merely): both matriculated at "Cambridge" (Harvard College in Cambridge, Massachusetts, in Eliot's case; Cambridge University in Coleridge's); both at one time were sages in Highgate (Eliot taught in the junior school there); both had friends named Mary Hutchinson; both were afraid of cows!

As psychological entities, Eliot and Coleridge were prone to instability, lassitude, anxiety, and depression. There is continuous evidence of a marked lack of self-confidence in each case; they seem to have been constantly dependent on external support and esteem. They were unusually adept at imitation and assimilation, frequently turning to other writers' works as a necessary stimulus to their own (and both, in the process, at some time or other incurring charges of plagiarism). In both men's histories there is a lengthy record of books, lectures, collections, and other projects that were planned and announced but never carried out. There are elements of the trickster in both characters; they were inventors of comic pseudonyms (compare the rhythm and appearance of Eliot's "Charles Augustus Conybeare" with Coleridge's "Silas Tomkyn Comberbache").

As to their careers and general achievements, Eliot and Coleridge are important to us today for a small canon of poetic masterpieces and for a larger body of influential critical writings that made them, while they were alive, the leading theorists of their time. Their single best-known poems—*The Waste Land* and *The Ancient Mariner*—share some principal themes and symbols: sickness of soul, emotional barrenness, spiritual death, inability to connect, the terror of isolation, the arrival of life-giving rain, with only partial recovery at the end; as Florence Marsh writes in the first paragraph of an extended comparison of the two works, "both are essentially religious poems concerned with salvation. In both, the protagonist needs to recover from a living death, from spiritual dryness."[4] In their prose, Eliot and Coleridge wrote memorably (if not always coherently) about Shakespeare, the history of literature, the functions of poetry and criticism, and organic unity and its converse, the dissociation of sensibility. Among many other activities, they both contributed plays to the London theater.

Of all the major writers of the nineteenth century, Coleridge is the one with whom Eliot should have most identified and sympathized, and there is plentiful evidence that he did make such an identification. The following, for example, from his paragraph-long "potted biography" of Coleridge written in the 1920s (the decade of *The Waste Land*) for a National Portrait Gallery postcard is empathically both censorious and admiring: "His life was ill-regulated; weak, slothful, a voracious reader, he contracted an unhappy marriage and much later the habit of taking laudanum. . . . The greatest English literary critic, he was also the greatest intellectual force of his time."[5] Something of the same sort of self-reflexivity pervades Eliot's December 1932 Norton lecture on Wordsworth and Coleridge:

> Coleridge was one of those unhappy persons . . . of whom one might say, that if they had not been poets, they might have made something of their lives, might even have had a career; or conversely, that if they had not been interested in so many things, crossed by such diverse passions, they might have been great poets. It was better for Coleridge, as poet, to read books of travel and exploration than to read books of metaphysics and political economy. He did genuinely want to read books of metaphysics and political economy, for he had a certain talent for such subjects. But for a few years he had been visited by the Muse . . . and thenceforth was a haunted man. . . . he was condemned to know that the little poetry he had written was worth more than all he could do with the rest of his life. . . . Sometimes, however, to be a "ruined man" is itself a vocation.

His identification with Coleridge is again signaled in the final sentence of the concluding Norton lecture (31 March 1933): "The sad ghost of Coleridge beckons to me from the shadows."[6] A few years later, Virginia Woolf noted in her diary that Eliot had acquired the habit of beginning sentences, "Coleridge and I. . . ."[7] And in a lecture of 1955, he told his audience that "Coleridge . . . was rather a man of my own type."[8]

While there are not nearly so many circumstantial similarities between Coleridge's *miglior fabbro,* Wordsworth, and Ezra Pound, those that exist are fundamental. Like Wordsworth at the time of *Lyrical Ballads,* Pound was centrally concerned with the reform of poetry (especially the language of poetry). As with Wordsworth, his most important work is a long unfinished poem on (to borrow Wordsworth's description for *The Recluse*) man, nature, and society. In standard literary history, each is a (and frequently is *the*) pioneering figure in a major movement—Romanticism and Modernism, respectively. Most to the point, however, is Pound's personality. Egotistical and self-willed, Pound can be thought of as a twentieth-century version of what Keats called "the wordsworthian or egotistical sublime";

his bumptious aggressiveness and strong sense of purpose contrast sharply with Eliot's indecision and self-doubts. While actually born not quite three years before Eliot, Pound in biographical retrospect *seems* to have been much older, and must have seemed so at the time to Eliot; Wordsworth was two and a half years older than Coleridge, and one suspects a similar disparity between the real and the perceived differences in their ages (and there was more involved than just age: Coleridge in a letter of late 1801 describes himself and "W. & his sister" as "three persons . . . but one God," the god being, of course, Wordsworth).[9]

In his 1932 Norton lecture on Wordsworth and Coleridge, Eliot comments only briefly on the question of which character was the more dominant: "Their influence upon each other was considerable; though probably the influence of Wordsworth upon Coleridge, during their brief period of intimate association, was greater than that of Coleridge upon Wordsworth." A few paragraphs later he adds, "I doubt whether the impulse in Coleridge would have been strong enough to have worked its way out, but for the example and encouragement of Wordsworth."[10] Whether or not Eliot himself was conscious of the parallel that I am proposing here, this last statement has an uncanny appropriateness as a description of Pound's help in the production of *The Waste Land*.

2

The complete chronology of *The Waste Land* is somewhat uncertain, but a number of facts are by now well established.[11] Eliot's earliest recoverable references—to a "long poem" that he has been planning for some time and hopes to begin writing shortly—occur in letters of November and December 1919 to John Quinn (the American lawyer and arts patron) and to Eliot's mother. By early February 1921 he had shown Wyndham Lewis some parts of it, and on 9 May he told Quinn that it was "partly on paper."[12] Part 3, "The Fire Sermon," seems to have been the earliest section completed, at London and perhaps also Margate in September and October 1921. The rest—the bulk of the lines of both the surviving manuscripts and the much reduced printed text—was written in a rush in London and Lausanne in November and December. Pound read and marked parts of the manuscripts on two occasions, first in the middle of November 1921, when Eliot stayed with him in Paris on his way to Lausanne for a month's "rest re" in the care of the analyst Dr. Roger Vittoz, and a second time in early January 1922, when he again stopped in Paris on his way back to London. The manuscripts extant in the Berg Collection and published in the facsimile edition of 1971 are a hodge-podge of holograph drafts, fair copies, and typescripts, fifty-four leaves in all, including a title leaf and marked and revised carbon copies of some of the typescript portions. Though Eliot called these sheets "all of the manuscript in existence" just before he shipped them off to Quinn in the fall of 1922,[13] a great deal else has been lost or destroyed—draft versions of material that we have only in fair copy or typescript, fair copies (and American and British printer's copies) of some of the text that we have only in draft, and no doubt other manuscript materials that we now know nothing about. The main items that survive in this batch, which Eliot sent to his benefactor Quinn almost as if he were offering a private display of multiple authorship in process, are the following:

1. "He Do the Police in Different Voices: Part I. The Burial of the Dead," 130 lines on three pages of typescript (rectos of three leaves). Eliot canceled the whole of page 1 (lines 1–54 in the facsimile edition numbering) in pencil; pages 2 and 3 (55–130), which Pound marked for revision, are an early version of the printed text lines 1–76.

2. "He Do the Police in Different Voices: Part II. A Game of Chess," 98 lines on three pages of typescript (rectos of three leaves) marked by both Pound and Eliot's wife, Vivien, and a carbon copy of the typescript with some holograph notations by Eliot—the equivalent of the printed text lines 77–172.

3. "The Fire Sermon," 240 lines on five pages of typescript (rectos of five leaves) plus holograph draft on the verso of leaf 1, a carbon copy of the typescript, and further holograph draft for this section of the poem on four other leaves (*Facsimile* pp. 28, 36, 48, 50, 52)—early versions of the printed text lines 173–311. Pound marked both the original typescript and the carbon, as well as the recto of the last leaf of draft in this section (p. 50).

4. "Part IV. Death by Water," 93 lines on four rectos of holograph fair copy and again (shortened to 92 lines) on four rectos of typescript. The last 10 lines in both versions are the equivalent of the printed text lines 312–21. Pound commented on the first page of the fair copy and marked the typescript throughout.

5. "What the Thunder Said," 117 lines on six rectos of untitled pencil draft and again (shortened to 113 lines) on four rectos of typescript—the equivalent of the printed text lines 322–434. Pound commented at the top of the first page of draft and made a few markings in the typescript.

6. Twelve additional leaves of lyrics and fragments, some dating from as early as 1914 to 1916, that contributed toward, or (in the case of the three typescript items) were once considered for inclusion in, the early text of the poem (*Facsimile* pp. 90–122): a holograph draft and fair copy of "The Death of Saint Narcissus" (containing early versions of the printed text lines 26–29); typescripts of "Song" (originally "Song for the Opherion"), "Exequy" (with draft of part of an additional stanza on the verso), and "The Death of the Duchess" (containing early versions of the printed text lines 108–10, 136–38), all three marked by Pound; a 13-line draft beginning "After the turning of the inspired days" (containing a version of the printed text line 322); a 5-line holograph fragment beginning "I am the Resurrection and the Life"; a 33-line draft fragment beginning "So through the evening, through the violet air" (containing early versions of the printed text lines 378–85); holograph drafts of short poems entitled "Elegy" and "Dirge"; a fair copy of "Dirge," with a comment by Pound; and a 5-line draft fragment beginning "Those are pearls that were his eyes. See!" (which became the printed text line 48).

These are the main materials, amounting to a thousand lines of verse (not counting the carbon copies and some other repetitions of passages), out of which Pound and Eliot excavated the world-famous *Waste Land,* published in both the *Criterion* (in London) and the *Dial* (in New York) in the middle of October 1922. It is of course impossible to consider the drafts objectively. Many readers know the printed poem by heart (indeed, one can almost collate the manuscripts against the standard text without book); the discarded passages of the manuscripts, some 300 lines in items 1–5 in the preceding list and another 260 in item 6, cannot be other than decidedly unfamiliar by comparison. Though every now and then a critic professes to admire, and even prefer, the flatter, more sprawling version of the manuscripts,[14] the majority view is that the 434 lines of *The Waste Land* as we know it were lying hidden from the beginning in the 1000 lines of draft, rather in the manner of one of Michelangelo's slumbering figures waiting to be rescued from the block of marble. But Michelangelo, in this analogy, was both artist and reviser simultaneously. In the case of *The Waste Land,* it took one poetic genius to create those 434 lines in the first place, and another to get rid of the several hundred inferior lines surrounding and obscuring them.

Part 1 in the manuscripts begins with a 54-line monologue on pub-crawling and Boston low life:

> First we had a couple of feelers down at Tom's place,
> There was old Tom, boiled to the eyes, blind,
> (Don't you remember that time after a dance,
> Top hats and all, we and Silk Hat Harry,
> And old Tom took us behind, brought out a bottle of fizz,
> With old Jane, Tom's wife; and we got Joe to sing
> "I'm proud of all the Irish blood that's in me,
> "There's not a man can say a word agin me").
> Then we had dinner in good form, and a couple of Bengal lights.
> When we got into the show, up in Row A,
> I tried to put my foot in the drum, and didn't the girl squeal,
> She never did take to me, a nice guy—but rough;
> The next thing we were out in the street, Oh was it cold! . . .

This is "language really used by men" in a way that Wordsworth never dreamed of. The descriptions and dialogue are tedious throughout; there is nothing of the earthy liveliness of the ladies discussing Albert and Lil in the pub scene of part 2 (printed text lines 139–72), and no telling point achieved by the unrelieved inanity of the passage. Eliot made deletions and marginal revisions in several lines and then canceled the entire page (and passage) with vertical strokes in pencil. In this instance it is uncertain whether the wholesale deletion was his or Pound's idea. In tonal inaccuracy and uselessness to the project as a whole, the passage is very much like some others that we know Pound objected to in later parts of the manuscripts; since Eliot was thoroughly dependent on Pound at this time in matters of literary judgment, the better likelihood is that the decision was Pound's.[15]

With the next two pages of the opening section, beginning with "April is the cruellest month, breeding / Lilacs out of the dead land," we are on solid and very familiar ground, the seventy-six lines that, after minor revisions by Pound and Eliot (and then by Eliot or an editor at a later stage), became part 1 of the printed poem. Pound marked, underlined, circled, queried, and deleted several lines in the six paragraphs and wrote "Marianne," "J.J." (for James Joyce), and "Blake. Too often used" in the margins. Eliot kept (or restored) three lines that Pound deleted—the printed text's lines 48, 67–68—and dropped two others: the parenthetical "I John saw these things, and heard them" between lines 56 and 57, and "I have sometimes seen and see" following "Unreal City" in line 60.

In the extant typescript of part 2, "A Game of Chess," Pound changed Eliot's original wording in nineteen lines. He commented marginally on the regularity of the meter ("3 lines too tum-pum at a stretch," "too penty"), ridiculed the phrasing in Eliot's original "one tender Cupidon" (" 'one' wee red mouse," Pound scrawled), seemingly faulted the overly accurate realism of several lines of speech ("photography," "photo."), objected to certain vaguenesses ("had is the weakest point," "dogmatic deduction but wobbly as well"), and again, as in part 1, noted echoes of other writers ("Beddoes," "J.J."). Pound's deletions and revisions are responsible for the printed text's wording in lines 80, 91–92, 94, 105, 109, 121–22, and comments and other markings by him brought about changes in lines 78, 98, 103–4, 106–7, 125, 136, 139, 149–50. Vivien Eliot, whose marginal pencilings show that she especially liked this section of the poem ("WONDERFUL," "Splendid last lines"), contributed the printed text's lines 153 and 164 and part of 159.

Part 3, "The Fire Sermon," originally opened with seventy lines of Popian couplets (plus an additional seventeen lines of couplets and triplets on an inserted sheet) describing a Belinda-like Fresca at her toilet:

> Admonished by the sun's inclining ray,
> And swift approaches of the thievish day,
> The white-armed Fresca blinks, and yawns, and gapes,
> Aroused from dreams of love and pleasant rapes.
> Electric summons of the busy bell
> Brings brisk Amanda to destroy the spell;
> With coarsened hand, and hard plebeian tread,
> Who draws the curtain round the lacquered bed,
> Depositing thereby a polished tray
> Of soothing chocolate, or stimulating tea. . . .

It is extremely shallow imitation, as Pound indicated by his comments on the carbon copy—"Too loose," "rhyme drags it out to diffuseness," "trick of Pope etc not to let couple[t] diffuse 'em"—and by his cancellation of the entire passage in the original typescript. Pound also worked over the rest of this section in both the typescript and the carbon, censuring Eliot's tentativeness ("dam per'apsez," "Perhaps be damned," "make up yr. mind," "you Tiresias if you know know damn well or else you dont"), commenting on circumlocutions ("B—ll—S," presumably for "Bullshit," beside Eliot's "London, the swarming life you kill and breed, / Huddled between the concrete and the sky," and "Palmer Cox's brownies" as a humorous illustration of Eliot's "Phantasmal gnomes, burrowing in brick and stone and steel"), and finding fault with most of the lines describing the typist and the clerk ("verse not interesting enough as verse to warrant so much of it," "inversions not warranted by any real exegience of metre," "Too easy," "mix up of the couplet & grishkin not good," "probaly over the mark").

Besides canceling the seventy-odd lines at the beginning of the section, Pound deleted twenty lines after the printed text's 214, single lines after 217 and 229, two lines after 248, and three lines after 258. His markings and comments prompted Eliot to reduce twelve lines describing the typist to half that number in the final text (222–27) and twenty lines describing the clerk to a mere four (231–34). Other markings produced (or helped produce) the final version of lines 207, 208, 212, 214, 215, 251, 252, 254. All told, in one way or another Pound changed more than 130 lines of Eliot's draft in this section.

On the first page of Eliot's holograph fair copy of part 4, "Death by Water," ninety-three lines describing a fisherman's voyage and shipwreck off the New England coast, Pound wrote, "Bad—but cant attack until I get typescript." When he subsequently had the typescript in hand (it was typed on his own typewriter in Paris), Pound marked through the first eighty lines so vigorously that Eliot considered removing the entire section. "Perhaps better omit Phlebas also???" he asked Pound, referring to the final ten lines, to which Pound replied: "I DO advise keeping Phlebas. In fact I more'n advise. Phlebas is an integral part of the poem; the card pack introduces him, the drowned phoen. sailor, and he is needed ABSoloootly where he is. Must stay in."[16] In this case, while Eliot is demonstrably the author of part 4 of the printed text, Pound is responsible both for the continuing existence of the Phlebas lines that constitute this part and for the deletion of the eighty-plus lines that originally preceded them.

In part 5, "What the Thunder Said," the errant and indecisive Eliot suddenly attained a degree of self-assurance nowhere evident in the preceding parts, and the lines, even in first draft, flowed in near-perfect form. No further excavation was needed. Pound, reading both the holograph draft and the typescript (again typed on his own

typewriter—in this instance, scholars have suggested, poss
Pound himself), made only a handful of markings—"OK from neiᴠ
on I think" at the top of the first page of draft, and small markings
that altered the typescript to produce the final text in lines 337 and
392.

As for the rest, principally the three poems that Pound read and
marked in typescript at the end of the manuscripts ("Song," "Exequy," and "The Death of the Duchess," *Facsimile* pp. 98–106),
Pound's role was mainly to say no. "I think your instinct had led you
to put the remaining superfluities at the end," he wrote to Eliot; "I
think you had better leave 'em, abolish 'em altogether or for the
present. . . . The thing now runs from April . . . to shantih without
[a] break. . . . Dont try to bust all records by prolonging it three
pages further." Eliot did as he was told ("Certainly omit miscellaneous pieces," he replied),[17] and *The Waste Land* as we know it was
the sensational result. In the process of shaping the poem, Pound had
altered or stripped away some 350 to 400 of Eliot's lines (either 2 or
56 in part 1; 19 in part 2; 130 or so in part 3; 83 in part 4; 2 in part 5;
and 118 in the three separate pieces at the end). Eliot in return, when
he included the poem in his first collected edition, *Poems 1909–1925*
(1925), added a dedication that has been part of the work ever since:
"For Ezra Pound / *il miglior fabbro*." The Italian phrase, from
Purgatorio 26.117, is Dante's tribute to a Provencal troubadour
whom Pound also admired and translated, Arnaut Daniel—"the better poet" (*fabbro,* or "maker," the literal meaning of Greek *poiētēs)*
in both love songs and prose romances ("versi d'amore e prose di
romanzi").

3

While he shows considerable ambivalence about the survival of the
manuscripts and the consequent possibility of public exposure of his
rough drafts as well as Pound's markings, Eliot's private and public
statements concerning the extent of Pound's contribution to the poem
are forthright and generous. Writing on 21 September 1922, he tells
Quinn,

> In the manuscript of *The Waste Land* which I am sending you, you will
> see the evidences of [Pound's] work, and I think that this manuscript is
> worth preserving in its present form solely for the reason that it is the

only evidence of the difference which his criticism has made to this poem.[18]

In an article in the April/June 1938 issue of *Purpose,* explaining the wording of his dedication to Pound, he says that he meant to "honour the technical mastery and critical ability manifest in [Pound's] own work, which had also done so much to turn *The Waste Land* from a jumble of good and bad passages into a poem."[19] His best-known remark on the matter is a parenthetical aside in a September 1946 essay on Pound in *Poetry:*

> It was in 1922 that I placed before him in Paris the manuscript of a sprawling, chaotic poem called *The Waste Land* which left his hands, reduced to about half its size, in the form in which it appears in print. I should like to think that the manuscript, with the suppressed passages, had disappeared irrecoverably: yet on the other hand, I should wish the blue penciling on it to be preserved as irrefutable evidence of Pound's critical genius.[20]

This last sentiment is reiterated in a comment by Valeric Eliot in an interview published in *Esquire* in 1972: "We never thought [the manuscript] would turn up, but Tom told me that if it did, I was to publish it. 'It won't do me any good,' he added, 'but I would like people to realize the extent of my debt to Ezra.' "[21]

Recognition of that debt has come rather slowly and grudgingly. In her 1971 transcription of the manuscripts, Valerie Eliot printed Pound's markings and comments in red ink, thus highlighting them as the most prominent feature of the facsimile edition. On the face of it, in Eliot's words of 1938, Pound turned "a jumble of good and bad passages into a poem." Yet a large contingent of Eliot scholars, even with this plain evidence before them, have insisted on minimizing Pound's contribution. Here is a brief sampling of assessments, mostly from the years immediately following publication of the facsimile:

> . . . the author of "The Waste Land" knew from the beginning *exactly* what he wanted to express, even if at times the poetic persona was unsure of the voice by which to express it. . . . The manuscripts, of course, show how little Pound altered the poem and that his role of "il miglior fabbro" was mainly to advise on stylistic, technical improvements, as any good teacher might comment on a pupil's work. (Gertrude Patterson, 1972)

Eliot . . . exercised full control over that [published] text. . . . Since the publication of the facsimiles, there can be no doubt that *The Waste Land* was controlled by Eliot's architectonic skill at every stage of composition: Eliot responded to Pound's criticisms by modifying the text, not by altering his own purpose. (Grover Smith, 1972)

Much of Pound's advice Eliot himself had in mind anyhow. (D. E. S. Maxwell, 1972)

For both Pound and Eliot, the business of revision seems to have been largely a matter of surface craftsmanship. (Richard Sheppard, 1972)

Pound's criticism tightened the poem, but did not otherwise alter its movement. (Denis Donoghue, 1974)

Eliot evidently conceived *The Waste Land* from the start as an "ideogrammic" collage, and any obstetrics Pound may have performed did nothing to change the original nature of the brainchild. . . . Not only must we conclude that the "editorial policy" in the composition of *The Waste Land* was Eliot's and not Pound's, but we must also seriously question whether Pound had a sympathetic understanding of Eliot's ultimate intentions. . . . Eliot is scrupulously independent in his judgment of Pound's advice. (Gareth Reeves, 1975)

[Pound] *edited* the poem, he did not determine or influence the poem's basic form and content: in concept and expression it is distinctly Eliot's own. Pound freed the drafts of weak, at times poor lines; he tightened the poem's dramatic structure and rhythmic flow and speeded its movement. He suggested changes, drew attention to weaknesses, but always left the final decision to Eliot. (Ruth Pulik, 1977)

As it turned out, Pound altered [the poem] relatively little. . . . In his revision Pound concentrated on local infelicities more than on the integrity of the whole and kept Eliot from brooding about his lack of outline for several crucial days or weeks. (Ronald Bush, 1983)

I do not . . . believe that Pound was responsible for the innovations in *The Waste Land*. An examination of the manuscript shows that, apart from a few minor revisions in diction, Pound's contributions were the removal of two long sections beginning "The Fire Sermon" and "Death by Water" and rather extensive revisions of the teatime episode in "The Fire Sermon." . . . But the strategy of the poem and the most powerful passages in the poem are not disturbed by Pound. (Harriet Davidson, 1985)[22]

Patterson's "*exactly* . . . of course" and Smith's "there can be no doubt" are clues to the precariousness of their positions; each had published a substantial book on Eliot, and naturally they were resistant to the idea of a second author for the most famous and influential poem in their poet's canon. Maxwell is indulging in mind reading. And the rest of the critics cited here, from Sheppard through Davidson, concur in the opinion that the poem represented in Eliot's manuscripts was *essentially* unchanged by Pound's deletion of several hundred of its lines and significant alteration of many others. Phrases like "surface craftsmanship," "did nothing to change the original nature," "always left the final decision to Eliot," "concentrated on local infelicities"—demonstrably wrong according to the biographical and textual evidence—are typical of their rhetoric.

Critics who argue that Pound's contribution made an essential difference are proportionately fewer. Glauco Cambon, in one of the earliest reactions to publication of the facsimiles, speaks of Pound's "radical abridgment" and "drastic excisions, so instrumental to the attainment of *The Waste Land's* final shape," and adds a personal anecdote:

> I remember Austin Warren's remark, in a conversation we had many years ago in Ann Arbor, that but for "violent" Pound, basically "academic" Eliot might have missed out on his high goal of literary achievement. Thirteen years ago one had few hopes of ever recovering the original drafts of *The Waste Land,* but now that they have been unearthed, they bear Austin Warren out. Nobody can deny that Pound's aggressiveness managed to bring forth a deeper coherence from Eliot's own creative resources.

Bernard Bergonzi's summary comment in his short biography of 1972 strikes a kindred note: "All in all, Pound's treatment of *The Waste Land* showed his intense feeling for what Eliot was trying to do. . . . Without Pound's attentions *The Waste Land* would still have been impressive, but it would have appeared, and remained, much more clearly a group of separate poems." Russell Kirk, another writer of 1972, says that "Pound mightily improved the poem. . . . Pound's taste was then superior to Eliot's, and what was deleted would have diminished the explosion of this bomb. . . . All of Pound's smaller changes . . . were for the better." The strongest statement of Pound's share in the collaboration is Lewis Turco's of 1979:

> If anything is clear about *The Waste Land,* it is that the poem had two
> authors, not one. Pound had as much to do with the making of the
> poem as did Eliot. . . . we ought at least to insist that all future editions
> of the work bear the names of both authors.[23]

Writers of the 1980s have tended to give Pound the credit that
Eliot (in the remarks quoted at the beginning of this section) said he
deserved. In his 1983 book devoted to the poem, Grover Smith has
somewhat revised his earlier estimate of Pound's importance: "Without [Pound] this poem would have been impossible: this *Waste Land*
is the best of all possible *Waste Lands.* . . . It did require Ezra Pound
to bring it to conclusion." The 1984 standard biography by Peter
Ackroyd gives a reasonably balanced account of the effect of Pound's
changes:

> When Ezra Pound began working on it, he removed most of the ele-
> ments of stylistic reproduction—he considered the sequence in the
> manner of Pope to be simply parodic—and curbed the tendency of the
> poem towards dramatic and fictional exposition. Pound was, perhaps,
> the purer poet of the two; certainly he was never much interested in
> Eliot's skill as a dramatist. . . . And it might fairly be said in retrospect
> that he quite misunderstood the essential nature of Eliot's genius. . . .
> But Pound had an extraordinarily good ear, and he located in the
> typescripts of *The Waste Land* the underlying rhythm of the poem—the
> music of which Eliot was so distrustful and which he surrounded with
> more deliberate and dramatic kinds of writing. Pound heard the music,
> and cut away what was for him the extraneous material which was
> attached to it. . . . In other words, Pound mistook or refused to recog-
> nize Eliot's original *schema* and as a result rescued the poetry.

Whether Pound mistook Eliot's genius or (like Keats's helpers) to
some degree ignored it in pursuit of his own goals, Ackroyd's description makes clear that *The Waste Land* without Pound would not have
been the "same" poem. And the 1985 and 1989 editions of the most
standard of American literature anthologies have already informed
thousands of undergraduate and graduate students that Eliot "cut
huge chunks out of the poem on Pound's advice. Indeed . . . study of
the manuscript before and after Pound's suggestions were incorporated has led some critics to suggest that we should think of *The Waste
Land* as jointly authored."[24]

4

I would offer three brief points by way of provisional conclusion to this example of multiple authorship. The first concerns my opening speculation that the Eliot–Pound collaboration, for which we have detailed evidence in the manuscripts in the Berg Collection, might by analogy throw light on the less solidly documented collaboration 120 years earlier between Coleridge and Wordsworth. The conclusion has to be, I think, that the later relationship cannot illuminate the earlier in any way that a majority of scholars could agree on. Indeed, as a more particular examination of the scholarship would show, the Eliot and Pound critics disagree with one another concerning the two writers' responsibility for nearly every aspect of *The Waste Land*—structure, style, tone, dramatic voice, themes, philosophy—even with the evidence of the manuscripts before their eyes. There is no reason to think that Coleridge and Wordsworth scholars would be any closer to unanimity, and every reason to think that if we had, say, a set of manuscripts of *The Ancient Mariner* with Wordsworth's comments and revisions, the critics would just as avidly declare Coleridge's independence of Wordsworth, or, conversely, his heavy indebtedness to Wordsworth, according to their subjective interpretations of the documentary evidence. Although I still think that the Eliot–Pound and Coleridge–Wordsworth parallels are interesting and suggestive, I would not use the one case to prove anything about the other.

More generally, or theoretically, just as it is historically inappropriate to assume a single author for a single text, so it is inappropriate to assume a given form of multiple authorship for a text. In every instance, recovery of the circumstances of literary production can proceed only on the assumption that each case is historically specific. Although Coleridge was something like Eliot, and Wordsworth something like Pound, it is virtually certain that no poem in *Lyrical Ballads* was constructed by Wordsworth carving out something from a mass of lines presented to him by Coleridge.

The second point concerns the fragility and elusiveness of any concept of authorial intention in *The Waste Land*. In spite of the confidence of some of the pro-Eliot critics quoted above ("knew . . . *exactly* what he wanted to express," "exercised full control"), the biographical evidence—especially the letters and other documents quoted by Valerie Eliot in her introduction to the facsimiles—shows

Eliot to have been in the most precarious of mental states during the
year in which he produced the drafts that he handed over to Pound
(Ackroyd's chapter covering 1921 and 1922 is titled "The Collapse").
He wrote the greater part of the manuscript text while undergoing
psychiatric treatment in Switzerland, and not least among the many
elements of pure chance that had their effect were the facts that Paris
lay between London and Lausanne, that Pound was in Paris, and that
Eliot therefore would see Pound both going and returning just at the
time when he was writing large passages of the poem. Eliot seems to
have been entirely dependent on, and to have followed in every
major detail, Pound's advice concerning what to keep and what to get
rid of in the manuscripts. We know that there were fundamental
differences between the two writers' aims, tastes, and ideas in poetry,
but on this occasion Pound had his own way, with Eliot first acquiesc-
ing and then objectively admiring the result.[25]

The drafts that Pound worked over were unquestionably the
product of genius; nobody has ever suggested that Eliot did not write
the great lines and passages for which he is most famous. But the
biographical evidence raises serious doubts about Eliot's consciousness of what he was doing, apart from the basic business of writing
great passages and hoping for Pound's approval. Ackroyd makes a
good point about the openness of the finished product:

> Pound imposed an order on it which it did not originally possess; as a
> result of his removal of the original context of the poem, it has become
> much easier for readers and critics to provide their own—to suggest a
> "theme" which the abbreviated sequences might be claimed to fit. *The
> Waste Land* provided a scaffold on which others might erect their own
> theories; so it is that it has been variously interpreted as personal
> autobiography, an account of a collapsing society, an allegory of the
> Grail and spiritual rebirth, a Buddhist meditation. Thus *The Waste
> Land* began a process of which Eliot has been the principal beneficiary,
> or victim. In the absence of philosophical or religious certainties, his
> poetry has been invested with a gnomic or moral force which it can
> hardly carry. A thin wash of "great truths" has been placed over *The
> Waste Land* and over Eliot's succeeding work. The poet himself was to
> be treated as a kind of seer, a position most unsuited to him.[26]

And several critics have quoted a remark from Eliot's 1953 National
Book League Lecture, "The Three Voices of Poetry," as the poet's
reflection on the way in which *The Waste Land* took shape:

In a poem which is neither didactic nor narrative, and not animated by any other social purpose, the poet may be concerned solely with expressing in verse—using all his resources of words, with their history, their connotations, their music—this obscure impulse. He does not know what he has to say until he has said it; and in the effort to say it he is not concerned with making other people understand anything. He is not concerned, at this stage, with other people at all: only with finding the right words or, anyhow, the least wrong words. He is not concerned whether anybody else will ever listen to them or not, or whether anybody else will ever understand them if he does. He is oppressed by a burden which he must bring to birth in order to obtain relief.[27]

In the drafts of *The Waste Land* Eliot may have been expressing just such an "obscure impulse"—not knowing "what he has to say until he has said it"—and Pound, far from helping Eliot find out what he had to say, may have further obscured the impulse so that it is no longer evident or recoverable. Who, then, is the author of *The Waste Land* published in October 1922? Eliot wrote the drafts; Pound is responsible for the principal revisions. But the *authorship* underlying any particular sequence, or passage, or detail is still very much up in the air.

My third point concerns the extent to which the myth of single authorship enters into the critical analysis of this obvious collaboration: *The Waste Land*, if it were perceived to be a jointly authored poem, would inevitably become a lesser work than it is now taken to be. At present, critical appreciation of a masterwork requires it to be the product of a single organizing mind. If multiple authorship were accepted as the norm of literary production, then no critic would need to appropriate a work for one or another author; indeed, the multiplicity of contributors to a work could even be considered a mark of its significance!

7

American Novels: Authors, Agents, Editors, Publishers

With the novel and (in the next chapter) plays and films, we at last encounter literature as commercial enterprise. Apart from timely loans from his publishers, Keats never received a penny from his poetry (and neither did the publishers). Mill and Wordsworth supported themselves as civil servants, offering their works principally for the edification of readers—then and, they hoped, for all time. Coleridge, who survived mainly on donations from patrons and friends, actually lost several hundred pounds when he published *Sibylline Leaves* and *Biographia Literaria* with the firm of Rest Fenner, which went bankrupt two years afterward. Eliot received all of $150, plus a prize of $2000, for the first publication of *The Waste Land*. To be sure, Eliot later became a shrewd businessman of letters, driving a hard bargain as a director of the London publisher Faber and Faber; but when he produced *The Waste Land,* he and his publishers were still operating in a nineteenth-century tradition of poetry writing and publishing primarily for the sake of art and fame.

Of course, there have been best-sellers all along in English and other literatures. Shakespeare, nowadays chief presider over the immortals "among the English Poets," was in his own time a reckonable figure at the box office. Pope and the mid-century novelists— Richardson, Fielding, and Smollett—came closest to being best-selling, or at least self-supporting, British authors in the eighteenth century, and among the Romantics Byron and Scott are obvious examples. But it was with the rise of the novel in the nineteenth century, intimately connected with the development and growth of a mass readership—itself the product of accelerated growth in population, widespread educational reform, the increase of literacy, the institution of commercial and public lending libraries, and a host of technological improvements in printing and publishing—that literature for the first time became big business.[1] Just as one would expect, commercial considerations more overtly began mixing with the artistic, and, as publishers turned an eye toward consumer response and sales figures, collaborative production became a frequent practice of authorship.

J. A. Sutherland has documented a number of early collaborations (and collaborative situations) between publishers and writers in Victorian fiction. They include, among others, Richard Bentley's offer to Melville to have *Pierre* rewritten by a "judicious literary friend . . . in a style to be understood by the great mass of readers"; Longman's alterations of the manuscript of Trollope's *Barchester Towers* to get rid of "vulgarity" and "exaggeration"; Bentley's persuading Anne Manning to enhance sales appeal by adding two chapters to *The Ladies of Bever Hollow* ("to give each volume a respectable girth"); George Smith's more pervasive influence, ultimately for the same reason, on the structure of Thackeray's *Henry Esmond;* the Macmillans' detailed advice to Charles Kingsley affecting the point of view, style, and tone of *Westward Ho!* ("I am aiming altogether at popularity," wrote Kingsley, "and am willing to alter or expunge wherever aught is likely to hurt the *sale* of the book"); and Dickens's revisions (in his capacity as editor of *All the Year Round*) to make the serialized version of Bulwer Lytton's *A Strange Story* more conformable to readers' expectations.[2]

These are, for the most part, famous names, but while the quality of the output may vary, the Victorian practices that Sutherland describes are not categorically different from a great deal of book production today. Take, as an extreme modern example, the activities of Lyle Kenyon Engel, founder in 1973 of Book Creations, Inc., a "fiction factory" in Canaan, New York, that has "created" several thousand books in the last dozen or so years, with over 100 million copies in print. According to his *New York Times* obituary (13 August 1986),

> Engel originated ideas for series of books, usually about a family or community through many generations, prepared a detailed outline, hired writers to flesh out the characters and plot, then sold publication rights to paperback houses. . . . A close friend of Pearl S. Buck, he created a series of hard-cover nonfiction books by the Nobel Prize–winning author, including "Tales of the Orient," "People of Japan," an Oriental cookbook, Bible stories and a Christmas book.[3]

Engel and Book Creations were themselves not publishers, but their role in authorship has obvious parallels both with that of the Victorian publishers in some of Sutherland's examples and with what has become standard practice of editors working for twentieth-century publishers.

Probably the routine presence of multiple authorship in the novel and film is so well known as to make rehearsal of details somewhat superfluous. Maxwell Perkins is already sufficiently famous as the editor and in effect collaborator in the works of Thomas Wolfe, Hemingway, Fitzgerald, and others; Hollywood screenwriters are in general decidedly *not* famous as authors of the films that their names are sometimes attached to. But some reminders, here and in the next chapter, of the collaborative character of modern commercial literature may be appropriate nevertheless. The present chapter will deal mostly with editors, though agents and others, as I show in the final section, also get into the business. Let us begin with the creation of a couple of twentieth-century best-sellers, Grace Metalious's *Peyton Place* and Jacqueline Susann's *Valley of the Dolls*.

1

Though some of the people who knew her expressed doubts, including her high-school English teacher, and though on one occasion her husband publicly claimed credit as a collaborator, there is really no question about Grace Metalious's principal authorship of *Peyton Place,* which sold 104,000 copies in the first month of its publication in 1956, stayed on the *New York Times* best-seller list for twenty-six weeks, and ultimately sold more copies than Margaret Mitchell's *Gone with the Wind* and Erskine Caldwell's *God's Little Acre,* becoming one of the best-selling novels ever published. Metalious spent parts of five or six years conceiving and drafting the work, and a carbon copy of her manuscript, with the original title "The Tree and the Blossom," is extant in the library of the Pennsylvania State University. The bulk of the evidence assembled by her biographer, Emily Toth, establishes Metalious as a dedicated amateur who, through a series of lucky circumstances—the nearly random choice of an agent who sent the manuscript to an unlikely publisher whose reader happened to mention it in a job interview with another publisher—became famous (and infamous) almost in spite of her intentions.

The centrality of Metalious in the work and the seriousness of her original effort do not, however, mean that *Peyton Place* had no coauthors. The published title of the novel (a place name intended to parallel that of Henry Bellamann's *Kings Row,* which sold well in both book and movie versions) was thought up by Aaron Sussman, head of the agency handling its advertising, who declared that "The Tree and the Blossom" was "too poetic." The text itself was substantially worked over by editors—initially by Leona Nevler, the free-lance reader who discovered the work in the first place and agreed to undertake the editing for the house that accepted it, Julian Messner, Inc., and subsequently by the publisher's president and editor-in-chief herself, Kitty Messner.

Nevler, entering critical comments, queries, and alterations directly on the manuscript, was concerned mainly to eliminate clichés and reduce scenes and descriptions that she judged were stilted, sentimental, and (as she wrote of one lovemaking episode) "unreal & a little embarrassing." Metalious was outraged at the markings, telling her agent that Nevler had turned her work into "somebody else's book. If it can't be mine, I don't want any part of it!" At this point Messner took over, treating the author more gently but actually effecting much more substantial changes than Nevler had called for. These include, among others, stylistic alterations throughout; the deletion of long philosophical passages, satirical comments, "unnecessary foreshadowings," a long anecdote, and at least one character (a minister who went insane); bowdlerizing changes in descriptions; the elimination of an incestuous rape (both as motif and as a significant element of plot); the wholesale rewriting of the unrealistic dialogue that Metalious had invented for her New York City characters; the request for an additional love scene between two of the principal characters; and some major changes in the development and career of the heroine, Allison MacKenzie, who in the manuscript text is to a considerable extent a fictional rendering of Metalious herself but in the editing, as Toth demonstrates, was stripped of most of her autobiographical features.

Oddly, but at the same time predictably, Toth prefaces her account of these alterations by saying that Messner "actually made few changes" and that though Metalious "found the editing painful, the book remained her own." Toth's recital of the details suggests otherwise, and so does her account of the author's reactions. A friend recalled that Metalious "felt her book was destroyed" by certain of the deletions (a strong statement, even when we make adjustment for normal authorial vanity and sensitivity); and after Messner's changes in the character of the heroine, Metalious, in Toth's words, "told many people . . . that *Peyton Place* wasn't the book she had wanted to write."[4]

Jacqueline Susann had no such illusions about artistic or authorial integrity. According to her biographer, Barbara Seaman, Susann first thought of writing a "gossipy, soap-opera kind of a novel" after seeing Metalious interviewed on television by Mike Wallace (Susann herself was in the studio producing commercials for the program) and thinking that she could do a much better job of promoting a book than the "chunky, depressed, and colorless" author of *Peyton Place*.[5] What she most wanted to accomplish as a writer was make the *New York Times* best-seller list, and with *Valley of the Dolls,* published by Bernard Geis Associates in 1966, she succeeded superlatively. The book was on the *Times* list for twenty-eight weeks and sold close to 7 million copies in the first six months of publication. To date, it is the best-selling novel of all time; according to the 1989 *Guinness Book of World Records,* cumulative sales through 26 May 1988 amounted to 29,104,000 copies.

The publisher's initial reaction to the manuscript of *Valley of the Dolls,* which Susann seems to have drafted in a few months sometime in 1964 or 1965, is that it "was a bad, bad book . . . hardly written in English."[6] Geis's executive editor, Don Preston, reported in part as follows:

> [Susann] is a painfully dull, inept, clumsy, undisciplined, rambling and thoroughly amateurish writer whose every sentence, paragraph and scene cries for the hand of a pro. She wastes endless pages on utter trivia, writes wide-eyed romantic scenes that would not make the back pages of *True Confessions,* hauls out every terrible show biz cliché in all the books, lets every good scene fall apart in endless talk and allows her book to ramble aimlessly. . . . [The book] will lend itself to lively promotion but it will be roasted by critics, not for being salacious but for being badly done, dull. . . .
>
> If, however, the decision is to publish this book despite the great odds against it, then what can editing do? If a competent editor is given carte blanche to cut, compress, and edit (interlinear as well as surgical), some of the faults of organization can be corrected and the story can be given greater pace and sharpness. This would mean drastic cutting, since most of the first 200 pages are virtually worthless and dreadfully dull and since practically every scene is dragged out flat and stomped

on by her endless talk. Some whole scenes should be dropped, a few characters should all but vanish . . . many drawn-out explanations would be compressed into paragraphs. . . . I really don't think there is a page of this ms. that can stand in its present form.

One might suppose that the manuscript would have been rejected at this point, but Geis also sought his wife's opinion, and she told him he had to publish it: the work made her feel "as if I'd picked up the telephone and was listening to two women telling how their husbands are in bed. You can't hang up on a conversation like that." Geis turned the manuscript over to Preston—"We're going to publish this book"—and Preston, whose report almost seems to beg for the assignment ("every sentence . . . cries for the hand of a pro"), spent the next six weeks rewriting it.

According to Geis, "This was not normal editing [Preston] did. This was reconstruction." Preston says that he "worked like hell, cutting and restructuring, rewriting in spots, moving things around. Scenes weren't in proper order. A couple of key scenes weren't there at all, and I had to block them out and convince [Susann] to write them." Seaman gives as one example a pivotal scene where two women get into a fight in the powder room of a nightclub and one grabs the other's wig and tries to flush it down a toilet: "Preston rough-drafted the first version of the scene. [Susann] rewrote it, drawing heavily on a similar episode from [Clare Boothe Luce's] *The Women*. Preston rewrote her rewrite, she rewrote him, and so on. The scene was one of Preston's many contributions toward focusing *Valley*'s action and strengthening its plot." Subsequently Susann came to resent the many compliments that she got for this scene, "galled by the knowledge that it wasn't pure Susann being praised, but something that was at least one-third Preston and one-third Clare Boothe Luce."

Metalious is (in intention, at least) the more serious writer in these brief examples, while Susann stands out as a genius at self-promotion—a combination of tireless energy in interviews, correspondence, and telephoning, an uncanny ability in the art of selling, and full utilization of various practical stratagems (for example, personally signing every copy in a bookstore's stock—because autographed copies could not be returned to the publisher for a refund—and repeatedly buying up all copies in the specific stores whose sales were used in the weekly compilation of the best-seller lists). Regardless of their different interests and personalities, however, the two writers and their editors offer epitomizing instances of the collaborative production of books that, from a commerical point of view, were immensely successful.

2

What is more to the point of the present study is that these same collaborative methods have also been used in books that are not so successful commercially, and even in works that have canonical status in American fiction.[7] For all their cultural impact—which includes attracting large numbers of people into bookstores for the first time in their lives and creating new readers of fiction who had never before managed to get all the way through a book—*Peyton Place* and *Valley of the Dolls* have no current status in the history of American fiction. *The Oxford Companion to American Literature* and the standard literary histories ignore their existence, and one has to go to side specialties and subfields like popular culture to learn about them. But the editors who reshaped and rewrote *Peyton Place* and *Valley of the Dolls* were operating in a by-then well-established tradition in which editors routinely initiated and effected major revisions, all the while professing to be no more than practical mechanisms serving to realize their authors' intentions. Maxwell Perkins was the best-known editor in this tradition—indeed, Don Preston, Geis's editor who revised *Valley of the Dolls,* had come from Louisville to New York in the early 1950s with dreams, as he said, of becoming "the next Maxwell Perkins"[8]—and probably Perkins has been the single greatest influence of the past half-century on the way editors have worked with authors.

Perkins, ambiguously called "editor of genius" by his biographer, A. Scott Berg,[9] served as editor, ultimately vice president and editor-in-chief, of Charles Scribner's Sons from 1914 until his death in 1947, and was the promoter of F. Scott Fitzgerald, Ernest Hemingway, and Thomas Wolfe, among principal figures of modern American literature, and fosterer of a considerable list of other notable writers, including Ring Lardner, J. P. Marquand, Will James, Douglas Southall Freeman, Morley Callaghan, S. S. Van Dine, Edmund Wilson, Erskine Caldwell, Marcia Davenport, Nancy Hale, Allen Tate, Marjorie Kinnan Rawlings, Sherwood Anderson, Stark Young, Hamilton

Basso, Taylor Caldwell, Alan Paton, and James Jones. For some of these writers Perkins acted primarily as acquisitions editor (talent scout, recruiter, salesman of the special virtues of the House of Scribner), while for others he was father–confessor, psychiatrist, fishing and drinking companion, cheerleader, financial manager, legal consultant, publicist, even literary executor. For many of them he was also provider of subjects, themes, plots, and titles of their books, as well as astute critic (and sometimes line-by-line reviser) of the structures, characterizations, descriptions, dialogues, and much else comprising the substance of their writings.

Perkins's most publicized accomplishment, both at the time and more recently (in connection with a dispute over scholars' use of the Thomas Wolfe manuscripts at Harvard), was the virtual creation of *Look Homeward, Angel* (1929) and *Of Time and the River* (1935) out of huge masses of manuscript that Wolfe had brought him in despair. Wolfe was an author who could produce, seemingly effortlessly but in fact uncontrollably, immense quantities of prose—frequently ten or fifteen thousand words at a time describing a scene or a character's feelings—but who never developed any sense of organization, structure, plot, or (even though he began as a dramatist) dramatic effect, and was pathologically unwilling to discard anything he had written. The saddest fact about Wolfe as a writer was his inability to remedy these shortcomings even while his teachers, his friends, and finally his editors repeatedly pointed them out to him. His characteristic response to a request for cutting was to eliminate a hundred words in one place but then add a couple of thousand words in another; his characteristic response to the demand for more plot in his works, more action and reader interest, was instead to produce more pages of description and lyricism. Here, if ever, was a writer who needed editors.

Perkins's principal task in Wolfe's first two books—not unlike that, on a much smaller scale, done by Pound on Eliot's manuscripts for *The Waste Land*—was cutting. But he was also responsible for dividing Wolfe's manuscripts into separate books (it was all one novel, from Wolfe's point of view) and for much of the restructuring and line-by-line rewriting, which, toward the end of their "collaboration" (Wolfe's term), took place at Perkins's office in two- or three-hour sessions nightly, six or seven nights a week, for several months. Here, as an example of the scope and character of Perkins's ministerings, is a set of instructions that he drafted for initial work on a series of "scenes" that became part of *Of Time and the River:*

THINGS TO BE DONE IMMEDIATELY IN FIRST REVISION

1. Make rich man in opening scene older and more middle-aged.
2. Cut out references to previous books and to success.
3. Write out fully and with all the dialogue the jail and arrest scene.
4. Use material from Man on the Wheel and Abraham Jones for first year in the city and University scenes.
5. Tell the story of love affair from beginning to end describing meeting with woman, etc.
6. Intersperse jealousy and madness scenes with more scenes of dialogue with woman.
7. Use description of the trip home and the boom town scenes out of the Man on the Wheel. You can possibly use the trip home and boom town scene to follow on to the station scene. Play up desire to go home, feelings of homesickness and unrest and then develop idea that hometown has become unfamiliar and strange to him and he sees he can no longer live there.
8. Possible ending for book with return to the city, the man in the window scenes and the passages, "some things never change."
9. On the Night Scene which precedes the station scene, write out fully with all dialogue the episodes of night including the death in the subway scene.
10. Cut out reference to daughter.
11. Complete all scenes wherever possible with dialogue.
12. Fill in memory of childhood scenes much more fully with additional stories and dialogue.[10]

Wolfe had strong and conflicting feelings about the way his novels were produced. He dedicated *Of Time and the River* to Perkins with an inscription recognizing "the loyal devotion and the patient care which a dauntless and unshaken friend has given to each part of it, and without which none of it could have been written," and he publicly described their work together in a lecture at the University of Colorado in 1935 and again in expanded versions of the lecture published in the *Saturday Review* (December 1935) and in book form by Scribner's as *The Story of a Novel* (1936). Such acknowledgments, since they obviously signal growing doubts about his authorial identity, unquestionably were tied up with anger and resentment. Almost at the very time that he published *The Story of a Novel* he was also actively seeking a new publisher—to prove, the novelist Marcia Davenport recalls him telling her, "that he was not, as he claimed the literary world believed, the creature of Max Perkins."[11] In the event, he proved nothing of the sort. Upon leaving Scribner's and signing

with Harper's in December 1937, he unloaded his crates of manuscripts on his new editor, Edward Aswell, just as he had earlier on
Perkins. Aswell, after Wolfe's death in September 1938, "shaped"
several posthumous books out of the remaining manuscripts—*The
Web and the Rock* (1939), *You Can't Go Home Again* (1940), and *The
Hills Beyond* (1941).[12] Wolfe's stories and other short pieces in print
had all along been quarried from his manuscripts, and freely revised,
by his agent, Elizabeth Nowell. The fact is that every one of his
published works was to some extent a collaborative production.

With none of his other authors was Perkins's cumulative contribution so extensive as his work with Wolfe, but he exerted significant
influence in some of the same ways on hundreds of books that were
published under his editorship. His extant letters in print and in the
Scribner's archives at Princeton are full of routine suggestions for
omitting material that seemed to him out of place or detrimental to
reader interest—four chapters amounting to 15,000 words from E. H.
Sothern's reminiscences published as *The Melancholy Tale of "Me"*
(1916), for instance, and more than a third of the first part of Arthur
Train's novel *The World and Thomas Kelly* (1917). On other occasions he would request additions rather than cuts—several further
chapters in Edward Bok's *Twice Thirty* (1925), for example. He proposed the topics and stories for works as varied as John W. Thomason, Jr.'s *Jeb Stuart* (1930), Douglas Southall Freeman's *Robert E.
Lee* (1934–35), Marjorie Rawlings's *The Yearling* (1938), and several
tales by Will James; persuaded Ring Lardner to write the humorous
introductions that made a best-seller out of his *How to Write Short
Stories* (1924); devised, arranged, and sometimes titled numerous
collections of short fiction (by Hemingway and Fitzgerald, among
others); and gave S. S. Van Dine substantial help with the characterization of his enduring detective hero, Philo Vance. A number of his
letters to authors are considerably longer and more detailed than the
list quoted above that he made for Wolfe of "things to be done immediately" in revising the scenes for *Of Time and the River*.[13] Berg
describes "a series of letters, one of them thirty pages long" to Marcia
Davenport about the manuscript of *The Valley of Decision* (1942):

> He started at the beginning and picked out the most important story
> lines, those he felt should run through the entire novel; anything that
> weakened those strands had no business in the book. Ignoring Mrs.
> Davenport's divisions, he separated the novel into three major parts
> and told her the principal purpose of each. Then he provided an exten-

sive chapter-by-chapter breakdown, with detailed commentary. Finally, he clarified the characters for the author, sharpening their definition in short summaries of their traits—all this for a novel he was never quite sure would prove publishable.[14]

Perkins's efforts with Scott Fitzgerald include prompting the thorough rewriting of the manuscript of his first novel, *This Side of Paradise* (1920), with a change from first-person to third-person narrative; the toning down of a flippant speech about the Bible in his second, *The Beautiful and Damned* (1922); some changes in the characterization of the hero in his third, *The Great Gatsby* (1925); and a basic restructuring of the fourth, *Tender Is the Night* (1934), in a revised version that Fitzgerald intended for inclusion in Random House's Modern Library series (it was ultimately published by Scribner's, with a preface by Malcolm Cowley, in 1951).[15] In the case of *Gatsby,* Perkins wrote to Fitzgerald on 20 November 1924, describing a series of "actual criticisms":

> One is that among a set of characters marvelously palpable and vital . . . Gatsby is somewhat vague. The reader's eyes can never quite focus upon him, his outlines are dim. Now everything about Gatsby is more or less a mystery i.e. more or less vague, and this may be somewhat of an artistic intention, but I think it is mistaken. Couldn't *he* be physically described as distinctly as the others, and couldn't you add one or two characteristics like the use of that phrase "old sport",—not verbal, but physical ones, perhaps. . . .
> The other point is also about Gatsby: his career must remain mysterious, of course. But in the end you make it pretty clear that his wealth came through his connection with Wolfsheim. . . . It did occur to me . . . that you might here and there interpolate some phrases, and possibly incidents, little touches of various kinds, that would suggest that he was in some active way mysteriously engaged. You do have him called on the telephone, but couldn't he be seen once or twice consulting at his parties with people of some sort of mysterious significance, from the political, the gambling, the sporting world, or whatever it may be. . . .
> There is one other point: in giving deliberately Gatsby's biography when he gives it to the narrator you do depart from the method of the narrative in some degree. . . . I thought you might find ways to let the truth of some of his claims like "Oxford" and his army career come out bit by bit in the course of actual narrative.

Fitzgerald responded with gratitude ("Your criticisms were excellent & most helpful," "With the aid you've given me I can make 'Gatsby' perfect") and also with lengthy lists of the revisions he had made in the proofs and the admission that "*I myself didn't know what Gatsby looked like or was engaged in* & you felt it. . . . But I know now—and as a penalty for not having known first . . . I'm going to tell more."[16] The remark of Madeleine Boyd, Wolfe's first literary agent, that Perkins was "the sole and only excuse . . . for Scott Fitzgerald having been successful as he is"[17] is gross exaggeration, of course, but Perkins's influence has to be reckoned considerable nonetheless.

Throughout his career, Perkins professed a philosophy of editorial self-effacement, consistently maintaining, as he remarked to a group of extension students at New York University a year before he died, that "an editor does not add to a book. At best he serves as a handmaiden to an author. Don't ever get to feeling important about yourself, because an editor at most releases energy. He creates nothing." In his work with authors, Perkins told his wife, he wanted to be "a little dwarf on the shoulder of a great general advising him what to do and what not to do, without anyone's noticing."[18] But these and similar comments may be as much smoke screen as pathology. Perkins actually did much more than release energy and whisper advice. His influence in the aggregate was pervasive: virtually none of his authors would have had the same careers without him, and it is possible that some of them, like Wolfe, would hardly have had published writing careers at all. There are today, of course, very few active students of Wolfe's artistry. But *Gatsby,* to refer back to the most recent example here, is currently the most widely read American novel in our colleges and universities. Some of the good effects of plot, characterization, and description that readers attribute to Fitzgerald were in fact partly the work of Perkins. The "little dwarf" unquestionably made permanent contributions to American literature.

3

After Perkins, probably the editor exerting the most influence on our major literature was Saxe Commins, who worked at Liveright from 1931 to 1933 and then at Random House from 1933 until his death in 1958. His authors include three Nobel Prize winners— Eugene O'Neill, Sinclair Lewis, and William Faulkner—as well as such varied types as S. N. Behrman, John O'Hara, James A. Michener, Budd Schulberg, Henry Steele Commager, Robinson Jeffers,

William Carlos Williams, W. H. Auden, Irwin Shaw, Walter Van Tilburg Clark, and Isak Dinesen.[19]

Commins was not above ghostwriting when he had to. He wrote each of the forewords signed by O'Neill in the twelve-volume Wilderness Edition of *The Plays of Eugene O'Neill,* published by Scribner's in 1934 and 1935, and was single-handedly responsible for virtually all of Parker Morell's biography of Lillian Russell—producing some 75,000 words in less than three weeks of April and May 1940—which he had been assigned to "whip into shape." More important, he frequently provided the same kind of page-by-page response to manuscripts that Perkins gave his authors, as in this 1958 commentary on a partial draft of Behrman's biography of Max Beerbohm, the work published after Commins's death as *Portrait of Max* (1960):

> Page 1. It seems to me that much more can be made of Max's and Herbert's background by elaborating on Julius, Constantia, and Eliza, more or less as you did with the forebears of Duveen.
>
> Also on this page, could there be a little expansion of Max's attitude toward the "theatrical columnists" and why he wouldn't deign to point his silver dagger at them?
>
> Page 2. Would it be possible to convey a little of the prevailing atmosphere in America, particularly in Chicago, when Tree put on *An Enemy of the People.* Here Max's attitude toward his brother's showmanship is clear enough, but what about Herbert and the act he was putting on.
>
> Page 3. Harry Paine's shot at Max suggests the reaction to "In Defense of Cosmetics," but do you give enough of the flavor of the essay itself to make the reader aware of what the shooting was all about?
>
> Page 4. Would it be out of place to write in a sentence or two about *The Yellow Book.* It had quite a history. On this page you do give a little of the flavor of the essay, but I think it would profit by a few more comments almost in Max's own vein.
>
> Page 5. The references to Scott Fitzgerald and Ned Sheldon are dangling in midair. Unless you specify some of the similarities I'm afraid the comparison will be lost. And why not more about Aubrey Beardsley? . . .

Commins's remarks continue at length, with questions and suggestions for most pages of the manuscript.[20]

Commins's specialty was marathon sessions with his authors, frequently in his home in Princeton, New Jersey, in which editor and author would work together over a manuscript, line by line, for days and even weeks until the project was perfected and ready for the printer. Faulkner, whom Commins edited from 1936 (the year of *Absalom, Absalom!*) through the middle of 1958 (when they were working on *The Mansion*, published in 1960), was one of several authors who regularly showed up for such sessions. Commins's wife provides a pleasant reminiscence of the two men making revisions in the first part of the manuscript of *The Town* (1957):

> The two went off for an early walk. When they got back and had some coffee, Saxe extended the large oak table in the living room, which serves as a dining table as well. Saxe then brought in his brief bag, which contained what there was of the new Snopes manuscript, soon to be given the title *The Town*. The pages of the manuscript soon covered most of the table, leaving just enough room to make notes. Many pages were already spread on the floor. What a sight that was to see Bill [Faulkner] and Saxe on their knees, moving from one page to another, marking, deleting, transferring passages here and there!
>
> Following lunch, Bill, at Saxe's suggestion, lay down for an hour's nap. Then, in the early twilight, they went for another short walk. When they returned, we had dinner, and after that the table was quickly cleared and the work resumed. I left the room as Saxe was going over a portion of the manuscript and Bill was sitting in his favorite spot near the fireplace. Suddenly I heard Saxe pound the table with his fist.
>
> "Bill," he said, "this won't do! You've said it before! It's redundant, and you are only weakening your premise."
>
> Bill didn't say a word. Later, when Saxe turned in for the night, he said to me, "I wish Bill had talked back to me. He could have said, 'Goddamnit, this is my book; I want it that way!' Instead, he just sat there with his pipe."
>
> In the morning, when I went into the kitchen, I noticed that Bill had already had his coffee and toast and that in Saxe's place at the table there were four newly typed pages with the old version pinned underneath. Evidently Bill had stayed up half the night revising the pages. When Saxe read them, he was delighted.[21]

Perkins and Commins were clearly our most distinguished twentieth-century American editors, but numerous others have contributed to the tradition as well—for example, Harold Strauss (editor-in-chief at Covici–Friede and then Alfred A. Knopf), Henry W. Simon (vice president and senior editor at Simon and Schuster), John Farrar (editor and chairman of Farrar, Straus), Pascal Covici (editor at Viking), Burroughs Mitchell (a successor to Perkins at

Scribner's), William Targ (editor at World Publishing and G. P. Putnam's Sons), Betty A. Prashker (vice president and editor-in-chief at Crown Publishers), Samuel S. Vaughan (vice president and editor-in-chief at Doubleday), Faith Sale (a senior editor at Putnam's) and, to mention a trio of magazine editors, Harold Ross (of the *New Yorker* from 1925 to 1951), Ellery Sedgwick (of the *Atlantic Monthly* from 1908 to 1938), and Edward Weeks (Sedgwick's successor from 1938 to 1966).[22]

Consider, as a representative recent example of the same editorial methods used by Perkins and Commins, this account from an interview with Helen Wolff, cofounder of Helen and Kurt Wolff Books, published by Harcourt Brace Jovanovich. Wolff is describing her work on a book that had been commissioned on the strength of an outline and a sample chapter:

> It sounded like a foolproof project, and the author had a considerable reputation. Everybody in our office was excited about it. With all this excitement, the contract was signed and a sizable advance agreed upon. The final manuscript, alas, did not live up to expectation and reputation. The treatment of a rich subject turned out to be skimpy, the facts alarmingly inaccurate, the general tone one of condescending flippancy. I showed it to a colleague who had originally been the most encouraging. His reaction was crushing: "Helen, you are in deep trouble." After I had absorbed the blow, my first step was to draw up a list, chapter by chapter, of what did not work. My second, to go to the author, rather than beg her to come to me. The bearer of bad news had better be considerate. Next, I asked the author to spend another six months on a book she had considered finished. She was virtually on her way to Europe, so this was quite a blow. I also suggested that we discuss each rewritten chapter as it came out of the typewriter. In one case, a chapter was expanded from four to twenty-four pages, giving it the integrity and substance it had lacked. As we worked together, I became aware of various strengths and weaknesses—no sense of place, a great sense of people. We proceeded to discard entire chapters that had never come to life. She added some that were more in tune with her gifts. In the meanwhile, facts and names were discreetly checked. My worry throughout was how to keep her spirits up, through the tedious process of rewriting. I can still see the stacks of manuscript, corrected in various inks, cut and pasted, shuffled, reshuffled, retyped. Maddening though the work was, I considered myself lucky. I was dealing with an intelligent, coöperative professional, not with a bundle of nerves. Eventually, this book was published, was widely and favorably reviewed, and more than earned its advance, which had caused me

many nightmares. The author and I still exchange sincerely amiable Christmas greetings.[23]

An editor who gives this much help to an author is ultimately responsible for the difference between the existence and the nonexistence of a book. Small wonder that numerous authors and publishers (if not literary scholars) have recognized the central importance of editors to their success. For some time now, editors' names have been appearing on title pages—"A Helen and Kurt Wolff Book," or, in the especially appropriate instance of Scott Berg's biography of Max Perkins, "Thomas Congdon Books"—in a size of type equal to that of the publishers' imprint. And not surprisingly, authors have made crucial decisions in choosing publishers on the basis of their past or anticipated relationships with editors. Joseph Heller's move from Alfred A. Knopf to G. P. Putnam's Sons is a recent prominent example. When Robert Gottlieb, Heller's editor for *Catch-22* and other novels, left Knopf to become editor of the *New Yorker* in March 1987, several rival publishers approached Heller with offers for his works in progress. Heller, in signing a two-book contract with Putnam's for a new novel plus a sequel to *Catch-22,* chose Putnam's, as he told the *New York Times,* "because the price was right" but also because he had enjoyed working with one of Putnam's editors, Faith Sale, in a book of nonfiction published the preceding year. Sale, the *Times* explains, will edit both of Heller's new novels.[24]

The one recurring oddity in all the evidence concerning their relationships with authors is the editors' continual insistence on the supreme importance of the author and the downplaying of their own contributions to the works in which they are, in fact, collaborators. I have already mentioned Perkins's concept of editorial self-effacement at the end of the preceding section. The same idea runs like a litany through Gerald Gross's *Editors on Editing:* "a book . . . is first and last the author's"; "the author is God"; "I don't believe that an editor's part in a book is a creative act. The writer performs that act"; "all credit belongs to the authors"; "[Maxwell Perkins would] probably be shocked to hear himself classified as a virtual co-writer"; "the final responsibility for the book is the author's. It's his idea, his baby"; "I see my role as helping the writer to realize his or her intention. . . . I never want the book to be mine"; "We believe that the editor has one primary responsibility, one loyalty, and that is to the *author's book*. . . . No editor should labor under the delusion that he or she is a collaborator"[25]—all this from a group of professionals who in other comments in the same collection make quite clear that they are themselves initiators of many of the subjects, themes, and plots of the books they work on and of revision and improvement in virtually every aspect of the writing. It would appear that the myth of the author's preeminence is strongly cherished by the very people who have the greatest knowledge of authors' failings and needs for assistance.

One could speculate at length about the psychology involved (the "pathological" self-effacement referred to earlier), but there is one obvious practical explanation for this reiterated party line. It is that editors *have* to say such things—in letters to authors and in public statements like those in Gross's collection—in order to appease the natural vanity of their authors. However moving their professions of gratitude (in dedications, prefaces, and other forms of acknowledgment), writers almost without exception resent the idea that other people are even partially responsible for the works supposed to be the products of their unique genius. An editor who made much of a claim as collaborator would very quickly find the authors giving their manuscripts to rival publishers. The fact is that authors themselves are among the most ardent believers in the myth of single authorship.

4

Many others besides editors working with authors have played a collaborative role in the creation of literary texts. There are, in the first place, editors *not* working with authors, as in posthumous books that are put into publishable shape from authors' incomplete manuscripts—for example, Hemingway's *The Garden of Eden* (1986), a novel produced by the Scribner's editor Tom Jenks, who combined parts of three manuscripts and reduced forty-eight chapters and 200,000 words to thirty chapters and 65,000 words (fewer than 250 printed pages), and Hermann Broch's *The Spell* (1987), a mingling of draft and revised text from two manuscripts that Broch left unfinished at his death in 1951. According to Scribner's "Publisher's Note" at the front of *The Garden of Eden*, "In preparing the book for publication we have made some cuts in the manuscript and some routine copy-editing corrections. Beyond a very small number of minor interpolations for clarity and consistency, nothing has been added. In every significant respect the work is all the author's." But one critic who has compared the printed text with the manuscripts in the Kennedy Library, Boston, strongly disagrees:

> Hemingway's publisher has committed a literary crime. . . . To paraphrase the publisher, in almost no significant respect is this book its author's. With all its disfigurements and omissions, its heightening of the trivial and its diminishment of the significant, its vulgarization of the great themes of Hemingway's final years, this volume is a travesty.[26]

Literary agents have frequently assumed some of the same duties as editors, and usually for the same practical reasons. Elizabeth Nowell, Thomas Wolfe's agent for his short fiction, routinely revised and compressed the material that she quarried from his manuscripts and sent out to periodicals.[27] Ben Wasson, acting as Faulkner's agent for the manuscript of his third novel—the first of the series about Yoknapatawpha County—cut out some twenty thousand words, containing significant characters and incidents, to make the work acceptable by Harcourt, Brace, which published it as *Sartoris* in 1929. The uncut version, with Faulkner's original title, "Flags in the Dust," was finally published, again with editorial help and alterations, in 1973.[28]

Publishers (where they can be considered independently of their editors) exert influence of all sorts. Richard Wright's best-selling *Black Boy* (1945) is merely a piece of the autobiography that Wright originally wrote; the drastically truncated version, with a new title and a different ending, was dictated and shaped by the directors of the Book-of-the-Month Club.[29] John Barth made major changes in the original version of his first novel, *The Floating Opera* (1956), to meet the demands of the publisher, Appleton-Century-Crofts.[30] In the American edition of Anthony Burgess's *A Clockwork Orange*, published in England in 1962, W. W. Norton purposely omitted the final chapter, an unconvincing (in the publisher's view) account of the formerly vicious protagonist's sudden acceptance of morality and social responsibility.[31] And even before agents, publishers, and editors get their hands on the works, friends and colleagues also are frequent collaborators, as (to give but a single instance) in the well-known circumstance of Fitzgerald's persuading Hemingway to drop the first fifteen pages of the original opening of *The Sun Also Rises* (1926)—two chapters of meandering biographical background for Brett Ashley and some others ("careless & ineffectual," "flat as hell," "elephantine facetiousness," wrote Fitzgerald)—so that the novel could instead begin with Jake Barnes's description of the antagonist, Robert Cohn.[32]

In this final section I wish to develop briefly, as an epitomizing example, a case of collaborative authorship involving several kinds of helpers. The work in question is Theodore Dreiser's *Sister Carrie* (1900), drafted in the first place by Dreiser; revised at various stages by Dreiser's wife, Sara, his friend Arthur Henry, and Dreiser himself; and additionally altered by typists, editors, printers, and proofreaders in the usual processes of transcription and publication. The example is of special interest because of a scholarly controversy that has arisen as a consequence of the 1981 publication of a new edition of the work by the University of Pennsylvania Press.[33] The controversy concerns a number of issues, but the principal one comes down to the question: Which, of several recoverable versions, is the "real" *Sister Carrie?*

The novel, 557 pages long in the first edition, was produced in an amazingly short time.[34] Dreiser started drafting it, in pencil on coarse yellow half-sheets, in September 1899, continued through the middle of October, wrote some more between the middle of December and late January, resumed again in February and made steady progress until he reached, as he noted in the draft, "The End. / Thursday, March 29—1900—2.53 P.M." All told, he appears to have spent about five months writing the initial version. He began having his draft copied (by a typing agency) when he was three-fifths of the way through the work, and, because the typists quickly caught up with him, he had a complete typed version very soon after finishing the draft and thus was able to submit it to a publisher, Harper and Brothers, almost immediately, in early April. Harper rejected it three weeks later—because it was too long, was too realistic, and would not be sufficiently interesting to "the feminine readers who control the destinies of so many novels"—and then, after further revision and cuts in reaction to Harper's criticism, the work was submitted to Doubleday, Page and Company, in May. Doubleday's first reader, the novelist Frank Norris, responded enthusiastically, and Walter Hines Page, the junior partner of the firm, accepted the work in mid-June. In the following month the senior partner, Frank Doubleday, who had been abroad, returned to New York, read the typescript with dismay, and tried to get Dreiser to withdraw it. But Dreiser stood his ground, and the firm reluctantly went ahead; galleys and pages were ready in September, bound copies by late October, and official publication was on 8 November 1900—no more than fourteen months after Dreiser first inscribed his title, "Sister Carrie," at the top of a blank sheet of draft paper.

Dreiser's pencil manuscript, which is in the New York Public Library, and the typescript, which is in the Dreiser Collection of the University of Pennsylvania Library, tell us a great deal about the successive stages of revision; the differences between the typescript and the printed text of 1900, which was set from the typescript, constitute further material concerning changes that were introduced while the work was in press. Other hands than Dreiser's—the Pennsylvania editors refer to them as "nonauthorial" (pp. 577, 578, 580)—helped shape the text almost from the beginning. When Dreiser finished the first three chapters, he handed them over to his wife for comments, criticism, and polishing, and then to Arthur Henry for further improvements. Thereafter, he routinely gave his draft to both of them for revision and editing. As the Pennsylvania editors point out,

> This practice was by now habitual: during his apprentice years as a newspaper reporter, Dreiser had become accustomed to working with copy-editors and rewrite men, and he had never developed much sensitivity about his prose. He had always been a poor speller and an indifferent grammarian; Jug [Sara Dreiser's nickname], who knew the mechanics of the language from her teaching days, could correct demonstrable errors in his drafts. Henry's function was different; he was a published author with some feeling for the style and rhythm of English prose, and Dreiser allowed him to identify and revise awkward spots in the drafts. The manuscript of *Sister Carrie* therefore exhibits, in nearly every chapter, markings by both Jug and Henry. (p. 507)

The typists, who regularly added punctuation in the next manuscript version, were also responsible for substantive changes in places where they misread the original wording and Dreiser, in the process of correcting and revising, repaired the mistake by inventing new text rather than checking the draft for what he had written in the first place. Sara Dreiser and Arthur Henry continued their revising in the typescript, the former mainly attending to mechanics, factual details, the reduction of colloquialisms, and the censoring of overly physical description, the latter concerning himself with the improvement of style and syntax and the elimination of wordiness. Dreiser was also an active reviser in the typescript, sometimes rewriting in response to markings by his wife or Henry, sometimes adding and changing on his own.

When it was determined that the novel had to be cut and cleaned up (probably, as the Pennsylvania editors assume, in response to the rejection by Harper), Dreiser got Henry to do a preliminary marking of block cuts—for example, minute analyses of the heroine's thoughts, lengthy philosophical passages, factual details about the principal cities in the book, and passages of sexually offensive material—and Dreiser followed Henry's suggestions, eliminating some 36,000 words.[35] Other alterations were blue-penciled in the typescript by someone at Doubleday, Page—mostly the fictionalizing of real names and removal of profanity—and still more changes were made in response by Dreiser and Henry, including the addition of titles for the fifty chapters. And then numerous further revisions were introduced at proof-stage— corrections and tidyings by Dreiser and his wife, additional censorings by the publisher. This elaborate process of revision, pretty much continual from September 1899 through September 1900, took more than twice as long as the original drafting.

The Pennsylvania editors present all this information with admirable clarity and an abundance of supporting detail, taking special pains to emphasize that Dreiser was an active collaborator in the revisions, that he seems to have fully approved of the help he was getting, and that he never, during the forty-five years that he lived after the original publication of *Sister Carrie,* attempted to restore any of his original text in place of the revisions, even though he retained a manuscript version (the much revised typescript) almost to the end of his life. How strange, then, in view of their command of the facts, that the Pennsylvania editors should choose Dreiser's pencil draft—and especially a hypothetical state of the draft *before* Dreiser's wife and Henry began marking it—as the base-text for their new edition.

In fact there are four, and only four, actually existing versions of *Sister Carrie* that have theoretical claims to be considered authoritative: the final text of the pencil draft, extant in New York; the final text of the typescript, extant in Philadelphia; and the texts of the first edition, published by Doubleday, Page in 1900—the direct or indirect source of all subsequent printings before the Pennsylvania edition in 1981—and the abridgment of the Doubleday edition published by Heinemann in 1901. These are authoritative in the general sense that Dreiser (with his helpers) actively produced the first three and approved the production of the fourth; the typescript could be considered more authoritative than the draft, on the grounds that it was intended to supersede an earlier, inferior version, and the earliest

printed texts could be considered more authoritative than the typescript on similar grounds, with the addition that Dreiser certainly
wanted the novel to appear as a published book (and, in the case of
the 1901 abridgment, hoped to make some money from British royal-
ties). I specify "final text" for the two manuscripts because it is both
theoretically and practically impossible to prove that any combination
of earlier readings recoverable from one or the other manuscript ever
actually existed together as a textual entity. The revising was carried
on as a continual process in both manuscripts, with the text of any
given part always in a more advanced or less advanced state of revision than the text of some other parts (until the revising was finally
concluded, that is), and thus the reconstituting of a *single* earlier state
of manuscript text can be only a hypothetical ideal, like the flat map
of the entire world included in geography books or, to offer a home-
lier comparison, an account of how a person *would* have been dressed
had he (or she) not made a great many changes of intention in the
process of putting on the separate items of clothing one after another.

The Pennsylvania editors know all this. Their text, they boast, "is
much more than a new version of the novel. It is in fact a new work of
art, heretofore unknown" (p. 532). But tied as they are to the then-
prevailing "modern copy-text principles of scholarly editing," by
which they mean the theory of W. W. Greg as publicized and developed by Fredson Bowers,[36] they are obligated to choose an extant
manuscript over an early printed version for their copy-text, and
(carrying the theory to an extreme) a less revised early manuscript
over a more revised later one—and thus are obligated to construct an
eclectic text on the basis of Dreiser's pencil draft:

> The selection of copy-text for *Sister Carrie* is simple. Dreiser's manu-
> script of the novel automatically becomes the base text for this edition.
> No other choice is possible: the typescript was corrupted by Anna
> Mallon's typists and was revised and cut by Sara Dreiser and Arthur
> Henry. The first printing was further flawed by editorial interference
> and censoring by Doubleday, Page and Company. Only the manuscript
> preserves the original text of *Sister Carrie,* the text that was most nearly
> under Dreiser's complete control. A further distinction must be made,
> however: copy-text for the Pennsylvania *Sister Carrie* is the original
> form of the manuscript *before* Jug and Henry made revisions in it.
> Some of their changes have been accepted into the text of this edition,
> but for theoretical reasons the copy-text must be defined as Dreiser's
> original manuscript, before nonauthorial alterations were introduced.
> (pp. 577–78)

The result is indeed a "new" *Sister Carrie,* one that rejects not only the factual, stylistic, and narrative changes initiated by Sara Dreiser and Henry but also Dreiser's revised ending of the novel, his and Henry's chapter titles, and the block cuts made by Henry and approved by Dreiser. In this expanded form, now some 36,000 words longer than the version that for eighty years was our standard, *Sister Carrie* is, in the editors' opinion, "a more somber and unresolved work of art . . . [in which] the characters assume the original clarity of the artist's design," "infinitely richer, more complex, and more tragic than it was before" (pp. ix, 532). Such opinion is highly subjective, of course. One disapproving reviewer, describing the Pennsylvania methods as "a superficial editorial romanticism," pronounces the new text "principally longer, more cumbersome, and more explicit, with some of its explicitness . . . running counter to Dreiser's final sense of his characters' natures."[37]

There are several controversial features of the Pennsylvania edition (one could, taking sides, call them faults), not least of which is the arbitrariness with which the editors accept or reject individual revisions according to their conjectures about Dreiser's involvement in them or their critical assessment of the artistic or logical appropriateness of the readings. While totally opposed to the "nonauthorial" interference of Sara Dreiser, Henry, and the publisher, the editors are themselves at least equally nonauthorial in *their* interference, with the rather conspicuous difference that Dreiser was alive and in a position to work with his contemporary "nonauthors" but is totally removed from the possibility of influencing this posthumous picking and choosing.

I have already commented on the impossibility of extracting a "purified" Dreiser from the ongoing process constituted by the successive manuscripts and the first printings. The resulting distortion—the Pennsylvania text—is similar to what might result if we tried to separate Mill from the collaborative enterprise represented by the early draft of the *Autobiography,* as described in Chapter 3. At any specific point we can demonstrate, or surmise, that Mill or Dreiser did such-and-such, but it would be quite wrong, and accord with no one's intention (save, perhaps, the intention of some modern editor), to claim that an aggregate of such pieces of information is the equivalent of a onetime extant text. As a work of textual investigation, providing an immense collection of facts about the manuscripts, composition, revision, printing, and publication of *Sister Carrie,* the Pennsylvania edition is an invaluable contribution. But its text, an essentially fanciful construct, bears little relation to that mass of textual information.

Perhaps the greatest cause for concern is the likelihood that the Pennsylvania *Sister Carrie* will permanently replace the hitherto standard text, based on the first printed edition, and that Dreiser's reputation (as principal author) and the place of the novel in the history of American fiction will be diminished accordingly. Donald Pizer and others have contrasted the 1900 *Sister Carrie*'s status as historical artifact—the version that challenged, entertained, and influenced readers at the time and for the next eight decades and that put Dreiser, as it were, among the American novelists—with the Pennsylvania text's lack of this same kind of historical validity (it has its own historical status, of course, as an example of late-twentieth-century application of Greg–Bowers textual theory!). But the problem transcends historical considerations and is much like the textual primitivists' inadvertent standardizing of Wordsworth's early texts that I discussed in Chapter 4. The Pennsylvania text has already been reprinted in the Penguin American Library edition (also 1981) and may very well become the text regularly used by readers and students from now on. Just as in the case of the unwary reader happening upon an unpolished and undistinguished version of a famous poem in the Cornell Wordsworth, the innocent seeker of *Sister Carrie* may wonder how Dreiser—all the more clumsy and long-winded in the Pennsylvania text—got to be such a big name in American literature. Somebody, this innocent seeker may think privately, should have helped Dreiser revise his prose!

8

Plays and Films:
Authors, Auteurs, Autres

In general, plays and films are by nature more explicitly collaborative than any of the other kinds of production discussed so far in this book. They are *literally* "show business" and, as such, have to sell to audiences or they go out of existence. They involve many more people and much greater expense than books, and require the commitment of investors who expect a profit. And not only does it take enormous numbers of people to create plays and films (agents, studio executives, producers, directors, writers, actors, designers, stage and camera technicians, editors, publicists and marketing executives, to name some of the large groups who may be responsible to the backers of the enterprise), but there are potential conflicts of interest and authority among them at every crucial moment of production.

There is also the circumstance that plays and films are far more flexible than books in their processes of taking shape. A play is rehearsed for a period of trial-and-error experimentation and then, if it succeeds to the next level of production, may be performed repeatedly over months, years, or even (in the case of classics, standard repertory pieces, and revivals) centuries. Audience reactions can be (and sometimes actually are) monitored on a daily basis, and numerous revisions can be introduced in response to them. Films might be thought to be less pliable in this respect, but there is continual editing and reediting during production, and changes may be made at many different stages in response to preview audiences, rating agencies, influential reviews, and trends at the box office, not to mention the whims of producers, directors, actors, and the rest of the numerous company.

In their character as extreme types of multiple authorship, however, plays and films are theoretically different from one another in an important respect. In plays the "author" is still considered to be—

just as with poems, autobiographies, novels, and the rest of the writ-ten genres—the principal *named* writer of the work; while in films, at least for the last quarter of a century, the "author," to the extent that there has been a need for one, has more often been identified with the director rather than with any of the actual writers. In plays, therefore, all the collaborators are (or may be thought to be) collabo-rating with the named author who wrote the work in the first place; in films, the collaborators are usually considered to be working with the director.

Since so much of the collaborative nature of plays and films is already well known—from the extraordinary spate of popular and academic books during the past two decades, as well as newspaper and magazine articles and behind-the-scenes television documenta-ries about the creation of successful works—I shall provide just a handful of representative examples to make my points.

1

It may be difficult to believe, given our long familiarity with the major writers of sixteenth- and seventeenth-century British drama, that the first playbill identifying the author of a play performed in England dates from March 1699, a full century after Shakespeare was at the height of his powers.[1] In fact, however, ordinary playgoers of the seventeenth century had no more notion of dramatic authorship than we have today when we turn on the television to watch "L.A. Law" or "thirtysomething." Frequently playgoers did not even know the title of the play they were attending; they simply went to the playhouse to see a spectacle or a story (often both) and be enter-tained. The idea of the sacredness of an individual author's text was as yet unknown, and nothing in either law or sentiment stood in the way of adapting, cutting, rearranging, and even massive rewriting in the interests of spectacle, story, and entertainment. Adapting, cut-ting, and rewriting were, therefore, frequent and widespread.

Consider the numerous changes made over the years in the act-ing texts of Shakespeare, who for the last two centuries has perfuncto-rily been ranked as our most esteemed writer in English. Probably the best-known alteration of a Shakespeare play is Nahum Tate's adapta-tion of *King Lear,* first performed in 1680 or 1681, a version in which more than a thousand of Shakespeare's lines are omitted, most of the remaining two thousand lines are revised and flattened, Lear's Fool is entirely excised, Cordelia and Edgar are made lovers, Edmund's villainy is expanded to include an attempted rape of Cordelia, and the story ends happily with the defeat of Lear's enemies, the retirement of Lear and Gloucester (who also survives in this version) "to some cool cell," and the marriage of Cordelia and Edgar: "Our drooping country now erects her head," says Edgar in the final speech, "Peace spreads her balmy wings, and Plenty blooms."[2] Tate, as he explains in his dedication of the published text in 1681, viewed the original play as "a heap of jewels, unstrung and unpolished"; his aim was "to rectify what was wanting in . . . regularity and probability." In general, the critics have roundly condemned Tate's "rectification": "ribald trash," according to Charles Lamb, in his famous essay "On the Tragedies of Shakspeare"; "notorious vandalization," in the words of a reviewer in the *New York Times* 175 years later, when it was revived (in a further freewheeling adaptation) by the Riverside Shakespeare Company in March 1985.[3] Yet Tate's was the *standard* version of "Shakespeare's" play for nearly 160 years, from the 1680s through the 1830s, the very period in which Shakespeare rose to his present eminence among the major British writers. And Tate's liberties, in the long history of collaborative Shakespeare performance, are just the tip (perhaps one should say the bottom) of the iceberg.[4]

Sir William Davenant, said to have been Shakespeare's godson, played a chief role in the "improving" of Shakespeare. As director of the Duke's Men when theatrical performances were resumed with the restoration of Charles II in 1660, Davenant built in Lincoln's Inn Fields the first theater ever to have a scene house with proscenium arch and grooves for movable painted scenery. Originally, of course, Shakespeare's plays were performed entirely without scenery. Davenant's new design not only initiated the use of scenery but made possible increasingly elaborate and sensational visual displays, including machines that allowed characters (witches in *Macbeth,* spirits in *The Tempest*) to fly through the air. Ultimately it led to the suppression of some of Shakespeare's best descriptive writing (the logical result of *showing* a scene rather than depicting it via speech).

Davenant was busy also in "reforming" and "making fit" the individual plays, as in his adaptations of *Macbeth* and (with Dryden) *The Tempest* in the mid-1660s. His *Macbeth* introduces a ghost of Duncan to balance the ghost of Banquo, builds up the role of Lady Macduff as foil to Lady Macbeth, and, in pursuing an ideal of strict logic, does away with much of Shakespeare's distinctive poetic language. Davenant's Lady Macbeth enjoins her husband to "Bring . . .

your courage to the fatal place" (instead of "screw your courage to the sticking place"); his sleep "locks up the senses from their care" (instead of "knits up the ravell'd sleave of care"); and in the "To-morrow, and to-morrow, and to-morrow" speech, Shakespeare's "petty pace" becomes "stealing pace," "last syllable" becomes "last minute," and "The way to dusty death" becomes "To their eternal homes":

> To-morrow, to-morrow, and to-morrow,
> Creeps in a stealing pace from day to day,
> To the last minute of recorded time,
> And all our yesterdays have lighted fools
> To their eternal homes.[5]

The Davenant–Dryden *Tempest* likewise gave the audience new scenes, characters, and speeches, and a host of stage effects that not even Prospero's magic could accomplish.

Thomas Shadwell redid *Timon of Athens* (adding a love story); Dryden, *Troilus and Cressida* (turning Cressida into a romantic victim of circumstances); and Otway, *Romeo and Juliet* (emphasizing politics rather than the lovers' tragedy)—all in the late 1670s—and Colley Cibber rewrote *Richard III* (with seven additional soliloquies for the villainous principal) in 1700. Cibber's *Richard* continued to be staged well into the twentieth century and influenced (and provided part of the text of) Laurence Olivier's film of the play in 1955. There is even report of a *Romeo and Juliet* with a happy ending.[6] Because women were now (since 1660) allowed to act on the stage, virtually all these Shakespeare adaptations had both new and much expanded female roles. And early Shakespeare scholarship introduced yet another form of collaborative improvement when Nicholas Rowe, in the first *edited* text of the plays (1709), divided the works into acts and scenes and added stage directions.

Needless to say, these and other seventeenth- and early-eighteenth-century adaptations, the calculated product of the new tastes and technologies of their age, had the effect of driving (or keeping) the originals off the stage. Much of the history of Shakespeare performance in the nearly three centuries that followed—right up to our own time—is an account of professed attempts, and conspicuous failures, to restore the "true" Shakespeare to the stage. David Garrick, for example, the most influential actor–producer of the eighteenth century, claimed to stage *Macbeth, Lear, Romeo and Juliet,* and other plays "as written by Shakespeare" and yet, along with some partial restorations, made nearly as many changes as Davenant and the rest of the adapters had in the century just preceding. John Philip Kemble, presiding at Drury Lane in the last two decades of the eighteenth century and at Covent Garden in the first two of the nineteenth, had a reputation for scholarly accuracy in his productions but nevertheless restaged Tate's, Garrick's, and other adaptations, making his own contributions in such matters as historical costumes and stage architecture. Later in the nineteenth century, William Charles Macready advertised his efforts to "restore the true text" of Shakespeare and managed to get rid of many of the lines added by previous adapters, but, as Charles Shattuck describes it, the *Lear* that he produced was hardly closer to Shakespeare's than Tate's had been:

> His *King Lear,* which he brought out in 1838, contained no Tate, but only two-thirds of Shakespeare. He suppressed all lines which he thought unintelligible or sacrilegious or obscene. He suppressed the blinding of Gloucester, which would have been too painful for his audience to endure, and Gloucester's attempt to leap from the cliff, which probably seemed too eccentric and possibly comic. He almost suppressed the Fool, fearing that it would "weary or annoy or distract the spectator," but a few weeks before the opening his stage manager convinced him that this "fragile, hectic, beautiful-faced, half-idiot-looking boy" (so Macready conceived the Fool) might be realized if a woman played it. Accordingly the role was stripped of all its indelicacies and most of its comic touches and assigned to Priscilla Horton, whose Fool was all tenderness and pathos.[7]

After Macready came "the Fechter method" (Charles Albert Fechter's turning Hamlet and Othello into Pickwickians in 1861), "spectacular" Shakespeare (later nineteenth- and early-twentieth-century productions by Henry Irving and Beerbohm Tree in which the texts had to be rearranged and cut drastically to allow time for changing the elaborate scenery), and, especially in our own century, all varieties of modern-dress Shakespeare (Hamlet in a dinner jacket, for example), "stunts-and-games" Shakespeare (*All's Well* as a comic strip, *Troilus and Cressida* as a version of the American Civil War), and downright silly Shakespeare (the zany *Hamlet* productions of Charles Marowitz and Joseph Papp). In the summer of 1989, a "star-studded" Papp production of *Twelfth Night* featured a tap-dancing Gregory Hines and Jeff Goldblum playing Malvolio as a human fly. These details could be multiplied and elaborated at great length, but this sketchy recital should suffice as a reminder that "Shakespeare" on the stage has been a collaborative enterprise for the last three and a half centuries. The real (historical) Shakespeare supplied plots, characters, speeches, and descriptions; and subsequent playwrights, producers, directors, designers, actors, screenwriters, and the rest have made free use of these initial materials in works that bear the same titles as Shakespeare's plays and are usually presented with some mention of Shakespeare's authorship (though occasionally with an acknowledgment of collaboration in the credits, as in the 1929 film of *The Taming of the Shrew* "Written by William Shakespeare with additional dialogue by Sam Taylor").[8] But the works are not purely Shakespeare's any more than Shakespeare's original plays are equatable with the sources that we know Shakespeare drew on for *his* plots, characters, speeches, and descriptions. This is just as it should be in the performing arts, where the achievement often lies as much in the performance as in the text or score. Nobody should be surprised or alarmed by these manifestations of jointly authored "Shakespeare."

But what about the plays in Shakespeare's own time? Virtually all studies of the authorship of works written for commercial entertainment in the Elizabethan and Jacobean theaters emphasize the prevalence of collaborative authorship.[9] Cyrus Hoy's seven-part analysis of the Beaumont and Fletcher canon, for example, demonstrates that Beaumont and Fletcher together wrote fewer than twelve of the fifty-two plays in the canon, and that most of the rest are joint efforts of Fletcher with many other colleagues (including Philip Massinger, Nathan Field, William Rowley, Thomas Middleton, and James Shirley).[10] And G. E. Bentley, in his study of playwriting from 1590 to 1642, marshals abundant evidence from theater records, title pages, prefaces, and commendatory verses to support his contention that "as many as half of the plays by professional dramatists in the period incorporated the writing at some date of more than one man."[11] Philip Henslowe's diary (an account of financial transactions involving several companies) repeatedly records payments to two, three, four, and even five persons for the writing of a single play, and there are numerous entries of payments for rewriting, "mending," and adding to plays after they were initially purchased. A frequent practice of joint authorship was dividing up the work by individual acts; the commonest types of revision were cuts and other changes for the original production made by the prompter or "book-holder" of the company and then additions (new scenes, songs, prologues, and epilogues) made in connection with the revival of plays.[12]

Documentary evidence of this sort of collaboration is generally lacking for Shakespeare himself, who did not write for any of the companies financed by Henslowe. Still there are persuasive arguments for the likelihood of other hands besides Shakespeare's in *The Taming of the Shrew, Henry VIII, Pericles,* and *The Two Noble Kinsmen,* among others, and of Shakespeare's hand in the complexly authored *Booke of Sir Thomas More.* [13] Twenty-five of Shakespeare's plays show evidence of having undergone revision, and it is by no means certain that Shakespeare himself was the reviser in every instance. [14] And then there is the collaborative character of Shakespeare's own interactions with his sources—North's translation of Plutarch, Holinshed's *Chronicles,* Arthur Brooke's poem on Romeo and Juliet, romances by Lodge and Greene, tales by Boccaccio and Cinthio, and the rest of the array collected and pored over by specialists. We do not regularly think of Shakespeare as a reviser of other men's works, but in some parts of his plays he is as much an adapter of earlier material as Davenant, Tate, and Cibber, in their day, were of Shakespeare, or as modern screenwriters are of the novels and plays they turn into films.

What is most to the point, as Bentley emphasizes throughout his study, is simply that Shakespeare's professional activity was by nature a collaborative enterprise involving, just as dramatic production does today, the cooperation of writers, directors (in the early form of prompters and theater managers), actors, musicians, costumers, and even audiences. Authors wrote their plays with clear ideas of the number, types, and capabilities of the specific actors in their company, the size and design of the specific theater in which they worked, and, not least, the expectations of the audiences who would pay money to see the plays. Concerning this last, Alfred Harbage, who devoted a long career to the study of Elizabethan theaters and audiences, opens one of his late essays with these striking sentences: "Shakespeare's plays would not have been enjoyed if they had offended the moral and religious sentiments prevailing in the audience for which they were designed. A basic conformity with the current system of values must be assumed." [15] Understandably, no one in the interim has taken up the challenge to write a book titled *Shakespeare the Conformist.* But Harbage's words underscore the fact that Shakespeare as a professional dramatist could never in any practical sense have worked separately from the rest of the people on whom his effectiveness and success depended.

2

For the collaborative character of modern play production, where information is much more plentiful, consider the examples of Tom Stoppard's *Travesties,* first staged in London in the summer of 1974, and William Gibson's *Two for the Seesaw,* which opened in Washington and then went on to Philadelphia and New York in the winter of 1957/58. In the one instance, the writer accepted and responded to the help of his collaborators as a matter of course; in the other instance, the writer hated what was done to his play and wrote a passion-filled book to complain about it.

We have a sizable body of details about the production of Stoppard's *Travesties* because Philip Gaskell used the play as one of twelve chapter-long examples in his 1978 book, *From Writer to Reader: Studies in Editorial Method.* For each of the first eleven examples, which range from Sir John Harington's translation of *Orlando furioso* (1591) to Joyce's *Ulysses* (1922), Gaskell describes the principal manuscripts and printed texts, gives us the circumstances of composition, transmission of text, and publication, and then considers how the work might best be presented in a modern edition. For *Travesties,* Gaskell's main materials are Stoppard's "original script" of the play (actually a revised draft as fair-copied by a typing agency), a tape recording of a complete performance that Gaskell made toward the end of the first London run (24 July 1974), and the "reading" text that Stoppard published as a book in the spring of 1975. In addition, Gaskell made another recording of a performance during the second London run the following year (13 September 1975) and got further information from Stoppard himself concerning the New York production of the play in 1975 and 1976.[16]

After drafting and revising the script on his own, Stoppard attended rehearsals and worked with the director and the actors in making changes, which Gaskell describes as "both major and minor," to arrive at an acceptable performance text. During nine "preview" performances, further changes, partly suggested by audience response, were incorporated by agreement among author, director, and the actors. By the time that Gaskell took his first recording of the play, the text was of course considerably altered from the original script that Stoppard had handed to the company. The version that Stoppard published in 1975—"his own preferred text of *Travesties,* the version that he would like to have performed by an ideal cast," as Gaskell relates the author's comments—is yet another version, agreeing in some parts with the original script, in other parts with the changes introduced in the performance text, and embodying further revisions not in any of the previous texts. The version that Gaskell taped from the second run of the play, a year later, was a version closer to the first performance text than to the published reading text, but there were, as one would expect, new changes (including the deletion of four-fifths of a lengthy political lecture at the beginning of act 2) and some additional dialogue. (Gaskell observes that unless Stoppard publishes a revised reading text, these later changes will be lost in future productions, which will have *only* the published text of 1975 to work with.) Finally, still other major changes were made for the New York production of 1975 and 1976, including a five-minute cut from act 1 to accommodate what Stoppard calls (in a letter to Gaskell) "Broadway Bladder."

At the end of his discussion, Gaskell comments on "the remarkable flexibility of the performance text when the author collaborates in the production" and the "interesting implications in all this" concerning the author's intentions and the question of what constitutes "the text of this or any other play." It would appear that Stoppard, at least, is not much worried by these questions. Asked in a June 1974 interview whether he ever felt "a conflict between literary and theatrical pressures," Stoppard replied:

> I realized quite a long time ago that I was in it because of the theatre rather than because of the literature. I like theatre, I like showbiz, and that's what I'm true to. . . . I think it's vital that the theatre is run by people who like showbiz. "If a thing doesn't work, why is it there in that form?" is roughly the philosophy, and I've benefited greatly from [the director] Peter Wood's down-to-earth way of telling me, "Right, I'm sitting in J 16, and I don't understand what you're trying to tell me. It's not clear." There's none of this stuff about "When Faber and Faber bring it out, I'll be able to read it six times and work it out for myself." Too late.

Stoppard goes on to credit the director with "actually sav[ing] the play. The speech in which Joyce justifies his art wasn't in the text of *Travesties* that I gave to Peter. It was he who said it was necessary, and I now think it's the most important speech in the play."[17]

By contrast, William Gibson, characterizing himself as "an author who . . . had devoted an obstinate quarter of a century to an avoidance of collaborators," was frustrated by virtually every aspect of the staging of his *Two for the Seesaw*. He offers his chronicle of the production, drafted in log form while the events were occurring, as an account of the conditions under which plays in general (and not just his in particular) were being produced in the middle of the twentieth century. It is above all, he says, a record of "harass[ment] by the complexities of group action."[18]

Actually, although Gibson is curiously insensitive to this point, "group action" began during his very earliest attempts at composition, when he read each scene, as it was written, to his wife and some friends (one of whom, Arthur Penn, became director of the play) and then made deletions and revisions in draft after draft in response to their criticisms. When he had a complete manuscript, he read the play to a dozen people in New York—his lawyer and agent, among others—and read it twice again, in successive revisions, to gatherings of friends at home. He also, seeking further reactions, sent a dozen copies to friends and associates around the country. Altogether, the process of writing and trial-and-error revision lasted for three years before his agent secured a producer and the play was headed for what Gibson calls, in retrospect, "the collaborative gluepot of the theater" (p. 22).

Two for the Seesaw has only two characters, who were played in the initial run by Henry Fonda and Anne Bancroft. One of Gibson's first tasks in the group effort was to rewrite the man's part, expanding it by half an hour's worth of new lines, in order to get Fonda to do the role. Thereafter, in rehearsals, Gibson and Fonda wrangled endlessly about the character and his lines. Fonda claimed not to be able to understand the role, thought that it had "too many complexes," and insisted on playing it "his way," which Gibson describes as "slickly amiable"; "what struck my eye," he says of Fonda's simplification, "was how much of what I conceived as the play's innards was not on the stage. . . . the darker material was not being acted" (pp. 40, 42). Rewriting the character to fit the actor amounted to "wrecking the structure of the play" (p. 45).

Much of Gibson's complaint here stems from his notion that "serious" art and theatrical "entertainment" are fundamentally at odds; "the theater . . . was primarily a place not in which to be serious, but in which to be likeable" (pp. 94, 140). The opening of the play in Washington was a "rendezvous with still another, final, and most implacable collaborator, the paying audience" (p. 52). When producer and director insisted on further rewriting of the man's part because it "could not hold the audience unless it were made more appealing," Gibson acceded, but felt that he had "crossed a line between two worlds of writing: henceforth material was to be shaped less by what I had to say than by what the audience would listen to" (pp. 64–65). Every audience in the early performances "was watched like a multi-headed behemoth; when spellbound it was soundless, when not it rustled its scaly fabrics and emitted little coughs, striking terror to our hearts; and those moments were without exception changed. I often wished it would cough itself to death" (p. 84).

Because he is all on the side of serious art, he is unconsoled by the success of the play, which included rave reviews from the New York critics and sale of the film rights for $600,000 plus a percentage of the gross. "The play grew more and more effective, and I felt less fulfilled as a writer"; the fact was "unblinkable, after such reviews, that the hammering my script and head had undergone at the hands of [the director, the producer, and Fonda] had issued in a much better play"; "I was ungratified by the compliments on the writing, as though I had won a beauty contest by appearing in a falseface . . . a rich thing but not mine own" (pp. 85, 101, 139).

This is not exactly emotion recollected in tranquillity; Gibson makes no attempt to hide his resentment. But even though he is a biased reporter—perhaps because he is one—Gibson gives us little reason to doubt that his chronicle is a reasonably accurate picture of play production in recent decades. Toward the end of his account there is a striking contrast between the feverish activity, confusion, instability, and disgruntlement behind the scenes and the expertly smooth and coherent performance that the reviewers admired out front. In the reviewers' descriptions, the play is a tidy whole made up of several discrete and smoothly articulated units: Gibson's script (as if he had submitted it by mail from his home in Massachusetts); Arthur Penn's directing (as if he had dropped in one afternoon to give advice); Fonda's and Bancroft's acting; George Jenkins's settings; and so on.[19] There appears to be very little understanding of (or interest in) the *processes* of interaction leading up to the performance that they saw and enjoyed so much.

Possibly there is a lesson in this for academic critics, who, like Gibson, are also usually on the side of serious art and tend to write their interpretations as if the texts under scrutiny existed in some fixed, definitive form from the very beginning. The lesson is that, because the product comes to us as a whole entity, we have mistakenly assumed that it was created whole in the first place. In other words, the mythic author is a projection from the text that we see or read, rather than a historical reality. To the extent that we wish to focus only on the formal whole, therefore, we should probably omit references to the author altogether!

3

Woody Allen, who undoubtedly would sympathize with Gibson's lament over loss of authorial control in *Two for the Seesaw,* is our most conspicuous example of successful single-author creativity in present-day American filmmaking. Allen is consistently the self-conscious artist and is on record, in a recent piece inveighing against colorization (or "color conversion") of black-and-white films, as believing "that no one should ever be able to tamper with any artist's work in any medium against the artist's will."[20] Like others in the business, Allen has his team of actors and technicians, but his position as triple threat in most of his films—writer, director, *and* principal actor—guarantees him a high degree of artistic control over the work; in a sense, he is a collaborator with himself. Earlier examples of such comprehensive artistic activity readily come to mind—Charles Chaplin in this country, Jacques Tati in France, Federico Fellini in Italy, Ingmar Bergman (Allen's principal model) in Sweden—and there have been many films over the years in which the same person is both writer and director (a recent instance is James L. Brooks's *Broadcast News,* which won the New York Film Critics' award for best film of 1987).

As a rule, however, the authorship of films is so complicated and diffuse as to be, for all practical purposes, unassignable. Take as a typical case *Yankee Doodle Dandy,* the life story of the Broadway showman George M. Cohan produced for Warner Brothers by Hal B. Wallis in 1942. The first screenwriter on the project was Robert Buckner, who dug into clippings, reviews, and profiles of Cohan, as well as Cohan's published autobiography. Cohan himself, then in his sixties, early became a collaborator, specifying a long list of things to be left unmentioned, dictating the story line, and responding with suggestions and revisions to a succession of drafts by Buckner. The writers Julius and Philip Epstein were brought in to enliven Buckner's script, and Edmund Joseph to tinker and add some jokes. Both the leading actor, James Cagney, and the director, Michael Curtiz, rewrote dialogue and improvised stage business during the shooting. At the end, however, only two of these half-dozen or more contributors appeared in the credits, Buckner because he initiated the writing and Joseph reportedly because he needed the credit to boost his career.[21] Not unreasonably, the 1981 edition of the screenplay issued by the Wisconsin Center for Film and Theater Research carries no author's name on the title page. Librarians catalogue it (as they do screenplays generally) by uniform title rather than by author.[22]

A more complex instance, though again representative of the kind of multiple authorship I am concerned with in this section, is the writing of *Casablanca,* a quite different film made by the same studio (and same producer and director) in the same year as *Yankee Doodle Dandy.* The origins of *Casablanca* lie in a play by Murray Burnett and Joan Alison called *Everybody Comes to Rick's.* After the play had been turned down by the rest of the studios in Hollywood, Hal Wallis bought the screen rights for $20,000 and hired the Epstein brothers to do an adaptation. Aeneas MacKenzie, who earlier had been sought as an adapter, contributed some basic ideas concerning theme and likely problems with the censor (then the Breen Office). When the Epsteins left Hollywood to work in Washington on a series of government propaganda films, Wallis hired another writer, Howard Koch, to write an alternative screenplay—"to be on the safe side," says Wallis, in the event that the Epsteins failed to complete their version. Wallis himself decided on the film's title, and he, the director, additional writers, and the actors all had a hand in revisions of a composite and piecemeal script by the Epsteins and Koch. Further changes were insisted on by the Breen Office, and at a very late stage a new scene was written (though ultimately it was dropped) in response to criticisms by the audience at a preview. Two different endings were filmed, leaving it open to the last minute which of the men got Ilsa, and there is still some question about who is responsible for the famous closing line, "Louis, I think this is the beginning of a beautiful friendship." Wallis says he thought of it, while Julius Epstein claims the credit for himself and his brother.[23]

Such dispersal of authorship might be deemed appropriate in an artistic medium that approvingly calls itself an "industry." Obviously the film industry's products are different from those of assembly-line operations that turn out, say, automobiles. A major Hollywood studio of the 1930s, '40s, and '50s made perhaps fifty films a year, each one of them, for better or worse, unique. But screenwriters of the so-called Golden Age, the years between the introduction of sound and the ascendancy of television, did have a few things in common with the factory workers of Detroit.[24] In some studios the writers punched time clocks, worked shifts, and were held responsible for specified quantities of production in the form of so many pages of writing per 5½-day work-week ("script factory" and "assembly line" are recurrent terms in writers' reminiscences). Like the automobile workers, writers generally concentrated on a small, detached part of a project, without knowing (and frequently, it is clear, without caring) what the rest of the workers—the other writers, the directors, the actors— were doing. Writers had no legal claim to their writing, because their contracts routinely contained a waiver of rights of authorship.[25] It was not uncommon for writers actually to be barred from the sets where scenes that they may or may not have written were being filmed; if they wanted to view "their" movies, they had to buy a ticket at a theater, just as the worker in Detroit, if he wanted to drive one of "his" cars, had to make a downpayment on a purchase. Often the writers did not bother to see the films they wrote for. The writing was only a job.

Everybody who comments on their status agrees that writers were at the very bottom of the industry's hierarchy of authority. The larger studios, like Warner Brothers, RKO, Twentieth Century–Fox, and MGM, employed 75 or 100 or even 150 or more writers at a time. There was extravagant duplication of effort—several writers might be assigned to the same project, each unaware of the others' involvement— and most of the writing was simply scrapped. Early in the 1930s, writers' salaries rose to impressive figures for the time, and many distinguished writers—Faulkner, Fitzgerald, Nathanael West, Lillian Hellman, Maxwell Anderson, Clifford Odets, Robert Sherwood, among them—were able to maintain careers as novelists, story writers, and playwrights by being, in effect, subsidized by stints of work in Hollywood. But their scripts, just like those of the rest of the virtually anonymous writers, were reworked, raided, cannibalized, or, most often, simply tossed aside and forgotten according to the needs or whims of the producers, directors, and actors. Julius Epstein recalls that "no matter what you wrote, original or adaptation, it never wound up the way you wanted. It was always changed by the producer, the director, or the actor. . . . So you're getting paid anyhow; what's the difference?"[26] As another writer puts it, "They ruin your stories. They massacre your ideas. They prostitute your art. They trample your pride. And what do you get for it? A fortune."[27]

Most films are collaborative from the start, even before the screenwriters sit down to work, because most films begin as adaptations of "originals" in other media—novels, short fiction, plays, biographies, autobiographies, histories, newspaper stories, even television scripts—or else as original concepts or ideas or stories by people who are not primarily paid as writers. The screenwriters enter in, usually after a project is approved, by providing a series of versions that might take the form of a synopsis, a "treatment" (a short-storylike account in several pages of prose), a revised treatment (after an army of producers, executives, and staffers have reacted to the treatment), a preliminary screenplay (a kind of rough draft), a screenplay with dialogue, and a shooting script. Ordinarily several writers will have taken part in the project before completion of the shooting script, one of them specializing in treatments, another in screenplays, another in dialogue, and so on. Then, if the project has survived to this point, there follows a continual process of rewriting—again often by specialists such as (according to the needs of the project) continuity writers, "salvage and polish" workers, "troubleshooters," gag-writers, "fixer-uppers," "dialogue doctors," and "script doctors"—and also, as we have seen in the examples of *Yankee Doodle Dandy* and *Casablanca* at the beginning of this section, revision by non-writing contributors like producers, directors, and actors. A new role may by created at a late stage to accommodate the friend or spouse of a producer or an executive; dialogue may have to be drastically simplified because an actor cannot memorize or pronounce the lines; whole scenes may have to be cut or bowdlerized to meet the objections of the censors (two *reels* were dropped from *The Flame of New Orleans,* a 1941 film starring Marlene Dietrich, to get it by the Hays Office).[28]

While it is obvious that films, at least since the invention of talking pictures, could never have existed without writers, it is also true that the screenwriter has been, and to an extent continues to be, a largely unrecognized contributor to the process of filmmaking. The notorious unreliability of screen credits bears this out. Companions and relatives of producers and directors have been assigned credit for writing they never did, while the names of others responsible for the actual writing have frequently been omitted. Donald Ogden Stewart, a writer for George Cukor and others in the 1930s and 1940s, describes some techniques for career advancement in this respect:

> In those days the first thing you had to learn as a writer, if you wanted to get screen credit, was to hold off until you knew when they were going to have to start shooting. Then, your agent would suggest you might be able to help. The producers had the theory that the more writers they had to work on the scripts, the better the scripts would be.

It was the third or fourth writer that always got the screen credit. It wasn't beyond you to try to possibly screw up another writer's script so that your script would come through at the end. It became a game to be the last one before they started shooting so that you would not be eased out of the screen credit.[29]

For most films it is impossible, given the workings of such a system, to assign authorship to individual writers.

4

But critics do need authors; and just as literary critics for the last two centuries have posited one or another concept of authorship to validate their interpretations, so film critics, once movies were accepted as a serious intellectual and academic subject, have similarly required a concept of authorship in order to focus their studies. The screenwriters would not serve as a center of authorship: there were too many of them, and it was seldom known who did the writing of any specific scene in a film. As a solution to the problem, the *auteur* theory was invented in France in the 1950s by François Truffaut and other "New Wave" writers in *Cahiers du cinéma* and domesticated and publicized in the United States about the same time by Andrew Sarris and Eugene Archer in the journal *Film Culture*.[30]

In the commonest application of auteur theory, the director rather than any writer becomes the mastermind creator of a film, the most conspicuous single *identifiable* person associated with the work. As auteurism took hold, other entities were tried out: the producer as auteur, the studio, the actor[31]—almost any individual or body who did not write the film! But the director has fairly consistently been the main focus in the last three decades. Critics have established canons for the individual directors, have made much of cross-references and allusions, thematic continuities, recurrences of character, symbol, technique in the works, and in effect have granted directors the same kind of pervasive authority as literary critics have regularly assigned to the poets and novelists of English and American (and other) literature. Orson Welles, Alfred Hitchcock, John Ford, and Howard Hawks (to name four who figured prominently early on) were routinely treated as sole authors of their films, and the movement has been so influential that virtually all films these days, whatever their quality, are identified primarily with their directors.

But the idea of director as sole author will not hold up under scrutiny; it is simply not possible for one person, however brilliant, to provide the entire creative force behind so complex a work as a motion picture. Consider, as a final example in this chapter, Orson Welles's *Citizen Kane* (1941), the film most frequently assigned and studied in college courses, the film most often written about by critics and historians, and a central focus of the auteur movement from the beginning. "It is, above all, the creation of one man," wrote an early biographer of Welles;[32] but Robert Carringer, in his carefully researched pioneering study, *The Making of "Citizen Kane"* (1985), demonstrates conclusively that it is not. Carringer's sources include scripts, production records, letters and other documents, sketches, and storyboards from the Welles archives at RKO Pictures and the Mercury Theatre Collection now at Indiana University, as well as interviews with professionals and technicians who worked on the film, including Welles himself.[33] While respectful of Welles's genius throughout, Carringer makes clear that the film owes its eminence, and perhaps even its existence, to the combined efforts of several extraordinarily talented individuals.

Credit for the *Citizen Kane* screenplay, which won an Academy Award, was shared by Herman J. Mankiewicz and Welles (in that order), and there were other writers as well. It is not certain who first thought of doing a film about William Randolph Hearst; Welles said that it was his own idea, while others have claimed priority for Mankiewicz (who died in 1953). Mankiewicz with the help of John Houseman wrote a 268-page first draft (titled "American") between the beginning of March and the middle of April 1940, some 40 pages of revisions shortly afterward, and a complete second draft by 9 May. At this point Welles took over the script, and the individual responsibilities for writing become more difficult to sort out. Amalia Kent reworked the second draft into a continuity version that added visual and mechanical details—necessary for budget and production planning—and drafted a breakdown script containing scene designations with physical descriptions. After approval from the RKO executives and department heads, the script was further heavily revised during June and July, mostly by Welles but also by Mankiewicz, in four further drafts, the last of which was the shooting script. From his painstaking analyses of cuts and other changes from one version to the next, Carringer concludes, concerning the shares of Mankiewicz and Welles, that Mankiewicz's main contributions were the story frame (including the Rosebud gimmick), the characters, many of the individual scenes, and much of the final dialogue, while Welles, as he says, added "narrative brilliance—the visual and verbal wit, the stylistic fluidity, and such stunningly original strokes as the newspaper montages and the breakfast table sequence." Carringer comments that *Citizen Kane* "is the only major Welles film on which the writing credit is shared. Not coincidentally, it is also the Welles film that has the strongest story, the most fully realized characters, and the most carefully sculpted dialogue. Mankiewicz made the difference."[34] This part of the collaboration gets us as far as the shooting script.

Subsequently, the most important contributors were Perry Ferguson, the art director, and Gregg Toland, the cinematographer, both working closely with Welles and with each other to produce brilliant technical innovations in the settings and photography. (Some of these innovations—for example, Ferguson's use of large pieces of black velvet to cover empty spaces on the sets, thereby giving the impression of extreme depth—were the result of severe financial restrictions, and thus even the studio's budget officer could be included among the collaborators involved in the film's artistic effects.) Obviously the actors, led and directed by Welles, had a part in the film's quality.[35] And then there were the professionals responsible for various postproduction operations: special effects; sound rerecording (mixing and dubbing); composing, orchestrating, and recording the music; and the overall editing.

Welles chose these helpers, provided suggestions and supervision all through the project, and brought out the best in them to accomplish results that he had not achieved before and never achieved afterward, as Carringer points out in his analyses of Welles's earlier *Heart of Darkness* and his later productions, especially *The Magnificent Ambersons.* The conclusion is inescapable that the excellence of *Citizen Kane* is tied to this particular nexus of people whom he assembled and worked with. Welles was not pleased when Carringer explained to him the thesis of *The Making of "Citizen Kane."* "Collaborators make contributions," he told Carringer in response, "but only a director can make a film." Carringer agrees on this point but goes on to propose a corollary:

> The quality of a film is partly a measure of the quality of its collaborative talent. On *Citizen Kane,* Welles was fortunate to have collaborators ideally suited to his temperament and working methods and capable of performing at his level of ambition. The film could never have been what

it is without them. . . . Had it not been for this particular combination, we might not have *Citizen Kane* at all.[36]

Other pantheon auteurs are under critical scrutiny these days— in the recent work on Hitchcock by Donald Spoto and Leonard Leff, for instance[37]—but the example of *Citizen Kane* can serve to epitomize the problems inherent in attributing sole authorship of a film to the director (or to any other single individual, whether producer, screenwriter, or actor). Though there are enormous technical differences between films and plays, the problems in film criticism are much like those inherent in attributing sole authorship of a theatrical production to a professional playwright (or, again, to any other one person). The circumstances of film and play production are too complicated, require too many separate specialized abilities, and are hedged on every side with competing interests and influences: budgetary constraints, audience demands, conflicting egos of directors, actors, artists, and everybody else involved. In theory and practice alike, the auteur approach does not seem well suited to the study of films, and probably we have long been operating too simply using an auteur-*like* approach, without specifying "auteur," in our more traditional criticism and interpretation of the work of professional dramatists like Tom Stoppard and Shakespeare.

9

Implications for Theory

The foregoing chapters have illustrated multiple authorship in a variety of forms: the young Keats being refined, polished, and restrained by well-intentioned friends and publishers; the middle-aged Mill being spruced up by his wife for attractive autobiographical presentation; the old Wordsworth rewriting his younger self; Coleridge constructing his philosophy with lengthy extracts taken over verbatim without acknowledgment from the Germans; Eliot seizing on the revisions and excisions of his mentor; novelists routinely sharing their authorship with friends, spouses, ghostwriters, agents, editors, censors, publishers; playwrights and screenwriters disappearing in the ordinary processes of play and film production.

These illustrations are offered as representative rather than special or isolated. For some of the many others that could have been given in their place, see the Appendix. To be sure, numerous more subtle external influences also impinge on authors' authority and freedom—the simplest exigencies of genre, to mention just one class of such influences, where three-decker novels had to be three volumes in length (not two or four), a serially published part-issue of a novel had to be thirty-two pages (not thirty or thirty-four), and a movie had to be, and generally still has to be, around a hundred minutes long (not fifty or two hundred). Just as music has been composed for special circumstances—the range of a singer, the technical skills of an instrumentalist—and sculptures and paintings have been created to fill specific spaces of courtyards, rooms, walls, even ceilings (sometimes to match specific color schemes of interior decorating), so literature has been produced in response to a range of externally exerted requests, demands, and pressures, many of which in effect become intrinsic elements in the process of creation.[1] Scholars sometimes try to sort out and accommodate these influences by making a distinction between "serious" work on the one hand, viewed as stalwartly resisting such pressures, and (mere) entertainment on the other, viewed as giving way on every side—in short, between work that is "creative or literary" and work that is "popular fare."[2] But no such distinction is possible, either practically or theoretically, any more than one can draw a practical or theoretical line between "good" poems, novels, and plays and "bad" ones. Shakespeare, Wordsworth, Coleridge, Keats, Mill, and Dickens, who produced, or at one time or another would have been glad to produce, "popular fare," are firmly established among the "serious" writers of our literature.

Such disclosures and reminders of the complexities of authorship have an obvious place in biography and literary history. The romantic notion of single authorship is so widespread as to be nearly universal. In contrast, the accumulation of evidence for the prevalence of multiple authorship can support a more realistic account of the ways in which literature is created and, especially when the ordinary human motives of authors, editors, publishers, booksellers, readers, and the rest are brought into the picture all together, can contribute to the ongoing efforts of new and old historicists alike to connect literary works with the social, cultural, and material conditions in which they were produced.

My concern in the present chapter, however, is primarily the relation of multiple authorship to theories of interpretation and editing. Multiple authorship has implications for almost any kind of theory postulated on the existence (and possibly, in the thinking of author-banishing critics, even the *nonexistence*) of a unified mind, personality, or consciousness in or behind a text that is being studied, interpreted, or edited. Some of these implications will already have been made obvious in the discussions of individual works in Chapters 2 through 8. Here I shall offer a few summary observations concerning interpretation and editing.

1

A relevant question at the outset is whether "pure" authorship is possible under any circumstances—single authorship without any influence, intervention, alteration, or distortion whatsoever by someone other than the nominal author. William Blake might seem a likely candidate: he drafted and revised his poems, invented the "illuminations" to accompany them, etched the texts, pictures, and designs onto copper plates, printed them, hand-colored them, and stitched them into books entirely by himself. To test out this possibility, imag-

but Catherine collaborated in their creation!

ine that I am discussing Blake in a public lecture and, in order to illustrate some fine points of my discussion, have projected on a large screen behind me a color slide of the plate containing *The Tyger* from *Songs of Innocence and of Experience*. The picture on the screen is a beautiful and at the same time slightly comical design of text, tree, and puffy smiling tiger. Here, one might think, is Blake all by himself, the author–artist free of every kind of external intervention, an epitomizing example of single authorship.

One would, of course, be wrong. The audience is looking not at a page in a small book but at a huge picture on a screen, a spectacle that Blake himself could never have produced or even foreseen (since photography and the other standard processes of enlargement had not yet been invented). In this hypothetical example, I have made my color slide using incandescent lighting but without the corrective blue filter on my camera and, further, have photographed not a Blake original but a modern printed facsimile, so that the audience is getting several kinds of distortion of Blake's colors on the screen. In addition, I and the audience alike are totally ignoring the probability that Blake meant *The Tyger* to be read in a book (not on a screen), in its designated position as one of the Songs of Experience in the 1794 volume *Songs of Innocence and of Experience*, with textual and thematic relationships not only to its Songs of Innocence counterpart, *The Lamb,* but to other plates preceding and following in the volume. What we have at my lecture, instead, is the single plate, blown up to giant size, with the colors distorted, and an academic lecturer making decidedly un-Blakean noises in the foreground (not to mention shuffling of feet and other sounds of a roomful of people attending this hypothetical occasion).

Other examples of distortion by context and audience are easy to invent. Imagine that I am teaching *The Tyger* in a course in Romantic poetry in which the class is using a text with only a black-and-white reproduction of Blake's design or, what is much more likely, a text with no picture at all, perhaps in a 2500-page anthology printed on extra-thin paper and weighing three pounds. (The absence of picture may not be a bad idea. Students occasionally point out that if the extended hind legs of Blake's tiger were brought forward to a vertical position, the animal's rear end would be raised to an absurd height above the rest of its body.) Suppose I bring in some of the commentary of Northrop Frye, David Erdman, Harold Bloom, Ronald Paulson, and John Grant. Suppose that, in spite of my best efforts, some of the students have trouble understanding Frye and the rest, or draw a blank at "frame thy fearful symmetry," or fail to notice the difference between "Could frame" and "Dare frame" as the poem takes shape.

What kind of artistic control does Blake have over the way he is read, commented on, discussed in classes, and misunderstood two hundred years after he wrote *The Tyger?* Clearly very little, and the example may serve to suggest that, once a reader or a spectator is introduced into the transaction, no work whatsoever, even one by an artist as singly self-sufficient as Blake, is free from impingements that change and distort what the author created in the first place. There are plentiful materials in such considerations for a separate chapter (which I shall not include here) on the topic "Reader as Collaborator." No author can control every specific effect—or even, probably, a very large proportion of the specific effects—of a work in the mind of a reader. It takes at least two people, a sender and a receiver, to constitute communication; with a literary work, collaborative creative activity on the part of a reader is an absolute and unavoidable necessity. "Pure" authorship (as defined at the beginning of this section) *might* be theoretically possible when a writer's holograph manuscript is locked up unread in a library or an attic, but the "initial purity" of the text (Bowers's term)[3] would immediately begin to be altered if another person were to cast eyes on it.

In any case, there is another theoretical problem—at the writer's end of the creative process, rather than the reader's—in the myriad influences exerted on Blake by his time and place. He was unquestionably an original genius, but like other original geniuses was partly a product of historical and cultural circumstances beyond his control. He was (to use the simplest possible illustrations) a revolutionary at the time of the French Revolution and would have been a different kind of revolutionary had he lived a century earlier or later; he could rail at Newton and Locke, who wrote and became major intellectual forces before he was born, but not at Charles Darwin or Freud, who came afterward; he could rewrite Milton and Swedenborg but not, say, Yeats or Eliot. To separate "pure" authorship from the circumstances of time and place, one would have to lock up not only the manuscripts but the authors themselves (and, in the process, thereby deprive them of, among many other necessities, language itself). Since no writer aims to produce unread manuscripts or wishes to be locked up in the hypothetical manner I have just suggested, "pure" authorship seems out of the question. Yet it is something very much like this idea of "pure" authorship that both the interpretive and the editorial theorists have in mind when they think and write about authors and authorial intentions.

2

If a locked-up, unread manuscript (not to mention a locked-up author) sounds a little like Bishop Berkeley's tree in the forest, let us bring in Dr. Johnson to kick a stone or two. In our day-to-day practice—what W. J. T. Mitchell calls "slogging along in the routines of scholarship and interpretation"[4]—the facts of multiple authorship generally do not constitute an obstacle. Professional historians (by which I mean people who work in university history departments) routinely accept the composite authorship of official letters, speeches, documents, diplomatic agreements, and the like out of necessity, cheerfully attributing to single individuals (presidents, cabinet members, legislators, governors, mayors) words that they know were written by committees, staff assistants, and speechwriters.[5] In somewhat the same way, literary "practitioners" (teachers, critics, interpreters, improvers of reading) make constant use of individual attributions—"Keats," "Mill," "Dreiser," and so on—which likewise may actually be composite entities.

For practical purposes, perhaps the single most important aspect of authorship is simply the vaguely apprehended *presence* of human creativity, personality, and (sometimes) voice that nominal authorship seems to provide. Just as it would be unthinkable for a visitor to an art museum to admire a roomful of paintings without knowing the names of the individual painters and for a concertgoer to sit through a program of symphonies and concertos without knowing the names of the individual composers, so it is impossible to imagine *any* presentation of writings (even of writings in which Barthes and Foucault contest the existence of authors!) that does not prominently refer to authorship. Readers must have authors' names on the jackets, spines, and title pages of the books they read.[6] Book advertisements in the *New York Review of Books* and the *New York Times Book Review* regularly include pictures of the authors (especially in the form of large photographs or drawings of their faces alone), as do the featured reviews in these same periodicals, which of course are as much reviews of the authors as they are of the books; and publishers are now producing videos of authors plugging their books to be shown on monitors (near the cash registers) in bookstores. *Critical Inquiry,* advertising itself ("at the forefront of critical thought") in the pages of *New Literary History,* makes a point of its "important contributions from such *authors* as Stanley Cavell, Jacques Derrida, Stanley Fish. . . ."

A practical corollary is that nobody is satisfied with anonymous authorship. If books without authors' names seem unacceptable (not to mention unmarketable), try imagining a Norton anthology in which the authors' names are suppressed and the works are arranged entirely by chronology or by genre or (alphabetically) by title. The authors of the few anonymous and pseudonymous works that manage to hold a place in literature have, even in their anonymity, acquired specific individual identities in our minds and our literary histories; lacking their names, we designate them by the works they wrote—the "*Pearl* poet," "Junius," the weather-wise "Bard . . . who made / The grand old ballad of Sir Patrick Spence."

Obviously, the myth of single authorship is a great convenience for teachers, students, critics, and other readers, as well as for publishers, agents, booksellers, librarians, copyright lawyers—indeed, for everyone connected with the production and reception of books, starting with the authors themselves. The myth is thoroughly embedded in our culture and our ordinary practices, including the ordinary practices of criticism and interpretation, for which, I would argue, it is an absolute necessity.[7] The countering reality of multiple authorship is no threat to the continuing existence of the myth, nor, except for deconstructionist theorists, is there any compelling reason for wanting the myth to cease to exist. Although a deconstructive approach to interpretation might take comfort in the idea of a plurally altered text, the behavior of deconstructionists as authors of their *own* texts shows that the myth is in no danger from that quarter. And for the historicist, the mythical author certainly has exerted a shaping force on literary production even when the text in question was produced by several hands.

In practical criticism, moreover, the particulars of multiple authorship can frequently be illuminating, even when one is pursuing the meanings of a mythical single author. In my first two chapters, I suggested ways in which distinguishing between Keats's contributions and those of his friends and editors tends to highlight Keats's intentions—for example, in *Isabella* and *The Eve of St. Agnes*—and some interesting situations where these intentions were in conflict with the tastes and moral ideas of people whom he depended on for help in getting the works into print. Clearly, such information may improve our understanding of Keats's poems, and the same is true of the more accurate representations we get of Mill's self-deprecation in the canceled passages of the *Autobiography,* Wordsworth's developing concepts of self-presentation in *The Prelude,* Coleridge's methods of writing philosophy and literary theory, Eliot's and Pound's contributions to the fragmentariness of *The Waste Land,* and the numerous ways in which editors and so many others have participated in the shaping of novels, plays, and films. This is useful information at a very basic level, rather like the help we sometimes get from textual variants in an author's manuscript—the "real grass" in Keats's draft and fair copy of *Endymion* (4.622), which points up the intended symbolism of the printed text's "grass," and "Was it a vision real" in the draft of *Ode to a Nightingale* (79), which gives us a hypothesis for distinguishing between "vision" and "waking dream" in the printed text. We can still, if we wish, assign these works solely to Keats, Mill, Wordsworth, and the rest, while taking advantage of our sharper grasp of the complex processes by which the works came into being.

3

It is when we come to interpretive theory, and especially theorists' understanding of the relation of interpretation to authorial intention, that the facts of multiple authorship may cause some complications. Traditionally—rather like the fabled medieval synthesis of God, nature, and humans—author, text, and reader existed in a perfect unity: the author put meaning in a text, the text represented the author's meaning, and the reader went to the text to find out what the author meant. Authors, readers, and critics (and teachers and students) still to a large extent depend on this traditional concept. But philosophers for at least a century and literary theorists in recent decades have been posing questions and arguing over the more specific locus of meaning in this once harmonious pristine triad: Does the meaning of a work exist primarily in the author's mind? (In which case, putting the theory into practice, we go to the text to read the author's mind.) Or in the text itself? (In which case we go to the text for *its* meaning, regardless of how it got there.) Or is it in the reader's mind in the act of reading? (In which case we just read, not worrying about the prior or ultimate sources of the meanings we get.)

A major influential statement of the second of these three positions (although it is not perfectly certain that the authors themselves, at the time, meant for it to be taken as such) was W. K. Wimsatt, Jr., and Monroe C. Beardsley's essay "The Intentional Fallacy" (1946).[8]

Initially Wimsatt and Beardsley set out to attack an outdated convention by which a work of art or literature was evaluated in terms of
what the artist or writer was trying to accomplish: one determined (as
best one could) first the aim and then the extent to which the work
approached fulfillment of the aim. The gist of their contention, as
stated in the opening paragraph of "The Intentional Fallacy," is that
"the design or intention of the author is neither available nor desirable as a standard for judging the success of a work of literary art."
They repeat the same point in almost the same words a page later—
"design or intention [will not do] as a *standard* by which the critic is to
judge the worth of the poet's performance"— and go on to argue that
the only possible evidence of intention is the work itself, that external
facts (biography, sources, allusions) are useless if not actually detrimental, and that, even if one could put questions about a work to a
living author, the author's answers would have no more bearing than
anyone else's based on a reading of the text. The poem "is detached
from the author at birth and goes about the world beyond his power
to intend about it or control it. . . . The poem belongs to the public."

This seems clear enough but actually is full of ambiguities, and
Wimsatt and Beardsley themselves are the first to become entangled
in the shifting senses of "intention" and "criticism" in the essay. In
their opening statement, "intention" signifies *aim, plan, purpose,
goal,* while "criticism" signifies *evaluation.* But very shortly (as in a
phrase that the authors quote from E. E. Stoll, "the author's meaning or intention"), "intention" starts to signify *meaning,* and by the
end of the essay "criticism" has come to signify something like *understanding* or *interpretation.* Thus Wimsatt and Beardsley's fairly in-
nocuous beginning—to the effect that an author's aim has no place
in the evaluation of a work—has been transformed into the quite
different and much more radical statement that an author's intended
meaning has no place in the interpretation of a work. It is this latter
formulation that constitutes our common understanding, over the
years, of "intentional fallacy" (an understanding probably based
more on the catchy wording of the title than on a close reading of
the essay itself), and both Wimsatt and Beardsley have encouraged
this view—Wimsatt saying pointedly, in a retrospective essay written
twenty-two years afterward, that the "statement in our essay of
[1946] should certainly have read: 'The design or intention of the
author is neither available nor desirable as a standard for judging
either the meaning or the value of a work of literary art.' "[9]

Subsequently there has grown up an enormous body of books

and essays on the concept of intention in art and literature, especially (for our purposes) on the place of authorial intention in literary criticism and interpretation. My account here is necessarily confined to a few of the more conspicuous contributions. Obviously, Wimsatt and Beardsley's essay was itself a landmark, and it continues to be a starting point for modern discussions, as in David Newton-De Molina's 1976 collection, *On Literary Intention: Critical Essays,* in which the first item is "The Intentional Fallacy" and most of the remaining fourteen essays are attacks against Wimsatt and Beardsley (and their influence), although with strikingly little agreement among the writers as to exactly where Wimsatt and Beardsley went wrong and why authorial intention should not be considered a fallacy.[10]

Three of the selections in *On Literary Intention* are by the preeminent opponent of Wimsatt and Beardsley, E. D. Hirsch, Jr., whose *Validity in Interpretation* (1967) is still, after more than twenty years, the centerpiece of any argument concerning authorial intention in criticism. Hirsch defends what he calls "objective interpretation" (the title of his 1960 *PMLA* article, which he includes as an appendix in *Validity*) by equating textual meaning with authorial meaning. His first chapter, "In Defense of the Author," lays the groundwork and sets the tone: "Meaning is an affair of consciousness not of words. . . . A word sequence means nothing in particular until somebody either means something by it or understands something from it." "The text [has] to represent *somebody's* meaning—if not the author's, then the critic's." "To banish the original author as the determiner of meaning was to reject the only compelling normative principle that could lend validity to an interpretation." "Re-cognitive interpretation ["rightly understanding what the author meant"] . . . is the only kind of interpretation with a determinate object, and thus the only kind that can lay claim to validity in any straightforward and practicable sense of that term."[11] Such "either/or" and "only" rhetoric invites dispute, of course, and Hirsch has been regularly assailed in reviews and symposia ever since *Validity in Interpretation* appeared.[12] His basic position seems, because of its persistence in the face of so much vigorous challenge, irrefutable, but the *practical* inaccessibility of an author's meaning in any sense in which it is separate from a text continues to be an obstacle to attaining the desired objectivity. Hirsch's main example of actual interpretation, a brief reading of Wordsworth's *A slumber did my spirit seal,* turns out to be of highly questionable validity.

In the early 1980s, what might be considered the third prominent wave of modern intentionalist controversy (Wimsatt and Beardsley having initiated the first and Hirsch the second) got under way with the publication of Steven Knapp and Walter Benn Michaels's "Against Theory" in the Summer 1982 issue of *Critical Inquiry*.[13] Setting out to attack theory in general—"If we are right, then the whole enterprise of critical theory is misguided and should be abandoned"; "Our thesis has been that no one can reach a position outside practice, that theorists should stop trying, and that the theoretical enterprise should therefore come to an end" (pp. 12, 30)—Knapp and Michaels find their "clearest example" of the failure of theory in the ongoing debate concerning the relation of authorial intention to the meaning of texts. Both intentionalists and anti-intentionalists—that is, Hirsch and Hirsch's opponents alike—are declared guilty of a fundamental mistake: treating intention and meaning as separable entities.

> Once it is seen that the meaning of a text is simply identical to the author's intended meaning, the project of *grounding* meaning in intention becomes incoherent. Since the project itself is incoherent, it can neither succeed nor fail; hence both theoretical attitudes toward intention are irrelevant. The mistake made by theorists has been to imagine the possibility or desirability of moving from one term (the author's intended meaning) to a second term (the text's meaning), when actually the two terms are the same. (p. 12)

Needless to say, since Knapp and Michaels not only faulted theorists' thinking but (in their whimsical straight-facedness) seemed to threaten theorists' very livelihood, there was quick and agitated response—seven pieces alone in the June 1983 issue of *Critical Inquiry* (to which Knapp and Michaels contributed an unrepentant "Reply to Our Critics"), two others in the March 1985 issue (to which Knapp and Michaels again replied),[14] and commentary in other journals besides *Critical Inquiry*. As with the earlier intentionalist attacks against Wimsatt and Beardsley and anti-intentionalist attacks against Hirsch, the criticisms from *both* sides against Knapp and Michaels set forth a variety of arguments and positions among which there is, again, very little agreement.

The debate persists on into the 1990s. William Schroeder, for instance, marshals a comprehensive list of older and newer objections to intentionalism in "A Teachable Theory of Interpretation," the opening piece in Cary Nelson's collection entitled *Theory in the Classroom* (1986).[15] And three other essays by philosophers in Anthony Cascardi's *Literature and the Question of Philosophy* (1987) also are relevant to the issue. Denis Dutton, in "Why Intentionalism Won't Go Away," weighing the arguments of Wimsatt, Beardsley, Hirsch, and Barthes (among others), thinks that the place of authorial intention will never be settled among theorists but also that it will continue to be an indispensable element in interpretation:

> Granted, to be sure, that the meanings of texts are hardly exhausted by what they meant to their authors, it remains nevertheless that, since words and texts are used by authors for myriad purposes, their intentions will never be found generally irrelevant to some of the interesting and legitimate things that critics may sometimes wish to say about some texts.

Stanley Rosen, in "The Limits of Interpretation," pursues a more radical tack, rather like that of Knapp and Michaels, maintaining that a theory of interpretation itself is impossible. "There is no theoretical substructure of reading *or* of writing; there is only the infrastructure of the reader and the writer." This allows a traditional existence to authors (in what Rosen calls "the domain of *phronēsis* or . . . the pretheoretical domain of common sense") but renders the usual question about authorial intention beside the point. Alexander Nehamas, in "Writer, Text, Work, Author," constructs in effect not one but two authors, expanding on his earlier argument for distinguishing between the historical writer outside the text and a "postulated author" speaking in the text.[16]

This abbreviated survey leaves out most of the argumentative detail and all of the subtlety of the handful of authors whom I have mentioned (yes, they *are* authors and, regardless of their view of authorial intention in the abstract, they insist, sometimes quite ferociously, that their own intended meanings be understood). I have been concerned mainly to suggest the scope and principal points of contention. As to the quality, there are several aspects of the discussion that might appear strange to an observer not trained in philosophy: the theorists' inability to agree on acceptable definitions of basic terms like "intention," "meaning," "significance," "understanding," "knowledge," "belief," and "theory"; their recurrent appeals, in support of abstract propositions, to concrete experience, common sense, human feeling, what "everybody knows" about authors or writing or intending; and their use of nonliterary analogies to make points about authors, texts, and interpretation—a touchdown in football, a piano concert by Vladimir Ashkenazy, a car running out of gas, Hopi Indian pottery decoration, a road sign on the New Jersey Turnpike, the television show "What's My Line?" For literary paradigms we have mostly (but not exclusively) newspaper misprints repeated as jokes in the *New Yorker,* Mark Akenside's "plastic arm," Shakespeare's plays dictated by a parrot to an amanuensis, and Wordsworth's *A slumber did my spirit seal* produced by a computer, by a wave on a beach, and by a monkey randomly pressing keys on a typewriter. As a reviewer of several theoretical works published in 1980 observes, if we can suppose that a monkey randomly typed Wordsworth's lines, we can suppose anything.[17]

In the context of the present study of multiple authorship, what these theoretical writings have in common, in their quite different ways of regarding the place of authorial intention in interpretation, is their virtually universal belief in the myth of the author as a single entity.[18] Anti-intentionalists like Wimsatt and Beardsley, intentionalists like E. D. Hirsch (and, if they would allow themselves to be categorized, Knapp and Michaels), and author-banishers like Barthes and Foucault all embrace or reject the traditional concept of the single author, the mastermind creator of whatever work is the occasion for thinking pro or con about authorship. And while the substitution of multiple author- ship in place of the traditional concept may not disconcert the anti- intentionalists (after all, it is as easy to reject the intentions of two or three authors as it is to reject those of the more usual single author), it does quite possibly throw a cloud of uncertainty over the single-author ideal on which the intentionalists theoretically depend.

Instead of E. D. Hirsch's formulation quoted above—"the origi- nal author as the determiner of meaning"— one may have to contem- plate an array of plural original authors, some of whom may be at odds with others. In Knapp and Michaels's breezy equation of "meaning of a text . . . to the author's intended meaning," one may have to accom- modate a complexity of plural authors' meanings, and possibly conflict- ing intentions among them. We have had several chapters illustrating actual or potential discord among the authors, and the Appendix at the back of this book lists many others, including works begun according to one person's intentions and completed posthumously, after the first author's death, by another person with another set of intentions. In situations of multiple authorship, the posited ideal of single-author intention seems a shaky foundation for general theory.

In the early draft of his *Autobiography,* John Stuart Mill recalls, from the time of his twelfth or thirteenth year, his father's "indigna- tion at my using the common expression that something was true in theory but required correction in practice: and how, after making me vainly strive to define the word theory, he explained its meaning and shewed the fallacy of the form of speech which places practice and theory in opposition."[19] If Mill's father were right, and there were never any opposition between theory and practice, then we would have no real problem about the locus of meaning. Author, text, and reader would be interrelated in such a way that a view of any one of the elements would necessarily entail a view of the other two as well, or all three together. Author-centered critics would interpret a text according to the ideal of author's intended meaning; text-centered critics would inevitably incorporate authorial intention into their interpretations; and reader-centered critics would inevitably be studying readers' attempts to re-create authorial meanings in the process of reading. In all these statements, a plural "authors" can be substituted for the singular "author"—authors and text and reader, authors-centered critics, authors' meaning, and so on—and the argument is not essentially altered.

David Hirsch remarks, concerning the claims of text versus author versus reader:

> It is really a matter of little import whether a critic's rhetorical strategy is to say "The meaning of *The Waste Land* is that life is a completely joyous experience," or "In *The Waste Land* Eliot intended the meaning that life is a completely joyous experience," or "The reader responds to *The Waste Land* by feeling the sense of life as a completely joyous experience."[20]

And one can substitute "Eliot and Pound" for "Eliot" without changing Hirsch's point that the meaning transcends the separate compartmentalizations. But then perhaps Mill's father was not right after all about the compatibility of theory and practice. In this case the theorists still have a theoretical problem with multiple authorship.

4

Interpretation and editorial work alike are concerned with some very basic questions: what constitutes a text, what constitutes meaning and significance, and the connection of these to authorial intention. In editing, however, theory and practice are much more closely linked to each other than they appear to be in interpretation. On the evidence of the writings surveyed in the preceding section, interpretive theory rarely leads to the production (or even the theoretical validation) of actual interpretations. Editorial theory, on the other hand, is usually tied to the production of actual editions; while it is obviously possible to theorize without editing, as in general discussion of the Greg–Bowers and other theories of copy-text, most of the theorizing has been coordinated with editorial procedures in a specific project (the plays of Thomas Dekker, the novels of William Dean Howells, the poems of Keats). The theory exists primarily as justification of the practice.

Until fairly recently, all editorial theories without exception were based on a concept of single authorship and the ideal of "realizing"—approximating, recovering, (re)constructing—the author's intentions in a critical edition. Authorial "*final* intention," a narrowing of the broader notion of authorial intention (and sometimes further restricted with adjectives like "precise" and "exact"), is implicit or explicit in the writings of W. W. Greg, Fredson Bowers, and G. Thomas Tanselle, as well as in various official and semiofficial publications of the Modern Language Association;[21] it is mentioned so frequently as to be virtually equated with intention in general. As one might expect from a sampling of the difficulties faced by the intentionalists among the interpreters, editorial theorists have from the beginning run up against a serious problem in their appeals to authorial intention, final or otherwise: authors' intentions are no more available to editors than they are to interpreters.

In editing a work according to the author's intentions, the principal older method, more or less the standard in the nineteenth century and the first half of the twentieth, was to reproduce, or at least use as copy-text (the base-text of an edition), the latest version published during the author's lifetime. The method was considered appropriate for any work existing in a series of printed editions, each of which, after the first, was set from the one immediately preceding; the justification was that the author *might* have had a hand in the text of each successive printing. When a later edition showed changes in wording that could be attributed to the author, it was regularly assumed (such was the naïveté of scholars *then*) that the author had overseen and approved all the other particulars of the later text as well. A typical example is Dickens's *Little Dorrit*, which was published in monthly parts between 1855 and 1857 and in a first one-volume edition in 1857 and then reprinted in the Library Edition of 1859 (set from a copy of 1857), the Cheap Edition of 1861 (set from a copy of 1859), and the

Charles Dickens Edition of 1868 (set from an 1865 or 1866 reprint of 1861). The text of 1868, because of the accumulation of errors in the successive reprintings, is the most corrupt of all these versions, but because it was the last published before Dickens's death in 1870, it has long been deemed the most authoritative and, in consequence, has been the source of numerous texts printed in the twentieth century, including those of the Everyman, Penguin, and New Oxford Illustrated Dickens editions.

In the 1950s, textual theorists began to take a more realistic view of the relation of authors to their texts, and the result was general abandonment of the "latest text" principle. There was actually, as it turned out, very little evidence that authors supervised their texts beyond the initial printing of a work; and there was virtually no evidence that, when authors did make changes in a later version, they bothered to look over the parts of the later version that they left unchanged. On these grounds it was decided that an earlier rather than a later text was more likely to embody what the author intended to have printed, and therefore that the earlier should be considered more authoritative. The Greg–Bowers theory of copy-text—originally proposed by W. W. Greg in a 1949 paper entitled "The Rationale of Copy-Text" and championed and developed by Fredson Bowers in hundreds of books, essays, introductions, and reviews beginning in 1950[22]— called for use of a first edition as copy-text, or better still, if one was available, the author's fair-copy manuscript. The wording of the first edition or manuscript could be emended where there was reason to think that the author was responsible for substantive rewriting in a later version, but the punctuation, spelling, capitalization, word-division, and paragraphing would remain those of the first edition or manuscript. Thus the most recent editor of *Little Dorrit*, following Greg–Bowers principles, chooses the first one-volume edition of 1857 for his copy-text, emending substantively in some 120 passages, usually to restore Dickens's wording from the extant draft or the proof-sheets. The resulting text, correcting the original printer's errors and avoiding the progressive deterioration in the reprints issued while Dickens was alive, is superior to the formerly standard 1868 text and the modern editions based on it in 300 passages.[23]

The Greg–Bowers theory, initially developed as a method for editing sixteenth- and seventeenth-century English plays, was soon extended to the treatment of works of more recent periods—*Little Dorrit* in the example just given, the novels of Hawthorne and many others in American fiction, the philosophical writings of William

James and John Dewey—and became the subject of considerable controversy, especially where editors chose for copy-text a "prepublication" version of a work (that is, an author's manuscript). In simplest form, the essential question, which continues to be debated, is whether authorial intention is better represented in a manuscript or in a printed text. In the Centenary Edition of the works of Hawthorne (to mention a famous case), both *The Blithedale Romance* and *The Marble Faun* are edited from Hawthorne's fair-copy manuscripts rather than from printed texts. How do we know whether the manuscript or the first edition (with the publishers' house styling and other changes in printing) is closer to what Hawthorne had in mind for his contemporaries—or us—to read?[24] Adherents of the Greg–Bowers dogma sometimes appear overly rigid in their insistence that one side (favoring the manuscript) is right and the other (favoring the printed text) is wrong, settling the question by general rule rather than by an assessment of particular circumstances.

There is a further problem with the Greg–Bowers theory whenever we have two or more versions of a work. Early and later texts of Henry James's novels, Wordsworth's *The Prelude,* and Keats's *La Belle Dame sans Merci* are repeatedly mentioned as examples, but actually the situation is commonplace. Coleridge's *Monody on the Death of Chatterton* (a typical *unremarkable* instance) exists in at least ten distinct versions, written over a period of forty-four years, each of which is authoritatively Coleridge's.[25] "*Final* authorial intention" is usually invoked to solve the problem: Coleridge (or somebody) settled on *a* version for the *Poetical Works* of 1834, the year of Coleridge's death, and presumably the substantives of that text could be introduced into a matrix of punctuation, spelling, and other accidentals of an earlier version in accordance with the Greg–Bowers procedures. But it is not clear to everybody's satisfaction why final versions or latest substantives, merely because they are latest, should be considered more authoritative than any other that carry the writer's authority. Textualists of the Greg–Bowers school are geniuses at recovering the historical facts of composition, transmission, and publication but frequently are duffers in their attempts to factualize their authors' intentions. Nearly every textual history in the Greg–Bowers tradition has, at a crucial point, a weak stab at explaining what the author genuinely preferred, or actively intended, or passively accepted, or merely acquiesced in, or positively hated—matters of speculation that contrast rather sharply with the factual details everywhere else.[26]

The newest general theory about editing, coming into prominence in the 1970s and arising as a reaction to the kinds of problem just mentioned, is based on the idea that every separate version of a work has its own legitimacy. The Greg–Bowers theory generally aspired to produce, in a single text combining early accidentals and late substantives, the Platonically perfect realization of an author's final intentions in a work. But the results of this editorial eclecticism, "ideal" texts that never previously existed, came increasingly to look like the realization of editors' rather than authors' intentions; practically every advance of textual knowledge brought new evidence of works in progress rather than works perfected—evidence of revision, development by stages, authors changing their minds. As James Thorpe wrote in a pioneering essay that became chapter 1 of *Principles of Textual Criticism,* "authorial revision is embodied in multiple printed versions to an extent which seems to be almost limitless." With an impressive array of illustrations, Thorpe went on to question the much repeated notion that the goal of editing is to construct a text embodying the author's final intentions:

> It is a bit puzzling to know why this dictum should for so long have passed unchallenged. For it is much like saying that an author's last poem (or novel, or play) is, as a general rule, his best one; it may be, and it may not be.
> When several different works—or several versions of the same work—were written by the same author and communicated to his usual public, each is "authoritative." It is idle to . . . [talk] about which one is "the most authoritative." Likewise, any one of them might be said to "claim precedence." It all depends on where the procession is supposed to be going.[27]

Other scholars, with or without Thorpe's help, have been working toward the same conclusion. Donald Pizer, in an essay of 1971, is sharply critical of the application of Greg–Bowers principles to American literature, arguing that each revision of a text "constitutes a distinctive work with its own aesthetic individuality and character"; "to coalesce these versions into an eclectic text and its apparatus is to blur the nature of each version." Hans Zeller, reporting in 1975 on recent developments in German editorial theory arising out of problems with the texts of Goethe, elaborately defends the concept of versions, each with its separate authorial intention. Philip Gaskell, whose *New Introduction to Bibliography* (1972) raised the hackles of Greg–Bowers disciples by advocating the use of printed texts rather than manuscripts for copy-texts ("It would normally be wrong . . . rigidly to follow the accidentals of the manuscript, which the author would himself have been prepared—or might have preferred—to discard"), takes the line in his next book, *From Writer to Reader* (1978), that an editor "should not base his work on *any* predetermined rule or theory"; "every case is unique and must be approached with an open mind." Jerome McGann, in *A Critique of Modern Textual Criticism* (1983), builds on Thorpe and Zeller in particular to make a strong case for versions. Independently of McGann, James McLaverty, in an essay of 1984, arrives at a similar position by way of the intentionalist controversy in interpretive theory.[28]

These scholars write from a variety of motives. Thorpe and Gaskell mainly address practical problems of editing a text according to the author's intentions. Zeller and McLaverty are more interested in theory than in practice, though they too center their thinking on authorial intention; the author is guarantor of the authenticity of each separate version. Among Pizer's several concerns is the loss of historical artifacts: the Greg–Bowers eclecticism in effect obliterates (rather than preserves) the once-extant documents of the past. McGann wants to promote what he calls "a socialized concept of authorship and textual authority," a concept involving not only authors but publishers, editors, printers, booksellers, purchasers, readers, reviewers, critics, teachers, and students. "Literary production is not an autonomous and self-reflexive activity; it is a social and an institutional event." The "textual authority" of a work "rests neither with the author nor with his affiliated institution [by which McGann means the publisher]; it resides in the actual structure of the agreements which these two cooperating authorities [and, I would add, the rest of the participants as well] reach in specific cases."[29]

It is with these theories of versions, and above all with McGann's socialized concept of literary production, that the facts of multiple authorship are most compatible. The Greg–Bowers scheme, emerging as the result of major advances in our knowledge of printing and publishing practices, ought to have found room for at least some of the elements of collaborative creativity. Instead, the proponents of the system routinely view every alteration and revision by friends, relatives, copyists, editors, printers, publishers, and censors alike as impurity or contamination. Their object is to expunge the impurity when it is possible to do so (for example, by reversion to a prepublication form of a work), and the inevitable result, in the extreme instance of the Pennsylvania *Sister Carrie,* is Dreiser in his underwear.

When it seems not possible to remove the collaborative elements—as in *The Waste Land,* where almost no one admits to preferring the text of Eliot's draft before Pound went to work on it—they devise ingenious explanations to show that the collaborator was the author's "delegated" agent and the revisions merely carried out the author's intentions.

For a variety of practical reasons, I suggest (if we have to have general principles) that we drop the concept of an ideal single text fulfilling an author's intentions and put our money instead on some theory of versions. In a theory of versions, by contrast, multiple authorship is not some embarrassing blemish to be cleaned up or hidden away. Unlike the ideal creations of the Greg–Bowers school, versions are texts that, just like authors' collaborators, actually existed. And while currently there is no agreed-on definition of the degree of difference necessary to distinguish one version of a work from another (the possibilities range from a single variant of wording or punctuation to "major revision" that results in "a changed aesthetic effect"),[30] it is in the nature of the concept that the text of a version includes all the words of that version, regardless of how many authors contributed to the writing. Thus in a collaboratively authored version, each contributor to the collaboration has—by definition, if for no better reason—an intrinsic rather than an extrinsic place in the text. Removing one or more of the authors (as, in our recurrent example, the revisions by Dreiser's wife, or friend, or editor, or all of them together, in *Sister Carrie*) simply produces a different version.

As Thorpe observed nearly twenty-five years ago, textual constitution by versions makes possible a more realistic recovery of authors and their activity in the production of literary works. It answers Pizer's plea for preservation of the literary artifacts of the past. It is central to McGann's socialized view of authorship and textual authority. And it is hospitable to the circumstances of multiple authorship. It downplays (or rejects outright) the concept of single authorial intention, looking instead to a harmonious or discordant network of many separate intentions, starting with one or more nominal authors but expanding out to the printers, publishers, booksellers, and everyone else involved in the business. It is an idea that appears to be gaining ascendancy (as in Donald Reiman's 1985 MLA paper and 1987 essay "Versioning" and Peter Shillingsburg's thoughtful survey of alternatives to the Greg–Bowers theory in the 1989 issue of *Studies in Bibliography*).[31] Meanwhile, the partisans of Greg–Bowers principles, just like the single-author intentionalists among the interpreters, will continue to have a problem—in this case, both theoretical *and* practical—with multiple authorship.

To theorize is human, and quite possibly it is theory, even more than speech, that distinguishes human beings from the other species. But theory means different things to different theorists. In the physical and biological sciences, theory is most often a concept to explain what happened in the past, or what is happening in the present, or what will happen or may happen in the future. Thus theory in the sciences has explanatory and predictive power; it may in the beginning be speculative rather than verified, but an essential characteristic is that it is, sooner or later, verifiable. By contrast, some of the interpretive and editorial theory I have been examining in this chapter is neither explanatory nor predictive but is, instead, expressive of what *ought* to have happened in the past, or what ought to be happening in the present, or what ought to happen in the future—a body of opinion in the realm of ethics, morality, rhetoric, or politics rather than knowledge. It is probably recognition of this fundamental difference from science that now and then produces books with titles like *The Politics of Interpretation* and *Hermeneutics as Politics*.[32]

Interpretive and editorial theory also appears at times to confuse fact with speculation. The facts lie in such matters as the biographical circumstances of composition, the handwriting of a manuscript, the identity of a printer, the date of a first publication, the immediate source of a reprint, and so on; for example, Eliot wrote such and such, typed such and such, *and then* Pound did such and such—all matters for which there is (or can be) documentary evidence. The speculations lie in such matters as how an author felt, what an author wanted, and undocumented harmonies and conflicts among the authors, editors, revisers, publishers, and others involved in literary production; for example, Eliot desired such and such, but then Pound countered with such and such (either fulfilling or not fulfilling Eliot's intentions, or else using or not using Eliot to fulfill *his* intentions). The theorists do not treat facts as if they were speculation, but sometimes they treat speculations as if they were fact.

I cannot claim always to have avoided the appearance of this same kind of confusion myself. My (authorial) intention—the explanatory content of the present study—has been to show that multiple authorship is a frequently occurring phenomenon, one of the routine ways of producing literature all along. Because the phenomenon has occurred so frequently, my predictive content is that a piece of writing, past, present, or future, is likely to embody elements of multiple authorship—elements that (if they are now hidden) would become clear if we had more information about the circumstances, the texts, and the people engaged in the production. The hortative content (or implication) is that critics and editors ought to be more aware of the phenomenon and that interpretive and editorial theorists ought to rethink their theories in order to accommodate a plurality of authors. At present, there is a basic contradiction between the theorists' single-author standard for interpreting and editing and the way much of our literature has been, and continues to be, produced.

Appendix:
Multiple Authorship
from Homer to Ann Beattie

This brief Appendix provides—in two lists, one for British writers and the other for American—a sampling of instances of unacknowledged multiple authorship during the last two centuries, the historical period corresponding to the rise of the romantic myth of the author as solitary genius. These are examples that have come to hand (rather than products of an extensive search), and the writers and works are, for the most part, "serious," literary, and canonical.

Originally I began, and intended to present, an elaborate gathering from earliest times (represented by the vestigial "Homer" in the heading above) and from all possible literatures. But it soon became apparent that such a scope was too large and ungainly for a mere appendix. Early on, when I was explaining my project to lecture audiences, several medievalists independently of one another inquired, in tones of sympathetic concern, whether I intended to include every work originating before the invention of printing. Specialists in Renaissance drama raised the same question about an enormous quantity of early plays. Students of the long history of English prose, with or without reference to problems of the multiply authored *canon* treated in P. N. Furbank and W. R. Owens's *The Canonisation of Daniel Defoe* (New Haven, Conn.: Yale University Press, 1988), suggested further complications connected with works published anonymously or pseudonymously. And at a late stage of the proceedings I discovered that the *MLA International Bibliography* regularly includes "collaboration" as a heading in its Subject Index. Dustin Griffin's opening remark in "Augustan Collaboration"—"Literary collaboration is surprisingly common in Restoration and eighteenth century England"—turns out to be applicable to several centuries both before and after the Augustans (*Essays in Criticism* 37 [1987]: 1–10).

The pared-down results here are offered as representative examples that have been mentioned by scholars and for which there exists some kind of extrinsic (biographical or other documentary) evidence. The lists are chronological according to the birth dates of the nominal authors. I have used the following abbreviations in my parenthetical documentation:

Fraistat	Neil Fraistat, *The Poem and the Book: Interpreting Collections of Romantic Poetry* (Chapel Hill: University of North Carolina Press, 1985)
Madden	David Madden and Richard Powers, *Writers' Revisions: An Annotated Bibliography of Articles and Books about Writers' Revisions and Their Comments on the Creative Process* (Metuchen, N.J.: Scarecrow Press, 1981)
Parker	Hershel Parker, *Flawed Texts and Verbal Icons: Literary Authority in American Fiction* (Evanston, Ill.: Northwestern University Press, 1984)
Sutherland	J. A. Sutherland, *Victorian Novelists and Publishers* (Chicago: University of Chicago Press, 1976)
Thorpe	James Thorpe, *Principles of Textual Criticism* (San Marino, Calif.: Huntington Library, 1972)
West	James L. W. West III, *American Authors and the Literary Marketplace since 1900* (Philadelphia: University of Pennsylvania Press, 1988)

British

William Wordsworth: Collaboration with Coleridge in *Lyrical Ballads* (see esp. Paul Magnuson, *Coleridge and Wordsworth: A Lyrical Dialogue* [Princeton, N.J.: Princeton University Press, 1988]); *The Three Graves* a joint work by Wordsworth and Coleridge (Magnuson, p. 69 and n., citing Wordsworth's *Poetical Works* 1:308–12, 374, and Coleridge's *Complete Poetical Works* 1:267–84); Wordsworth's use of his sister's journals; Wordsworth's self-revision (see Chapter 4)

Samuel Taylor Coleridge: Collaboration with Wordsworth in *The Wanderings of Cain* (Magnuson, *Coleridge and Wordsworth*, pp. 69–70 n., citing Coleridge's *Complete Poetical Works* 1:285–92 and *Notebooks* 2: entry 2780 and n.); Wordsworth's contributions to *The Ancient Mariner;* collaboration with Southey in *The Fall of Robespierre* and *Joan of Arc* (Coleridge's *Collected Letters* 1:98 n., 106, 172 n.); Coleridge's appropriations from the Germans (see Chapter 5); collaborations with Joseph Henry Green and James Gillman (H. J. Jackson, "Coleridge's Collaborator, Joseph Henry Green," *Studies in Romanticism* 21 [1982]: 161–79; J. H. Haeger, "Coleridge's 'Bye Blow': The Composition and Date of *Theory of Life*," *Modern Philology* 74 [1976]: 20–41); Sara Coleridge's creative editing of *Biographia Literaria* and other writings

Jane Austen: Other hands in the MS of *Volume the Third* (B. C. Southam, "Interpolations to Jane Austen's 'Volume the Third,' " *Notes and Queries*, n.s., 9 [1962]: 185–87)

Lord Byron: Title of *Hours of Idleness* supplied by Byron's publisher, John Ridge (Fraistat, p. 200); most of the notes to *Childe Harold* canto 4 written by John Cam Hobhouse, who expanded them into a separate book, *Historical Illustrations to the Fourth Canto of Childe Harold* (*Lord Byron: The Complete Poetical Works*, ed. Jerome McGann, 2:316ff.)

Percy Bysshe Shelley: Collaboration with Thomas Jefferson Hogg in *The Necessity of Atheism* (E. B. Murray's forthcoming edition of Shelley's prose); Mary Shelley's editing of her husband's posthumous poems

Edward John Trelawny: Charles Brown's rewriting of *Adventures of a Younger Son* (MS at Harvard; see *The Letters of Charles Armitage Brown* [Cambridge, Mass.: Harvard University Press, 1966], p. 292 and n.)

John Clare: Extensive editing by John Taylor, who devised the title and plan for *The Shepherd's Calendar* (Tim Chilcott, *A Publisher and His Circle: The Life and Work of John Taylor, Keats's Publisher* [London: Routledge and Kegan Paul, 1972], pp. 86–128; Fraistat, p. 197, citing Ian Jack, "Poems of John Clare's Sanity," in *Some British Romantics: A Collection of Essays*, ed. James V. Logan et al. [Columbus: Ohio State University Press, 1966], pp. 189–232)

John Keats: Help from friends and publishers in *Endymion, Isabella, The Eve of St. Agnes, Lamia*, among others (see Chapters 1 and 2)

Mary W. Shelley: Help from Percy Shelley in *Frankenstein* (E. B. Murray, "Shelley's Contribution to Mary's *Frankenstein*," *Keats–Shelley Memorial Bulletin* 29 [1978]: 50–68; Anne K. Mellor, *Mary Shelley: Her Life, Her Fiction, Her Monsters* [New York: Methuen, 1988], pp. 57–69, 219–24)

Edward Bulwer-Lytton: Dickens's editing of works in *All the Year Round* (Sutherland, pp. 180–86)

John Stuart Mill: Collaboration with his wife in *Autobiography* and other works (see Chapter 3)

Anne Manning: The publisher Bentley's influence on *The Ladies of Bever Hollow* (Sutherland, p. 30)

Charles Dickens: The altered ending of *Great Expectations* influenced by Bulwer-Lytton (Sutherland, pp. 180–86)

Charles Reade: Editorial alteration of *The Woman Hater* (Thorpe, p. 17)

Anthony Trollope: *Barchester Towers* purged of "vulgarity" and "exaggeration" by the publisher Longman (Sutherland, p. 27)

Charles Kingsley: Continual advice from the Macmillans during the writing of *Westward Ho!* (Sutherland, pp. 124–26)

Thomas Hardy: Editorial alteration of novels in serialized form (Thorpe, p. 17; Dale Kramer, "Two 'New' Texts of Thomas Hardy's *The Woodlanders*," *Studies in Bibliography* 20 [1967]: 135–50, and "Revisions and Vision: Thomas Hardy's *The Woodlanders*," *Bulletin of the New York Public Library* 75 [1971]: 195–230, 248–82; Simon Gatrell, *Hardy the Creator: A Textual Biography* [Oxford: Clarendon Press, 1988]); the first *Life* of Hardy (purported biography) actually coauthored by Hardy and his second wife

George Moore: Collaboration in *Esther Waters* and other works (Barrett H. Clark, *Intimate Portraits* [New York: Dramatists Play Service, 1951], pp. 63, 90–104, 119–20, 123–24, 133–34, 146, 148–49; W. Eugene Davis, " 'The Celebrated Case of Esther Waters': Unpublished Letters of George Moore to Barrett H. Clark," *Papers on Language and Literature* 13 [1977]: 71–79, and "George Moore as Collaborator and Artist: The Making of a Later *Esther Waters: A Play*," *English Literature in Transition* 24 [1981]: 185–95)

Oscar Wilde: Other hands in *The Importance of Being Earnest* (Thorpe, pp. 23–24; James Barron, "Premiere of Original 'Earnest,' " *New York Times*, 18 November 1985, p. C15)

George Bernard Shaw: Early collaboration in *Widowers' Houses* (*Widowers' Houses: Facsimiles of the Shorthand and Holograph Manuscripts and the 1893 Published Text*, ed. Jerald E. Bringle [New York: Garland, 1981])

Joseph Conrad: Collaboration with Ford Madox Ford and Edward Garnett in *Nostromo* and other works (Arthur Mizener, *The Saddest Story: A Biography of Ford Madox Ford* [New York: World, 1971], pp. 89–91; West, p. 56)

Ford Madox Ford: Collaboration with Conrad on various works including *The Inheritors* and *Romance* (Raymond Brebach, *Joseph Conrad, Ford Madox Ford, and the Making of "Romance"* [Ann Arbor: UMI Research Press, 1985]; three articles by Brebach: "The Making of *Romance*, Part Fifth," *Conradiana* 6 [1974]: 171–81, "*Romance*: A Survey of Manuscripts and Typescripts," *Conradiana* 10 [1978]: 85–86, and "Conrad, Ford, and the *Romance* Poem," *Modern Philology* 81 [1983]: 169–72; Nicholas Delbanco, *Group Portrait* [New York: Morrow, 1982], pp. 98–99, 106–7, 117–18, 126–27)

James Joyce: Publisher's censorship in *Dubliners* (Madden, p. 85, citing Robert E. Scholes, "Some Observations on the Text of *Dubliners:* 'The Dead,' " *Studies in Bibliography* 15 [1962]: 191–205, and "Further Observations on the Text of *Dubliners*," *Studies in Bibliography* 17 [1964]: 107–22); verbatim use of another writer's sermon in *Portrait of the Artist as a Young Man;* other hands in the final chapter of *Ulysses*

D. H. Lawrence: Collaboration with Frieda Lawrence, Edward Garnett, and others in *The Rainbow, Women in Love,* and *Sons and Lovers* (Charles L. Ross, *The Composition of "The Rainbow" and "Women in Love": A History* [Charlottesville: University Press of Virginia, 1979]; Lois Palken Rudnik, *Mabel Dodge Luhan: New Woman, New Worlds* [Albuquerque: University of New Mexico Press, 1984], p. 197; West, p. 56)

Hugh MacDiarmid: Plagiarism in *A Drunk Man Looks at the Thistle* (Nancy K. Gish, *Hugh MacDiarmid: The Man and His Work* [London: Macmillan, 1984], pp. 59–64)

"Bryher" (Winifred Ellerman): *Two Selves* in collaboration with H.D. (Hilda Doolittle) (Susan Stanford Friedman, *Psyche Reborn: The Emergence of H.D.* [Bloomington: Indiana University Press, 1981], p. 35)

George Orwell: Extensive censorship by the editors of his novels (Jo Thomas, "New, Uncensored Edition of Orwell," *New York Times,* 8 March 1986, p. 13)

Samuel Beckett: Collaboration with Jasper Johns in *Fizzles* (Carol Shloss, *"Foirades/Fizzles:* Variations on a Past Image," *Journal of Modern Literature* 12 [1985]: 153–68)

Malcolm Lowry: Collaboration with his wife in *Under the Volcano* (Douglas Day, *Malcolm Lowry: A Biography* [New York: Oxford University Press, 1973], pp. 37, 270–73)

Barbara Pym: Editorial creation of the posthumous *An Academic Question* from two incomplete drafts, one a first-person novel, the other a version written in the third person

Anthony Burgess: Editorial alteration in the American issue of *A Clockwork Orange* (Edwin McDowell, "Publishing: 'Clockwork Orange' Regains Chapter 21," *New York Times,* 31 December 1986, p. C16)

D. M. Thomas: Plagiarism from A. V. Kuznetsov's *Babi Yar* in *The White Hotel* (various writers in the London *Times Literary Supplement,* 26 March, 2, 9, 16, 23, 30 April, 16 July 1982, pp. 355, 383, 412–15, 439, 463, 487, 766)

David Lodge: Original publisher of *Out of the Shelter* responsible for revisions and cuts amounting to 25 percent (see Lodge's introduction to the 1985 Penguin reprint)

American

Washington Irving: Help from nephew Pierre Irving in *The Life of George Washington* and other works (Wayne R. Kime, *Pierre M. Irving and Washington Irving: A Collaboration in Life and Letters* [Waterloo, Ont.: Wilfrid Laurier University Press, 1977])

Ralph Waldo Emerson: Later lectures constructed out of his journals and notes by his daughter Ellen and James Elliot Cabot (*The Letters of Ellen Tucker Emerson,* ed. Edith E. W. Gregg [Kent, Ohio: Kent State University Press, 1982], 2:283ff.; Nancy Craig Simmons, "Arranging the Sibylline Leaves: James Elliot Cabot's Work as Emerson's Literary Executor," *Studies in the American Renaissance* [1983]: 335–89; Glen M. Johnson, "Emerson's Essay 'Immortality': The Problem of Authorship," *American Literature* 56 [1984]: 313–30)

Nathaniel Hawthorne: Substantive contributions by his wife (Thorpe, p. 19); editorial construction of his three posthumous romances

Herman Melville: Editorial expurgations in *Typee* (Parker, p. 48); plagiarisms in *Moby-Dick* (Howard P. Vincent, *The Trying-Out of "Moby-Dick"* [Boston: Houghton Mifflin, 1949]); controversial editing of the posthumous *Billy Budd*

Lew Wallace: *Ben-Hur* and other works coauthored with his wife, Susan Arnold Wallace; *Lew Wallace: An Autobiography* completed by his wife

Emily Dickinson: Editorial rewriting of the poems (Thorpe, pp. 14–15)

Slave narratives: Numerous instances of rewriting by publishers (see, for example, *Puttin' on Ole Massa: The Slave Narratives of Henry Bibb, William Wells Brown, and Solomon Northup,* ed. Gilbert Osofsky [New York: Harper & Row, 1969]; William L. Andrews, *To Tell a Free Story: The First Century of Afro-American Autobiography, 1760–1865* [Urbana: University of Illinois Press, 1986]; and Alice A. Deck, "Whose Book Is This?: Authorial versus Editorial Control of Harriet Brent Jacobs' *Incidents in the Life of a Slave Girl: Written by Herself,*" *Women's Studies International Forum* 10 [1987]: 33–40)

Mark Twain: Collaboration with Charles Dudley Warner in *The Gilded Age* (Bryant Morey French, *Mark Twain and "The Gilded Age": The Book That Named an Era* [Dallas: Southern Methodist University Press, 1965], esp. chap. 3); collaboration with William Dean Howells on at least one play; editorial changes in magazine extracts from *Huckleberry Finn* (Thorpe, p. 16); editorial completion of *The Mysterious Stranger* (Thorpe, p. 20); substantive alterations in various works influenced by Twain's wife

William Dean Howells: Collaboration with Henry James and others in *The Whole Family,* published serially in *Harper's* in 1906 and then as a book in 1908 (reprint, New York: Ungar, 1986)

Henry Adams: Use of his wife's letters in *Democracy* and *Esther* (Eugenia Kaledin, *The Education of Mrs. Henry Adams* [Philadelphia: Temple University Press, 1981], p. 9)

Edward Noyes Westcott: *David Harum* fashioned out of Westcott's MS by Appleton editor Ripley Hitchcock (West, pp. 51–55)

Thomas Nelson Page: Editorial changes in his stories (Thorpe, p. 17)

Black Elk: *Black Elk Speaks* the product of Black Elk's dictation in Oglala

Sioux dialect, his son's oral translation of this into English, and the poet John G. Neihardt's transcribing and editing (the work was published "as told to"—later changed to "as told through"—Neihardt), with additions by other tribal elders who interrupted to correct Black Elk or were called on by Black Elk to contribute or fill in details (see 1972 Pocket Books reissue, pp. 235–38, "About This Book and Its Author"; Arnold Krupat, "The Indian Autobiography: Origins, Type, and Function," *American Literature* 53 [1981]: 22–42; Albert E. Stone, *Autobiographical Occasions and Original Acts: Versions of American Identity from Henry Adams to Nate Shaw* [Philadelphia: University of Pennsylvania Press, 1982], chap. 3, "The Soul and the Self: Black Elk and Thomas Merton," esp. pp. 61–76; G. Thomas Couser, *"Black Elk Speaks* with Forked Tongue," in *Studies in Autobiography,* ed. James Olney [New York: Oxford University Press, 1988], pp. 73–88)

Theodore Dreiser: *Sister Carrie* the product of several hands (see Chapter 7); *Jennie Gerhardt* edited and altered by Ripley Hitchcock (West, p. 55); posthumous work, *The Stoic,* cut and altered by editor with the approval of Dreiser's widow (West, p. 72, citing Philip L. Gerber, "Dreiser's *Stoic:* A Study in Literary Frustration," *Literary Monographs* 7 [1975]: 85–144, 159–64)

Stephen Crane: Other hands in *Maggie* and *The Red Badge of Courage* (Parker, pp. 39, 49, 147–79 passim—see Ripley Hitchcock in Parker's index)

Gertrude Stein: Possible substantive contributions by Alice Toklas to Stein's *The Autobiography of Alice B. Toklas* (Catharine R. Stimpson, "Gertrice/Altrude: Stein, Toklas, and the Paradox of the Happy Marriage," in *Mothering the Mind: Twelve Studies of Writers and Their Silent Partners,* ed. Ruth Perry and Martine Watson Brownley [New York: Holmes and Meier, 1984], pp. 122–39, and references there)

Sherwood Anderson: Works edited by Maxwell Perkins (A. Scott Berg, *Max Perkins: Editor of Genius* [New York: Dutton, 1978], pp. 379–82)

Upton Sinclair: Extensive revisions and cuts supposedly influenced by publishers and censors in *The Jungle* (new edition by Gene DeGruson—see Edwin McDowell, "Sinclair's 'Jungle' with All Muck Restored," *New York Times,* 22 August 1988, pp. C15, C20)

Wallace Stevens: Influence of Harriet Monroe on the first published text, five stanzas long, of *Sunday Morning* (*Letters of Wallace Stevens,* ed. Holly Stevens [New York: Knopf, 1966], pp. 183–84; Joan Richardson, *Wallace Stevens: The Early Years, 1879–1923* [New York: Morrow, 1986], pp. 436–37)

William Carlos Williams: Deletions in *Paterson* influenced by Richard Eberhart at Yaddo (Eberhart's recollection)

Edith Summers Kelley: *Weeds* significantly altered by a trade editor (West, p. 70)

H.D. (Hilda Doolittle): Editing of early poems (for example, *Hermes of the*

Ways) by Ezra Pound, who also devised her literary name, "H.D., Imagiste," and submitted the poems to *Poetry* (see H.D.'s brief descriptions in *End to Torment: A Memoir of Ezra Pound*, ed. Norman Holmes Pearson and Michael King [New York: New Directions, 1979], pp. 18, 40)

Robinson Jeffers: Saxe Commins's editing of Jeffers's final volume of poetry, *The Double Axe* (West, p. 65, citing James Shebl, *In This Wild Water: The Suppressed Poems of Robinson Jeffers* [Pasadena: Ward Ritchie Press, 1976], and a 1977 edition of Jeffers's *The Double Axe and Other Poems including Eleven Suppressed Poems*)

T. S. Eliot: The work of Pound and others on *The Waste Land* (see Chapter 6)

Eugene O'Neill: *More Stately Mansions* concocted from O'Neill's partially revised script by Karl Ragner Gierow (Thorpe, p. 20)

Archibald MacLeish: The work of Elia Kazan and others on *J.B.* (Thorpe, pp. 24–25, 30–31)

Pearl S. Buck: Several works of nonfiction, including *Fairy Tales of the Orient, The People of Japan, The Story Bible, Pearl S. Buck's Oriental Cookbook,* and *Pearl S. Buck's Book of Christmas* "created" by Lyle Kenyon Engel, the founder of Book Creations, Inc. (see Chapter 7)

Dashiell Hammett: *Red Harvest* changed significantly by a trade editor (West, p. 70)

E. E. Cummings: *The Enormous Room* changed significantly by a trade editor (West, p. 70)

John Dos Passos: *Three Soldiers* changed significantly by a trade editor (West, p. 70)

Marjorie Kinnan Rawlings: Subject and plot of *The Yearling* suggested by Maxwell Perkins (Berg, *Max Perkins*, pp. 297–300)

F. Scott Fitzgerald: Maxwell Perkins's influence on *The Great Gatsby* (see Chapter 7); Malcolm Cowley's work on *Tender Is the Night* (Brian Higgins and Hershel Parker, "Sober Second Thoughts: Fitzgerald's 'Final Version' of *Tender Is the Night*," *Proof* 4 [1975]: 129–52); Edmund Wilson's doctoring of *The Last Tycoon* (Matthew J. Bruccoli, "*The Last of the Novelists*": *F. Scott Fitzgerald and "The Last Tycoon"* [Carbondale: Southern Illinois University Press, 1977]); Fitzgerald's use of his wife's diaries and letters (Arthur Mizener, *The Far Side of Paradise: A Biography of F. Scott Fitzgerald* [Boston: Houghton Mifflin, 1951]; Nancy Milford, *Zelda: A Biography* [New York: Harper & Row, 1970], pp. 35, 44, 55, 58, 71, 76, 81, 89, 102, 177, 284–85)

William Faulkner: *Flags in the Dust* (early version of *Sartoris*) cut drastically by agent; various hands in *Sanctuary, Requiem for a Nun, Absalom, Absalom!*, stories, and films (Madden, pp. 52–60; Parker, pp. 47–48; West, p. 64; numerous articles and editions by Noel Polk)

Ernest Hemingway: Fitzgerald's influence on the beginning of *The Sun Also Rises* (see Chapter 7; *Antaeus*, no. 33 [Spring 1979]: 7–18; Parker, p. 43);

Mary Hemingway's concoction of *A Moveable Feast* (Kenneth S. Lynn, *Hemingway* [New York: Simon and Schuster, 1987], p. 585 and n.) and *Islands in the Stream* (West, p. 72, citing Michael S. Reynolds, "Words Killed, Wounded, Missing in Action," *Hemingway Notes* 6, no. 2 [Spring 1981]: 2–9); editorial production of *The Garden of Eden* (West, p. 72; Barbara Probst Solomon, "Where's Papa?" *New Republic,* 9 March 1987, pp. 30–34)

Thomas Wolfe: Editorial collaboration in all the works, lifetime and posthumous (see Chapter 7)

Zora Neale Hurston: Autobiography, *Dust Tracks on a Road,* altered by editor in such a way as to make it unsatisfactory to both author and audience (Robert E. Hemenway, *Zora Neale Hurston: A Literary Biography* [Urbana: University of Illinois Press, 1977], pp. 286–90)

Nathanael West: Collaboration with S. J. Perelman (see second item below)

Irving Stone: Collaboration with his wife in *Lust for Life* and other works (obituary, *New York Times,* 28 August 1989, p. B6)

S. J. Perelman: Collaboration with Nathanael West in a three-act play entitled "Even Stephen" (never produced, never published, extant in MS at Brown University—see Mel Gussow, "Perelman–West Play in New Trove at Brown," *New York Times,* 2 February 1987, p. C11)

Moss Hart: Performance changes in *Once in a Lifetime* (Thorpe, p. 24, citing Hart's *Act One*)

John O'Hara: Saxe Commins's editing of *A Rage to Live* and other works (West, p. 65)

James Michener: Large novels written in part by a research team (*Texas* a recent example)

Richard Wright: Participation of Wright's agent, editor, and others in the production of *Native Son* (Keneth Kinnamon, "How *Native Son* Was Born," in *Writing the American Classics,* ed. James Barbour and Tom Quirk [Chapel Hill: University of North Carolina Press, 1990], pp. 209–34); Book-of-the-Month Club creation of *Black Boy* out of the longer *American Hunger* (Janice Thaddeus, "The Metamorphosis of Richard Wright's *Black Boy,*" *American Literature* 57 [1985]: 199–214)

James Agee: Editorial creation of *A Death in the Family* (West, pp. 71–72, citing Victor A. Kramer, "*A Death in the Family* and Agee's Projected Novel," *Proof* 3 [1973]: 139–54)

Willard Motley: Editorial creation of *Knock on Any Door* (Madden, p. 103, citing Jerome Klinkowitz and Karen Wood, "The Making and Unmaking of *Knock on Any Door,*" *Proof* 3 [1973]: 121–37; William Proctor Williams and Craig S. Abbott, *An Introduction to Bibliographical and Textual Studies* [New York: Modern Language Association, 1985], p. 54; West, p. 70)

William Gibson: Performance changes in *Two for the Seesaw* (see Chapter 8)

Shirley Jackson: Contribution of her husband, Stanley Edgar Hyman, to

"The Lottery" (Judy Oppenheimer, *Private Demons: The Life of Shirley Jackson* [New York: Putnam, 1988], p. 130)

Robert Lowell: Influence of friends to produce "collective poetry" (Stanley Kunitz's comment quoted in Linda Bamber, "Writers *Can* Be Friends," *New York Times Book Review,* 14 December 1986, pp. 1, 40–41); Randall Jarrell's hand in *Lord Weary's Castle* (Bruce Michelson, "Randall Jarrell and Robert Lowell: The Making of *Lord Weary's Castle,*" *Contemporary Literature* 26 [1985]: 402–25)

Jacqueline Susann: Editorial creation of *Valley of the Dolls* by Don Preston and *The Love Machine* by "the Simon and Schuster editorial team" (see Chapter 7, citing Barbara Seaman, *Lovely Me: The Life of Jacqueline Susann* [1987], esp. pp. 285–89, 296–98, 322–24, 375)

James Jones: Extensive cuts and revisions by the publisher in *From Here to Eternity* (MS of the novel at the University of Illinois)

Jack Kerouac: Collaboration of editors, agents, and friends in *On the Road* (Tim Hunt, *Kerouac's Crooked Road: Development of a Fiction* [Hamden, Conn.: Archon Books, 1981])

William Zinsser: Editorial contributions to various of Zinsser's works (Zinsser, *On Writing Well: An Informal Guide to Writing Nonfiction,* 3rd ed. [New York: Harper & Row, 1985], pp. 227, 234–38)

Kurt Vonnegut, Jr.: Early book altered by editor, and then reissued in the form that Vonnegut wanted (West, pp. 70–71, citing Susan Schiefelbein, "Writers, Editors and the Shaping of Books," *Washington Post Book World,* 17 January 1982, pp. 1–2, 8)

Joseph Heller: Title of *Catch-22* the work of Robert Gottlieb (see Chapter 7)

Grace Metalious: Editorial rewriting of *Peyton Place* (see Chapter 7, citing Emily Toth, *Inside Peyton Place: The Life of Grace Metalious* [1981], pp. 96–109)

Truman Capote: Editorial creation of posthumous book, *Answered Prayers,* from Capote's partially complete MS (Edwin McDowell, "Publishing Manuscripts Posthumously," *New York Times,* 10 September 1984, p. C13)

Malcolm X: Collaboration with Alex Haley in *The Autobiography of Malcolm X* (Stone, *Autobiographical Occasions and Original Acts,* chap. 7, "Two Recreate One: The Act of Collaboration in Recent Black Autobiography—Ossie Guffy, Nate Shaw, Malcolm X," esp. pp. 246–64)

William Styron: Hiram Haydn's work on *Lie Down in Darkness* (West, p. 68, citing articles by Arthur D. Casciato and West)

John Barth: Publisher's alterations in *The Floating Opera* (Sherry Lutz Zivley, "A Collation of John Barth's *Floating Opera,*" *Papers of the Bibliographical Society of America* 72 [1978]: 201–12; West, p. 70)

John Updike: *Rabbit, Run* altered by editor in first published version, after which Updike was able to "repair the damage" in a later edition (West, pp. 70–71, citing Randall H. Waldron, "Rabbit Revised," *American Literature* 56 [1984]: 51–67)

Sylvia Plath: *Ariel* posthumously produced, arranged, and published by her husband, Ted Hughes (MSS at Smith College; Marjorie Perloff, "The Two *Ariels:* The (Re)Making of the Sylvia Plath Canon," in *Poems in Their Place: The Intertextuality and Order of Poetic Collections,* ed. Neil Fraistat [Chapel Hill: University of North Carolina Press, 1986], pp. 308–33)

Louise Shivers: *Here to Get My Baby Out of Jail,* originally a 700-page MS, reduced by editor to a 125-page printed book

Stephen King: Original publisher of *The Stand* responsible for cuts amounting to 150,000 words (Edwin McDowell, "Book Notes," *New York Times,* 31 January 1990, p. C20)

Ann Beattie: Title of *Love Always* (criticized by reviewers as inappropriate) supplied by Roger Angell, fiction editor of the *New Yorker*

Notes

1. What Is an Author?

1. This authorial "disappearance" in Barthes and Foucault should not be confused with a different concept expressed in the same words by English and American critics earlier in this century—the "disappearance of the author" behind a novelist's fictitious point of view; see the citations in Norman Friedman, "Point of View in Fiction: The Development of a Critical Concept," *PMLA* 70 (1955): 1160–84. For Barthes's "The Death of the Author," originally published in *Mantéia* 5 (1968), see *Image—Music—Text*, a collection of Barthes's essays selected and trans. Stephen Heath (New York: Hill and Wang, 1977), pp. 142–48. Foucault's "What Is an Author?"—delivered at the Collège de France on 22 February 1969 and then published in *Bulletin de la Société française de Philosophie* 63 (1969)—is available both in Foucault's *Language, Counter-Memory, Practice: Selected Essays and Interviews*, ed. Donald F. Bouchard (Ithaca, N.Y.: Cornell University Press, 1977), pp. 113–38 (translation, by Bouchard and Sherry Simon, of the printed text of 1969), and in *Textual Strategies: Perspectives in Post-Structuralist Criticism*, ed. Josué V. Harari (Ithaca, N.Y.: Cornell University Press, 1979), pp. 141–60 (translation, by Harari, of a revised version delivered at the State University of New York at Buffalo). I need hardly point out that my chapter title is intentionally taken over from Foucault, who thus at the beginning of this book becomes one of *my* coauthors.

2. I quote the first two definitions in *Webster's Ninth New Collegiate Dictionary* (Springfield, Mass.: Merriam-Webster, 1983). The unabridged *Webster's Third New International Dictionary* (1961) adds several others that, taken together, read like an outline for a study of multiple authorship: "one that compiles material (as for publication)," "one (as an author's agent) having the right to make author's alterations," "a printer's customer," "a corporate author." Other definitions in the larger dictionary include "one that fathers" [*sic*], "SOURCE, CREATOR; *esp:* GOD," "one that prompts to an action," and "the source of an opinion."

3. This is the point of Stanley Fish's "With the Compliments of the Author: Reflections on Austin and Derrida," *Critical Inquiry* 8 (1982): 693–721.

4. James's best-known pronouncements are conveniently collected in *Theory of Fiction: Henry James*, ed. James E. Miller, Jr. (Lincoln: University of Nebraska Press, 1972); see esp. chap. 9, part B, "Presence of the Author," and chap. 12, "Point of View," pp. 174–80, 234–56. For Booth and Barthes, see Wayne C. Booth, *The Rhetoric of Fiction* (Chicago: University of Chicago Press, 1961), esp. part 2: "The Author's Voice in Fiction," pp. 167–266, and Barthes, "Introduction to the Structural Analysis of Narratives," in *Image—Music—Text*, pp. 79–124 (quotations from p. 111).

5. *The Letters of Emily Dickinson,* ed. Thomas H. Johnson (Cambridge, Mass.: Harvard University Press, 1958), 2:412.

6. Patrick Cruttwell, "Makers and Persons," *Hudson Review* 12 (1959–60): 487–507; Ralph W. Rader, "The Dramatic Monologue and Related Lyric Forms," *Critical Inquiry* 3 (1976): 131–51. W. K. Wimsatt comments on Cruttwell and a number of other writers on personae and masks in "Genesis: A Fallacy Revisited," in *The Disciplines of Criticism: Essays in Literary Theory, Interpretation, and History,* ed. Peter Demetz et al. (New Haven, Conn.: Yale University Press, 1968), pp. 193–225 (reprinted with a different title, "Genesis: An Argument Resumed," in Wimsatt's *Day of the Leopards: Essays in Defense of Poems* [New Haven, Conn.: Yale University Press, 1976], pp. 11–39). See also Friedman, "Point of View in Fiction."

7. For comprehensive discussion of the Romantics' use of biography as a critical methodology, see Annette Wheeler Cafarelli, *Prose in the Age of Poets: Romanticism and Biographical Narrative from Johnson to De Quincey* (Philadelphia: University of Pennsylvania Press, 1990). Nineteenth-century American readers' interest in authors and genius is thoroughly documented in Nina Baym, *Novels, Readers, and Reviewers: Responses to Fiction in Antebellum America* (Ithaca, N.Y.: Cornell University Press, 1984), chap. 12, "Authors," pp. 249–69.

8. Charles Grosvenor Osgood, *The Voice of England: A History of English Literature* (New York: Harper, 1935), pp. xi, 246, 305.

9. Wimsatt and Beardsley's "The Intentional Fallacy"—discussed in Chapter 9—originally appeared in *Sewanee Review* 54 (1946): 468–88, and then was republished, in revised form, in Wimsatt's *The Verbal Icon: Studies in the Meaning of Poetry* (Lexington: University of Kentucky Press, 1954), pp. 3–18. See also Wimsatt's retrospective "Genesis: A Fallacy Revisited." Frye's "Literary Criticism" is in *The Aims and Methods of Scholarship in Modern Languages and Literatures,* ed. James Thorpe (New York: Modern Language Association, 1963), pp. 57–69 (quotation from p. 59). As Gerald Graff points out, Richards misinterpreted the evidence of his experiments at Cambridge; in the accounts in *Practical Criticism: A Study of Literary Judgment* (London: K. Paul, Trench, Trubner, 1929), it is the *lack* of biographical and historical contexts that caused students the greatest difficulties in reading. See Graff's *Professing Literature: An Institutional History* (Chicago: University of Chicago Press, 1987), pp. 174–77.

10. E. D. Hirsch, Jr., *Validity in Interpretation* (New Haven, Conn.: Yale University Press, 1967).

11. *The Poems of John Keats,* ed. Jack Stillinger (Cambridge, Mass.: Harvard University Press, 1978), pp. 363–64. The basic facts about the composition, manuscripts, and textual history of the poem are given in Stillinger, *The Texts of Keats's Poems* (Cambridge, Mass.: Harvard University Press, 1974), pp. 235–38, and the textual notes in *The Poems of John Keats,* pp. 646–47. For facsimiles of Keats's draft, see *Athenaeum,* 26 October 1872, p. 529, and *The Keats Letters, Papers, and Other Relics Forming the Dilke Bequest in the Hampstead Public Library,* ed. George C. Williamson (London: John Lane, 1914), plate 8.

12. See H. W. Garrod, ed., *The Oxford Book of Latin Verse* (Oxford: Clarendon Press, 1912), pp. 330, 495–500, and J. V. Cunningham, "Classical and Medieval: Statius, On Sleep," in *Tradition and Poetic Structure* (Denver: Alan Swallow, 1960), pp. 25–39.

13. *The Letters of John Keats, 1814–1821,* ed. Hyder E. Rollins (Cambridge, Mass.: Harvard University Press, 1958), 2:108.

14. See H. W. Garrod, *Keats,* 2nd ed. (Oxford: Clarendon Press, 1939), pp. 80–87; M. R. Ridley, *Keats' Craftsmanship: A Study in Poetic Development* (Oxford: Clarendon Press, 1933), pp. 196–209; Lawrence John Zillman, *John Keats and the Sonnet Tradition: A Critical and Comparative Study* (Los Angeles: Lymanhouse, 1939); and W. J. Bate, *The Stylistic Development of Keats* (New York: Modern Language Association, 1945), pp. 125–33.

15. On the language and theme of the sonnet, the most helpful critics are Claude Lee Finney, *The Evolution of Keats's Poetry* (Cambridge, Mass.: Harvard University Press, 1936), 2:605–8; W. K. Thomas, "Keats' 'To Sleep,' " *Explicator* 26 (1968): item 55; and Morris Dickstein, *Keats and His Poetry: A Study in Development* (Chicago: University of Chicago Press, 1971), pp. 18–28.

16. For the Burton and Dante passages, see Robert Gittings, *John Keats: The Living Year* (Cambridge, Mass.: Harvard University Press, 1954), pp. 126, 218, and *The Mask of Keats: A Study of Problems* (London: Heinemann, 1956), pp. 32–33, 151, 166.

17. Booth, *The Rhetoric of Fiction,* pp. 71–76; Foucault, "What Is an Author?"; Kendall L. Walton, "Style and the Products and Processes of Art," in *The Concept of Style,* ed. Berel Lang, rev. ed. (Ithaca, N.Y.: Cornell University Press, 1987), pp. 72–103; Alexander Nehamas, "The Postulated Author: Critical Monism as a Regulative Ideal," *Critical Inquiry* 8 (1981): 133–49.

18. A similar situation exists in the principal twentieth-century editions of Keats's poems, where the texts of the sonnet in H. W. Garrod's Oxford English Texts *Poetical Works* of 1939 and 1958 (based on Milnes's *Life*), Miriam Allott's Longman Annotated English Poets *Poems* of 1970 (based on Woodhouse's first transcript), and my own *Poems* of 1978 (based on Keats's album copy) again all differ substantively from one another. John Barnard's text in *Complete Poems* (Harmondsworth: Penguin) is also substantively unique in both the first edition, 1973 (based on the version in Milnes's *Life*), and the second edition, 1976 (based on Keats's album copy); Keats's "thy poppy" in line 7 is misprinted "the poppy" in both editions.

19. Keats's letter has no punctuation in line 11 and has "borrowing" (presumably a slip of the pen) for "burrowing" and "a" interlined above deleted "the" in line 12 (Keats's *Letters,* 2:105). Both of Woodhouse's transcripts have lowercase "conscience" altered to "Conscience" in line 11; his first transcript also has the pencil queries "q enshrouded" opposite "Enshaded" in line 4 and "q hoards" (written before he changed the word in his text) opposite "lords" in line 11. For facsimiles of Brown's transcript and Woodhouse's first copy, see *The Charles Brown Poetry Transcripts at Harvard* (p. 50) and *The Woodhouse Poetry Transcripts at Harvard* (pp. 276–77), both ed. Jack Stillinger (New York: Garland, 1988).

20. See the eight letters under the heading "A Line in Keats" in *Times Literary Supplement,* 8, 29 March; 12, 19 April; and 3 May 1941, pp. 117, 151, 179, 191, 215. Garrod repeats his paraphrase (along with several pieces of misinformation concerning the texts of the sonnet) in his Oxford Standard Authors edition, *The Poetical Works of John Keats* (London: Oxford University Press, 1956), p. 467. It was not known until much later, with the publication of *The Texts of Keats's Poems* in 1974, that Keats accepted Woodhouse's "hoards" when he wrote out the poem in the lady's album in 1820.

2. *Keats and His Helpers:*
   The Multiple Authorship of Isabella

1. The "little change . . . in my intellect lately" is in Keats's *Letters*, 1:214 (23 January 1818). For interpretation of the poem as antiromance, see Jack Stillinger, "Keats and Romance: The 'Reality' of *Isabella*," in *The Hoodwinking of Madeline and Other Essays on Keats's Poems* (Urbana: University of Illinois Press, 1971), pp. 31–45, and Susan Wolfson, "Keats's *Isabella* and the 'Digressions' of 'Romance,' " *Criticism* 27 (1985): 247–61. The facts concerning composition, manuscripts, and textual history are given in Stillinger, *The Texts of Keats's Poems*, pp. 182–86, and in the apparatus and textual notes in *The Poems of John Keats* (1978), pp. 245–63, 601–9.

2. Woodhouse figures prominently in four of the seven volumes of Keats facsimiles in the series Manuscripts of the Younger Romantics: vol. 1, *Poems (1817): A Facsimile of Richard Woodhouse's Annotated Copy in the Huntington Library;* vol. 3, *Endymion (1818): A Facsimile of Richard Woodhouse's Annotated Copy in the Berg Collection;* vol. 4, *Poems, Transcripts, Letters, &c.: Facsimiles of Richard Woodhouse's Scrapbook Materials in the Pierpont Morgan Library;* and vol. 6, *The Woodhouse Poetry Transcripts at Harvard: A Facsimile of the W^2 Notebook, with Description and Contents of the W^1 Notebook,* all ed. Jack Stillinger (New York: Garland, 1985, 1988). There is information about Woodhouse as scholar, collector, annotator, and reader of Keats in the introductions to the four volumes; his shorthand transcript of *Isabella* is reproduced in vol. 4, pp. 265–84, and his longhand W^2 transcript in vol. 6, pp. 36–87. A facsimile of Keats's fair copy of the poem (with Woodhouse's suggested corrections and revisions in pencil) is available in vol. 5 of the series, *Manuscript Poems in the British Library: Facsimiles of the "Hyperion" Holograph and George Keats's Notebook of Holographs and Transcripts* (1988), pp. 59–113.

3. One other Woodhouse shorthand transcript of a Keats poem is extant, that of *The Eve of St. Mark* (in the Adelman Collection at Bryn Mawr College), and a lost shorthand copy has been hypothesized as the first of Woodhouse's transcripts of *The Eve of St. Agnes* (see *The Texts of Keats's Poems*, pp. 215–18, and *Poems* [1978], pp. 626–28). There is, however, no ready explanation as to *why* Woodhouse made these initial copies in shorthand. He seems to have had plenty of time in which to make other copies of long poems (and sometimes more than one duplicate) in longhand, and he obviously was in no hurry when he made the shorthand transcript of *Isabella*, since he took the trouble to pencil (and, before he could pencil, compose) a great many revisions and suggestions in the holograph that he was copying.

4. Keats's *Letters*, 1:376–77.

5. They are listed in *The Texts of Keats's Poems*, pp. 184–85, and again, slightly more accurately, in *Poems* (1978), pp. 605–6 (and in the apparatus and textual notes to *Isabella*, passim).

6. In the introduction to my "reading edition," *John Keats: Complete Poems* (Cambridge, Mass.: Harvard University Press, 1982), esp. pp. xxii–xxviii.

7. Quite possibly Keats got his final wording from Woodhouse as well, since it is the same as Woodhouse's penciled alteration of the line in the W^2 transcript (to read "Three hours they labored . . ."). See note 9.

8. See *Keats: The Critical Heritage*, ed. G. M. Matthews (New York: Barnes and Noble, 1971), pp. 104, 113–14. Both reviews, in the August and April 1818 issues, respectively, actually appeared in September, about the time Keats was revising *Isabella* and getting ready to show it to Reynolds and probably to Woodhouse as well.

9. There is no clear evidence that Keats saw any of Woodhouse's queries, suggestions, and revisions in either the holograph fair copy or the W^2 transcript, but the two men were good friends and the markings may be taken as indications of problems that Woodhouse could have brought up in conversation. Keats did of course see the W^1 transcript when he was preparing his poems for the 1820 printer.

10. See Christopher Ricks, *Keats and Embarrassment* (Oxford: Clarendon Press, 1974), and, for the *Edinburgh Magazine* notice of *Poems* in October 1817, *Keats: The Critical Heritage,* ed. Matthews, p. 71.

11. These lines are all in very faint and partially erased pencil, and some of the readings are questionable. (For another set of transcriptions, with many differences from those given here, see H. W. Garrod's Oxford English Texts edition, *The Poetical Works of John Keats,* 2nd ed. [Oxford: Clarendon Press, 1958], pp. 217–18.) The first version in my arbitrary numbering is written above and beneath the original lines 55–56 in the transcript; versions 2–5 appear on the opposite verso, and the last is written at the end of the W^2 book, on fol. 241. The three versions given below from W^1, faint with age and deleted rather than erased, are similarly questionable.

12. *The Poems of John Keats,* ed. Miriam Allott (London: Longman, 1970), p. 330; *The Poetical Works and Other Writings of John Keats,* Hampstead Edition, ed. H. Buxton Forman (New York: Scribner's, 1938–39), 3:61.

13. The text of Keats's source (*The Novels and Tales of the Renowned John Boccacio,* 5th ed. [1684], pp. 182–85) is given in the notes to *John Keats: Complete Poems,* pp. 443–45.

14. Keats's *Letters,* 1:238, 270–71. Here and in the preceding paragraph I am drawing on my introduction to *Endymion: A Facsimile of the Revised Holograph Manuscript,* vol. 2 of the Keats series of Manuscripts of the Younger Romantics (New York: Garland, 1985). Taylor's changes and other markings in the manuscript are categorized and listed in the notes on pp. 377–78.

15. See *The Texts of Keats's Poems,* pp. 214–20, and *Poems* (1978), pp. 625–29. The September 1819 correspondence between Woodhouse and Taylor in the next four paragraphs is quoted from Keats's *Letters,* 2:162–63, 182–83.

16. See Keats's *Letters,* 2:157–59, 183. Mention should also be made of Keats's and Charles Brown's collaborative effort at playwriting, *Otho the Great,* for which Brown supplied the plot and characters and Keats the actual writing. Scholars who treat this work usually phrase their remarks as if Keats alone were the author.

17. *The Poems of John Keats,* ed. Allott, p. 330; *The Poetical Works and Other Writings of John Keats,* ed. Forman, 3:61.

18. *Modern Language Notes* 94 (1979): 988–1032. The essay is reprinted without significant change in McGann's *The Beauty of Inflections: Literary Investigations in Historical Method and Theory* (Oxford: Clarendon Press, 1985), pp. 15–65. My quotations in the next two paragraphs are from the latter source, pp. 32–39.

19. Majorie Levinson repeats McGann's errors and misplaced emphases in her chapter on *La Belle Dame* in *Keats's Life of Allegory: The Origins of a Style* (Oxford: Basil Blackwell, 1988), pp. 45–95 passim. Her aim, however, is to demonize rather than apotheosize the author. A good corrective to McGann's argument is Theresa M. Kelley's "Poetics and the Politics of Reception: Keats's 'La Belle Dame sans Merci,' " *ELH* 54 (1987): 333–62.

20. Jerome J. McGann, *A Critique of Modern Textual Criticism* (Chicago: University of Chicago Press, 1983), pp. 8, 42–43, 85–86. McGann cites James Thorpe, *Principles of Textual Criticism* (San Marino, Calif.: Huntington Library, 1972), p. 48.

3. *Who Wrote J. S. Mill's* Autobiography?

1. The basic facts concerning composition, transmission, and publication of the text are given and documented in three earlier accounts by the present author: "The Text of John Stuart Mill's *Autobiography,*" *Bulletin of the John Rylands Library* 43 (1960): 220–42, and the introductions to *The Early Draft of John Stuart Mill's "Autobiography"* (Urbana: University of Illinois Press, 1961), pp. 1–11—hereafter cited as *Early Draft*—and Mill's *Autobiography and Literary Essays,* ed. John M. Robson and Jack Stillinger, vol. 1 of *Collected Works of John Stuart Mill* (Toronto: University of Toronto Press, 1981), pp. xviii–xxx—hereafter cited as CW, 1. The text of the Early Draft manuscript is printed both in *Early Draft,* pp. 35ff., and—on pages facing the text of the revised manuscript at Columbia—in CW, 1:4–246 (with text of the rejected leaves on pp. 608–24).

2. Diary entry, 19 January 1854, in *The Letters of John Stuart Mill,* ed. Hugh S. R. Elliot (London: Longmans, Green, 1910), 2:361.

3. Nicholas Joukovsky, of Penn State, who has done a great deal of research in the archives of Mill's employer, the East India Company, tells me that Mill's method of drafting in the right-hand half of the page was standard practice for documents that he wrote at work. The space in the left-hand side of the page was reserved for revisions by a member of the Company's Board of Control. In the creation of the *Autobiography,* he suggests, Harriet Mill in effect became her husband's "Board of Control."

4. The two editions of the *Autobiography* most frequently cited from the 1920s through the 1960s add still more authors. Harold J. Laski's Oxford World's Classics edition (London: Oxford University Press, 1924), an unedited reprint of the first edition, has several additional mistakes in wording introduced by the World's Classics printer, and in issues after 1944, when some damaged type was reset, has a further substantive change made by the printer who repaired the damage; the number of authors in this version of the work has increased to nine. The Columbia University Press edition of 1924—*Autobiography of John Stuart Mill Published for the First Time without Alterations or Omissions from the Original Manuscript in the Possession of Columbia University,* with a Preface by John Jacob Coss—also, it turns out, has nine authors. Purportedly taken directly from the revised holograph manuscript, the text of the Columbia edition nevertheless incorporates readings of the same seven authors listed above (the editor used the 1873 printed text as a guide to deciphering Mill's handwriting!) and then adds further misreadings by the Columbia editor and new mistakes by the Columbia printer. ("Misreading" and "mistake" seem justifiable terms when the intent was to copy the text exactly.)

5. This has been done in the two most recent scholarly editings—that in the Riverside paperback *Autobiography,* ed. Jack Stillinger (Boston: Houghton Mifflin, 1969), also issued in the Oxford paperbacks series (London: Oxford University Press, 1971), and that in CW, 1.

6. Parenthetical numbers of this sort refer to pages in CW, 1 (the quoted words in the present instance appear three times—in the Early Draft text, the Columbia text, and one of the Early Draft rejected leaves transcribed in CW, 1, appendix G). More elaborate references in the form "6.4" (beginning in the third paragraph below) cite both page and line number in CW, 1. In quoting directly from the Early Draft manuscript, I follow the editorial practices outlined in CW, 1:xlviii.

7. For the most important of these passages in the various texts of the *Autobiography,* see CW, 1:196–97, 234–35 n., 250–59, 620–21. The phrases "joint product" and

"joint production(s)" occur seven times at CW, 1:250, 251, 256, 257, and another seventeen times in the extant transcript of Mill's personal bibliography (see *Bibliography of the Published Writings of John Stuart Mill,* ed. Ney MacMinn et al. [Evanston, Ill.: Northwestern University, 1945], pp. 59ff.).

8. The principal works include F. A. Hayek, *John Stuart Mill and Harriet Taylor* (Chicago: University of Chicago Press, 1951); Michael St. John Packe, *The Life of John Stuart Mill* (London: Secker and Warburg, 1954); H. O. Pappe, *John Stuart Mill and the Harriet Taylor Myth* (Melbourne: Melbourne University Press, 1960); my introduction in *Early Draft,* esp. pp. 22–28; Francis E. Mineka, "The *Autobiography* and the Lady," *University of Toronto Quarterly* 32 (1963): 301–6; John M. Robson, "Harriet Taylor and John Stuart Mill: Artist and Scientist," *Queen's Quarterly* 73 (1966): 167–86; Alice S. Rossi's introduction ("Sentiment and Intellect: The Story of John Stuart Mill and Harriet Taylor Mill") to her edition of the Mills' *Essays on Sex Equality* (Chicago: University of Chicago Press, 1970); and Phyllis Rose, *Parallel Lives: Five Victorian Marriages* (New York: Knopf, 1983), pp. 95–140, esp. pp. 127–37. See also Gertrude Himmelfarb, *On Liberty and Liberalism: The Case of John Stuart Mill* (New York: Knopf, 1974), and John C. Rees, *John Stuart Mill's "On Liberty"* (Oxford: Clarendon Press, 1985).

9. The *Political Economy* letters are extracted in appendix G of *Principles of Political Economy,* ed. John M. Robson, vol. 3 of *Collected Works of John Stuart Mill* (Toronto: University of Toronto Press, 1965), pp. 1026–37. On the *Logic,* see Robson, " 'Joint Authorship' Again: The Evidence in the Third Edition of Mill's Logic," *Mill News Letter* 6, no. 2 (Spring 1971): 15–20. A small additional piece of physical evidence has recently come to light in the five-page draft "What Is to Be Done with Ireland?" published for the first time in *Essays on England, Ireland, and the Empire,* ed. John M. Robson, vol. 6 of *Collected Works of John Stuart Mill* (Toronto: University of Toronto Press, 1982). Mill's manuscript, at the King's School, Canterbury, has several penciled revisions by Harriet Mill (detailed in Robson's textual apparatus, pp. 499–503), but in this instance he apparently never returned to the work and so never responded to her markings.

10. This and other numbers should be read as approximations. Any such tallying involves arbitrary decisions; three separate markings or alterations of a sentence, for example, could count as a single passage (her marking of the sentence) or as three passages (her markings of words and phrases in the sentence). Her pencilings in nearly two-thirds of the passages (about 185 of the 300) are recorded in the notes in *Early Draft;* a lesser number (approximately half) are described in the textual notes in CW, 1. Some 30 of the pencilings consist of erased or otherwise unintelligible markings and comments that, while they most probably were influential at the time, are no longer recoverable.

11. Mill's reference, in a letter to his wife of 10 February 1854 (quoted in CW, 1:xxi), to "passages which we marked for alteration in the early part of it [the Early Draft] which we read together" might suggest that some, most, or all of her markings and alterations actually originated with Mill while she, pencil in hand, acted as amanuensis. This does not, however, square with the evidence of the manuscript itself, where it is clear that a *written* dialogue took place in which first she marked, queried, or revised a passage and then he responded to her penciling (after which she sometimes further marked rewritten passages at left, and he sometimes further responded to her new suggestions).

12. It is not certain that every sentence of this reconstructed text stood together, in

a single version, as I am giving it here. At some point, possibly before his wife read the passage, Mill canceled the last thirty-five words of this sentence ("but all the common things . . .") and substituted a shorter conclusion at left: "but I never put even a common share of the exercise of understanding into practical things." And the fourth sentence before this ("I had hardly any use of my hands"), now canceled in the manuscript, perhaps was removed by him when he wrote the present more elaborate sentence on manual dexterity.

13. There is an analogous situation in the extant correspondence between the two, where, as I remarked in *Early Draft,* "It is notable . . . how seldom *ideas* are touched on" (p. 26). I would emphasize, however, that neither the Early Draft manuscript nor their letters give us much of a clue as to what they *said* to each other when they were together.

14. The "progress from private to public . . . voice" described in the introduction to *Early Draft* (p. 15) was in large part initiated by her.

15. Packe, *The Life of John Stuart Mill,* p. 33; W. H. Burston, *James Mill on Philosophy and Education* (London: Athlone Press, 1973), pp. 85–86; Peter Glassman, *J. S. Mill: The Evolution of a Genius* (Gainesville: University of Florida Press, 1985), p. 149; Jonathan Loesberg, *Fictions of Consciousness: Mill, Newman, and the Reading of Victorian Prose* (New Brunswick, N.J.: Rutgers University Press, 1986), p. 49.

16. *On Liberty,* in *Essays on Politics and Society,* ed. John M. Robson, vol. 18 of *Collected Works of John Stuart Mill* (Toronto: University of Toronto Press, 1977), p. 216.

17. Typical examples are Himmelfarb, *On Liberty and Liberalism,* esp. pp. 239–75 (pro-Harriet, as it were), and Rees, *John Stuart Mill's "On Liberty,"* esp. pp. 12ff., 109–15 (anti-Harriet).

18. I am much obliged to Ann P. W. Robson, of the University of Toronto, for sending me a photocopy of this unpublished letter. The original is in the Russell Archives at McMaster University.

4. *Multiple "Consciousnesses" in Wordsworth's* Prelude

1. See Mill's *Autobiography and Literary Essays,* CW, 1:149–53, 147. I have described parallels between Wordsworth's development and Mill's in my introduction to the 1969 Riverside edition of the *Autobiography,* pp. viii–xvii, and the influence on Keats in "Wordsworth and Keats," in *The Age of William Wordsworth: Critical Essays on the Romantic Tradition,* ed. Kenneth R. Johnston and Gene W. Ruoff (New Brunswick, N.J.: Rutgers University Press, 1987), pp. 173–95, 357–58.

2. Neil Fraistat, *The Poem and the Book: Interpreting Collections of Romantic Poetry* (Chapel Hill: University of North Carolina Press, 1985), esp. p. 52.

3. See Thomas McFarland, *Romanticism and the Forms of Ruin: Wordsworth, Coleridge, and Modalities of Fragmentation* (Princeton, N.J.: Princeton University Press, 1981), chap. 1, "The Symbiosis of Coleridge and Wordsworth," pp. 56–103, and Paul Magnuson, *Coleridge and Wordsworth: A Lyrical Dialogue* (Princeton, N.J.: Princeton University Press, 1988). Gene W. Ruoff, *Wordsworth and Coleridge: The Making of the Major Lyrics, 1802–1804* (New Brunswick, N.J.: Rutgers University Press, 1989), interprets the relationship as a dialogue of "intertextual genetics," and Lucy Newlyn, *Coleridge, Wordsworth, and the Language of Allusion* (Oxford: Clarendon Press, 1986), as a dialogue of literary allusion.

4. McFarland, citing resemblances with the discharged soldier of *The Prelude* 4, the drowned man of book 5, and the leechgatherer in *Resolution and Independence,* suggests that the Mariner is "a projection from the psycho-dramatic center of Wordsworth's fantasy more than from that of Coleridge" (*Romanticism and the Forms of Ruin,* p. 68).

5. *Collected Letters of Samuel Taylor Coleridge,* ed. E. L. Griggs (Oxford: Clarendon Press, 1956–71), 2:830. There is another relevant statement at 2:811. Wordsworth commented many years later, in a note in the manuscript of Barron Field's "Memoirs of the Life and Poetry of William Wordsworth" now in the British Library, "I never cared a straw about the theory—& the Preface was written at the request of Mr Coleridge out of sheer good nature. I recollect the very spot, a deserted Quarry in the Vale of Grasmere where he pressed the thing upon me, & but for that it would never have been thought of" (*Barron Field's Memoirs of Wordsworth,* ed. Geoffrey Little [Sydney: Sydney University Press, 1975], p. 62 n.).

6. *The Letters of William and Dorothy Wordsworth: The Early Years,* ed. Ernest de Selincourt, 2nd ed., rev. Chester L. Shaver (Oxford: Clarendon Press, 1967), p. 289.

7. *The Letters of William and Dorothy Wordsworth: The Middle Years,* ed. Ernest de Selincourt, 2nd ed., rev. Mary Moorman, part 1 (Oxford: Clarendon Press, 1969), pp. 298, 299, 319, 341–42. See also John E. Jordan, *De Quincey to Wordsworth: A Biography of a Relationship* (Berkeley: University of California Press, 1963), pp. 62–85.

8. See *Barron Field's Memoirs of Wordsworth,* pp. 39–47, 132–42, and Geoffrey Little, "A Lesson in the Art of Poetry: Barron Field and Wordsworth's Later Revisions," *AUMLA: Journal of the Australasian Universities Language and Literature Association,* no. 46 (November 1976): 189–205.

9. Christopher Morley, *The Middle Kingdom: Poems 1929–1944* (New York: Harcourt, Brace, 1944), p. 7. For some of the passages that Wordsworth seems to have drawn on, see *Journals of Dorothy Wordsworth,* ed. Mary Moorman (London: Oxford University Press, 1971), pp. 2, 4–5, 8, 26–27, 38, 42, 92, 109, 111, 150–51, 156. Wordsworth's poetic use of the journals is discussed by Frederick A. Pottle, "The Eye and the Object in the Poetry of Wordsworth," *Yale Review* 40 (1950): 27–42 (reprinted in *Wordsworth: Centenary Studies,* ed. Gilbert T. Dunklin [Princeton, N.J.: Princeton University Press, 1951], pp. 23–44); Rachel Mayer Brownstein, "The Private Life: Dorothy Wordsworth's Journals," *Modern Language Quarterly* 34 (1973): 48–63; W. J. Keith, *The Poetry of Nature: Rural Perspectives in Poetry from Wordsworth to the Present* (Toronto: University of Toronto Press, 1980), pp. 13–14, 19–21, 31–32; Thomas R. Frosch, "Wordsworth's 'Beggars' and a Brief Instance of 'Writer's Block,' " *Studies in Romanticism* 21 (1982): 619–36; and Eric C. Walker, "Dorothy Wordsworth, William Wordsworth, and the Kirkstone Pass," *The Wordsworth Circle* 19 (1988): 116–21. In their recent biography, *Dorothy Wordsworth* (Oxford: Clarendon Press, 1985), Robert Gittings and Jo Manton treat the matter circumspectly: "Several [journal] entries use almost the same words as Coleridge and William employ in their poems, and much has been written on the relation between Dorothy's journal and the poets' work. Apart from one or two instances, though, it is impossible to say which came first, or who can be said to derive one from the other. . . . The debt, as between the three friends, is practically impossible to determine" (pp. 79–80).

10. Compare Keats's remark, preserved by Woodhouse, that at times his own

verses "seemed rather the production of another person than his own" (*The Keats Circle: Letters and Papers, 1816–1878*, ed. Hyder E. Rollins [Cambridge, Mass.: Harvard University Press, 1948], 1:129). A recent example is provided by Donald Davie, who gave a reading at the University of Illinois on 11 November 1985. Speaking of his own poems written twenty years earlier, Davie remarked that their author was, to him, "a total stranger, an unknown person with the same name."

11. Unless another version is specified, my quotations of *The Prelude* are from the latest authoritative text (mainly that of MS. D) as edited by W. J. B. Owen, *The Fourteen-Book "Prelude"* (Ithaca, N.Y.: Cornell University Press, 1985). For the shorter poems I have generally quoted from *William Wordsworth: Selected Poems and Prefaces*, ed. Jack Stillinger (Boston: Houghton Mifflin, 1965), which gives more accurate texts from the same source that Ernest de Selincourt and Helen Darbishire used in their Oxford English Texts edition, *The Poetical Works of William Wordsworth*, 5 vols. (Oxford: Clarendon Press, 1940–49).

12. All writers of long poems are to some extent readers and revisers of themselves as they progress through a work. For recent discussion of a modern example, see Margaret Dickie, "Williams Reading *Paterson,*" *ELH* 53 (1986): 653–71.

13. The best sources of information concerning composition of the work are the introduction to Ernest de Selincourt's edition, *The Prelude*, 2nd ed., rev. Helen Darbishire (Oxford: Clarendon Press, 1959), esp. pp. xliii–liv; Mark L. Reed, *Wordsworth: The Chronology of the Middle Years, 1800–1815* (Cambridge, Mass.: Harvard University Press, 1975), pp. 11–15, 628–55; the sections on "Composition and Texts" in *The Prelude, 1799, 1805, 1850*, Norton Critical Edition, ed. Jonathan Wordsworth, M. H. Abrams, and Stephen Gill (New York: Norton, 1979), pp. 512–22; and the introductions to the Cornell Wordsworth *"The Prelude," 1798–1799*, ed. Stephen Parrish (Ithaca, N.Y.: Cornell University Press, 1977), and *The Fourteen-Book "Prelude,"* ed. Owen.

14. Mark Reed informs me that the two-part *Prelude* was put into print even earlier among selected works in an illustrated *Poems of William Wordsworth* that Jonathan Wordsworth got together for Members of the Limited Editions Club (Cambridge: University Printing House, 1973).

15. Jonathan Wordsworth, "The Five-Book *Prelude* of Early Spring 1804," *Journal of English and Germanic Philology* 76 (1977): 1–25.

16. The Wordsworths' *Letters: The Early Years*, p. 436.

17. Jonathan Wordsworth, "The Five-Book *Prelude* of Early Spring 1804," p. 1. Robin Jarvis has expressed reservations about the existence of this version in "The Five-Book *Prelude:* A Reconsideration," *Journal of English and Germanic Philology* 80 (1981): 528–51. At the least, Jonathan Wordsworth is here a collaborator with his ancestor in the production of this version.

18. Reed, *Wordsworth: The Chronology of the Middle Years*, pp. 628, 635.

19. *The Letters of William and Dorothy Wordsworth: The Later Years*, ed. Ernest de Selincourt, 2nd ed., rev. Alan G. Hill, part 2 (Oxford: Clarendon Press, 1979), p. 236.

20. The passages quoted here and in the preceding paragraph occur in the original edition (Oxford: Clarendon Press, 1926) on pp. xliv, xlviii–li, liv, lvi, lix–lxii. All of them, even the most fanciful and rhetorically extravagant, are repeated verbatim in the revised 2nd ed. (1959), pp. lvii, lxi, lxiii, lxiv, lxvi, lxviii, lxxi–lxxiv, a fault that I noted in my review in *Journal of English and Germanic Philology* 59 (1960): 161–64. Herbert Lindenberger's wistful suggestion of "a popular, composite edition of *The Prelude*, an

edition based principally on the 1805 text" but dropping some of its weaker lines and passages and incorporating some of the better lines and passages added in revision (*On Wordsworth's "Prelude"* [Princeton, N.J.: Princeton University Press, 1963], p. 299), rather closely resembles, especially in spirit, de Selincourt's "ideal text" of nearly four decades earlier. Again it should not be overlooked—though my focus in this chapter is elsewhere—that in any such "ideal text" Wordsworth would be jointly authored by himself and his editor(s).

21. "The 'Prelude': 1805 and 1850," *Times Literary Supplement*, 29 April 1926, pp. 309–10; Leslie Nathan Broughton, *Journal of English and Germanic Philology* 26 (1927): 427–32; Helen Darbishire, "Wordsworth's 'Prelude,' " *Nineteenth Century and After* 99 (1926): 718–31; G. C. Moore Smith, *Modern Language Review* 21 (1926): 443–46; George McLean Harper, "Growth," *Saturday Review of Literature*, 2 October 1926, p. 154; Henry King, "Wordsworth's Decline," *Adelphi* 4 (1926): 106–15. In reprinting the substance of her review in *The Poet Wordsworth: The Clark Lectures . . . 1949* (Oxford: Clarendon Press, 1950), Darbishire changed "They generally mar the poetry; they always disguise the truth" to "they often mar the poetry; they more often disguise the truth" (p. 123).

22. Osgood, *The Voice of England*, p. 396.

23. Edith C. Batho, *The Later Wordsworth* (Cambridge: Cambridge University Press, 1933); Mary E. Burton, *The One Wordsworth* (Chapel Hill: University of North Carolina Press, 1942); Raymond Dexter Havens, *The Mind of a Poet: A Study of Wordsworth's Thought with Particular Reference to "The Prelude"* (Baltimore: Johns Hopkins Press, 1941). For a more recent argument favoring a single Wordsworth, see Bernard Groom, *The Unity of Wordsworth's Poetry* (London: Macmillan, 1966).

24. For example (to select four), C. F. Stone III, "Narrative Variation in Wordsworth's Versions of 'The Discharged Soldier,' " *Journal of Narrative Technique* 4 (1974): 32–44; Richard Schell, "Wordsworth's Revisions of the Ascent of Snowdon," *Philological Quarterly* 54 (1975): 592–603; Peter J. Manning, "Reading Wordsworth's Revisions: Othello and the Drowned Man," *Studies in Romanticism* 22 (1983): 3–28; Susan J. Wolfson, "The Illusion of Mastery: Wordsworth's Revisions of 'The Drowned Man of Esthwaite,' 1799, 1805, 1850," *PMLA* 99 (1984): 917–35. For a handy guide to the recent scholarship on the *Prelude* revisions, see the index to Mark Jones and Karl Kroeber's *Wordsworth Scholarship and Criticism, 1973–1984: An Annotated Bibliography, with Selected Criticism, 1809–1972* (New York: Garland, 1985), pp. 302–4 (the *Prelude* entries that specify "revision") and 306 (the revision entries that specify "Prel.").

25. Schell, "Wordsworth's Revisions of the Ascent of Snowdon," p. 593; Jonathan Arac, review of three recent books on Wordsworth in *Studies in Romanticism* 22 (1983): 145–46. (Arac should not, however, be numbered among the primitivists; see his *Critical Genealogies: Historical Situations for Postmodern Literary Studies* [New York: Columbia University Press, 1987], chap. 2, *"The Prelude* and Critical Revision: Bounding Lines," pp. 57–80.) Similarly, Reeve Parker, in proposing that the "literary merits [of *The Excursion* book 1] . . . have been underestimated," feels obligated to add: "As I hope will be clear, this is not the same as saying that I prefer 'later' Wordsworth or that the poem espouses a 'philosophy' I find congenial" (" 'Finer Distance': The Narrative Art of Wordsworth's 'The Wanderer,' " *ELH* 39 [1972]: 90).

26. Philip Hobsbaum, *Tradition and Experiment in English Poetry* (London: Macmillan, 1979), pp. 180–205 (quotations from pp. 187, 190, 191, 193).

27. Jonathan Wordsworth, *The Music of Humanity: A Critical Study of Words-*

worth's "Ruined Cottage" (London: Nelson, 1969), p. xiii. The sentence has a stirring ring to it, and has been quoted many times, but neither of its clauses comes close to being literally true.

28. Jonathan Wordsworth, *William Wordsworth: The Borders of Vision* (Oxford: Clarendon Press, 1982), chap. 10 (quotations from pp. 328–31). These passages are not in the earlier version of the chapter, published as " 'The Climbing of Snowdon,' " in *Bicentenary Wordsworth Studies in Memory of John Alban Finch,* ed. Jonathan Wordsworth (Ithaca, N.Y.: Cornell University Press, 1970), pp. 449–74. Apparently critics are to be allowed their revisions, even while they attack poets for theirs! Jeffrey Baker has an amusing comment concerning Jonathan Wordsworth's zeal for earlier and earlier versions: "a reader who was determined to push the matter *ad absurdum* might claim that the greatest *Prelude* was probably known only to Wordsworth's dog, who heard the rambling poet's earliest, unrevised 'booings' " ("Prelude and Prejudice," *The Wordsworth Circle* 13 [1982]: 79–86 [quotation from p. 79]). After a promising start, however, Baker's essay ends up revealing just as much prejudice in the opposite direction, in favor of 1850.

29. I quote from the Wordsworth Summer Conference brochure for 1984. In *The Wordsworth Circle,* Jonathan Wordsworth reports good-humoredly on the debate: "Norman Fruman put the case for the early version, Bob Barth and Jeffrey Baker for the late. There was a large and lively audience, and a remarkably dispassionate Chairman. Both sides were clear that they had won. A transcript will be published so that readers of *TWC* may decide for themselves" (16 [1985]: 45). Subsequently the "transcript" occupied the whole of the Winter 1986 issue (17, no. 1); quite possibly readers will decide that both sides *lost.*

30. Jonathan Wordsworth's phrase (see note 27) is taken over in the title and opening sentence of Stephen Parrish's "The Worst of Wordsworth," *The Wordsworth Circle* 7 (1976): 89–91. Parrish is the originator and general editor of the Cornell Wordsworth, and this brief essay, along with his foreword to the first volume published, constitutes a rationale for the series (*The Salisbury Plain Poems* [Ithaca, N.Y.: Cornell University Press, 1975], pp. ix–xiii). See also Parrish's "The Editor as Archeologist," *Kentucky Review* 4 (1983): 3–14, esp. pp. 6–7 (on the "hardening" of Wordsworth's "social, religious, and political orthodoxies") and 12–14 ("ageing Tory humanist," "orthodox piety," "hardening crust of middle and old age," "crusted layers of revision"), and "The Whig Interpretation of Literature," *TEXT* 4 (1988): 343–50, esp. p. 346 (on the early Wordsworth's being "closer to the sources of his inspiration and less inhibited by the various orthodoxies—political, social, religious, and poetical—that he succumbed to in his later years").

31. Stephen Gill, "Wordsworth's Poems: The Question of Text," *Review of English Studies,* n.s., 34 (1983): 172–90 (quotation from p. 188). Given our present-day interest in narrative technique, the role of the narrator, and self-reflexivity, critics ought to prefer the more complicated later version—tale *plus* narrator in equal proportions—and surely would have preferred it all along if the chronology of versions had not biased the issue. See Philip Cohen, "Narrative and Persuasion in *The Ruined Cottage,*" *Journal of Narrative Technique* 8 (1978): 185–99.

32. Parrish, "The Worst of Wordsworth," pp. 90, 91.

33. It has worried others as well. For a recent statement of concern—though it dates from reports on the Cornell Wordsworth written for the MLA's Committee on Scholarly Editions in 1977—see Donald H. Reiman, *Romantic Texts and Contexts*

(Columbia: University of Missouri Press, 1987), chap. 8, "The Cornell Wordsworth and the Norton *Prelude,"* esp. pp. 135, 145–46.

34. James K. Chandler, in a lengthy review of five volumes of the Cornell Wordsworth, casually mentions that "this should . . . be an edition sufficiently long-lived so that libraries will not have to replace it for a while," and "this will be the way that many students and scholars read their Wordsworth for some time to come" ("Wordsworth Rejuvenated," *Modern Philology* 84 [1986]: 207, 208). Kenneth R. Johnston and Gene W. Ruoff comment approvingly in a recent *Chronicle of Higher Education:* "The de Selincourt and Darbishire editions have been replaced, particularly by the work of the Cornell University Wordsworth project, which seeks to restore the poems to their earliest forms and to set forth for examination all the revisions and encrustations to which Wordsworth subjected his canon throughout his long life. These and other studies have reached the college classroom, with the result that today students read poems and versions of poems by Wordsworth that were unknown in 1960" ("Wordsworth: Intimations of His Immortality," 28 October 1987, p. B52; the statement is repeated, in slightly revised form, in their introduction to *The Age of William Wordsworth,* pp. x–xi).

35. Gill, "Wordsworth's Poems," p. 181. It is worth noting that a companion Oxford Authors volume, *Samuel Taylor Coleridge,* ed. H. J. Jackson (Oxford: Oxford University Press, 1985), similarly offers a chronological arrangement but nevertheless prints the standard final texts throughout.

36. The Wordsworths' *Letters: The Early Years,* p. 34.

37. *The Prelude,* 2nd ed. (1959), p. lvii. I have used this edition for my quotations of the 1805 text.

38. The most extreme theorist of textual primitivism to date is Hershel Parker, who in *Flawed Texts and Verbal Icons: Literary Authority in American Fiction* (Evanston, Ill.: Northwestern University Press, 1984) sounds very much like the Wordsworthian primitivists, even though he never mentions our poet: for example, "revising authors very often betray or otherwise blur their original achievements in ways they seldom intend and seldom become aware of"; "In revising or allowing someone else to revise a literary work, especially after it has been thought of as complete, authors very often lose authority, with the result that familiar literary texts at some points have no meaning, only partially authorial meaning, or quite adventitious meaning unintended by the author or anyone else" (pp. ix, 4). Parker studies the revision of works by Twain, James, Crane, and Mailer and finds the later texts vitiated by mistakes, inconsistencies, and incoherences. He uses words like "wreck," "damage," "deface," "violate," "destroy," "sabotage," and "drain" to describe the process of rewriting, and in one place contrasts "a clear and consistent" original version with a "hopelessly confusing" revision (pp. 29, 37, 39, 40, 41, 74, 173, 184, 207). Parker's basic premise, that "genuine art is coherent" (p. 23), seems extremely dubious. See Gary Davenport's review of Parker, "Necessary Fictions," *Sewanee Review* 93 (1985): 499–504.

39. Thorpe, *Principles of Textual Criticism,* pp. 32–47; Hans Zeller, "A New Approach to the Critical Constitution of Literary Texts," *Studies in Bibliography* 28 (1975): 231–64.

40. Raymond Carney, "Making the Most of a Mess," *Georgia Review* 35 (1981): 631–42 (quotations from pp. 634–35); Robert Young, "A Reply: To 'Prelude and Prejudice,' by Jeffrey Baker," *The Wordsworth Circle* 13 (1982): 87–88; Clifford Siskin, "Revision Romanticized: A Study in Literary Change," *Romanticism Past and Present*

7, no. 2 (Summer 1983): 1–16 (quotations from pp. 10, 7–8); Wolfson, "The Illusion of Mastery," p. 918.

5. *Creative Plagiarism: The Case of Coleridge*

1. Keats may again serve as the handy (and typical) example. As I have pointed out elsewhere, writers on Keats explicitly or implicitly invoke sources on practically every occasion, sometimes without awareness of doing so, as in commenting on a phrase (e.g., relating "tongueless nightingale" in *The Eve of St. Agnes* to the classical myth of Philomel), or a character (relating Angela in the same work to Juliet's Nurse in *Romeo and Juliet*), or a motivation (comparing that of Isabella's brothers in Keats's poem with that in the English translation of Boccaccio that Keats used), or a style (Leigh Huntian in Keats's early *Calidore,* Miltonic in *Hyperion,* "Drydenian heroic" in *Lamia*): "Keats criticism carried on without reference to sources is almost unthinkable" ("John Keats," in *The English Romantic Poets: A Review of Research and Criticism,* ed. Frank Jordan, 4th ed. [New York: Modern Language Association, 1985], pp. 698–99).

2. *The Prose Works of William Wordsworth,* ed. W. J. B. Owen and Jane W. Smyser (Oxford: Clarendon Press, 1974), 3:82.

3. *Biographia Literaria,* ed. James Engell and W. J. Bate (Princeton, N.J.: Princeton University Press, 1983), 1:304.

4. John Livingston Lowes, *The Road to Xanadu: A Study in the Ways of the Imagination* (Boston: Houghton Mifflin, 1927).

5. All quotations of the poems are taken from *The Complete Poetical Works of Samuel Taylor Coleridge,* ed. E. H. Coleridge (Oxford: Clarendon Press, 1912), still the standard edition.

6. *Collected Letters of Samuel Taylor Coleridge,* 3:355–61. The real subject of the letter, as becomes clear after the first four pages, is a more immediate occasion, the discovery of "coincidental" resemblances of idea and illustration between Coleridge's lectures on *Romeo and Juliet* in December 1811 and A. W. von Schlegel's lectures on Shakespeare delivered in Vienna in 1808 and published in Germany in December 1810.

7. Engell remarks in part 2 of the editors' introduction to *Biographia Literaria,* "Nothing quite like this problem, both in degree and in kind, exists for any classic comparable to the *Biographia* in importance" (1:cxv). Herman Melville "borrowed" extensively, but his practice has not been perceived as problematic in the same way, perhaps because his sources were mainly ephemera.

8. I have discussed this last in " 'Kubla Khan' and Michelangelo's Glorious Boast," *English Language Notes* 23, no. 1 (September 1985): 38–42.

9. I quote E. H. Coleridge's text, which is based on the poet's latest revisions in the *Poetical Works* of 1834. The two earliest versions differ considerably in their equivalent of the last five lines of the passage, but in such expressions (recorded in the textual apparatus) as "Idle thought," "fantastic playfulness," "curious toys / Of the self-watching subtilizing mind" (quarto text of 1798) and "wilful playfulness," "Smiles, as self-scornful," "wild reliques of our childish Thought," and "subtle toys / Of the self-watching mind" (*Poetical Register* text of 1812) the elements that I wish to emphasize are there from the beginning.

10. See M. H. Abrams, "Structure and Style in the Greater Romantic Lyric"

(1965), reprinted most recently in Abrams's *The Correspondent Breeze: Essays on English Romanticism* (New York: Norton, 1984), pp. 76–108.

11. Wordsworth provides an interpretive gloss to the poem along these lines in *The Prelude* 6.264–305, especially the lines describing Coleridge's "self-created sustenance of a Mind / Debarred from Nature's living images, / Compelled to be a life unto herself" (301–3).

12. *The Poetical Works of William Cowper*, ed. H. S. Milford, 4th ed. (London: Oxford University Press, 1934), pp. 188–89. Presumably the passage was well known to Coleridge's contemporaries. The connection between Coleridge's and Cowper's lines was first made by a scholar in Alois Brandl's "Cowpers 'Winter Evening' und Coleridges 'Frost at Midnight,' " *Archiv für das Studium der Neueren Sprachen und Literaturen* 96 (1896): 341–42, and is prominently discussed by Humphry House, *Coleridge: The Clark Lectures 1951–52* (London: Rupert Hart-Davis, 1953), pp. 71–73, 78–82, and Norman Fruman, *Coleridge, the Damaged Archangel* (New York: Braziller, 1971), pp. 305–9 (to whom I owe the reference to Brandl's 1896 note). On Coleridge's reading of Cowper more generally, see Michael J. Kelly, " 'Kubla Khan' and Cowper's *Task*: Speculation amidst Echoes," *Bulletin of the New York Public Library* 78 (1975): 482–89, and Ann Matheson, "The Influence of Cowper's *The Task* on Coleridge's Conversation Poems," in *New Approaches to Coleridge: Biographical and Critical Essays*, ed. Donald Sultana (London: Vision Press, 1981), pp. 137–50.

13. "My First Acquaintance with Poets," in *The Complete Works of William Hazlitt*, ed. P. P. Howe (London: Dent, 1930–34), 17:120. Joseph Johnson, the publisher of the first printed version of *Frost at Midnight*, in the *Fears in Solitude* quarto of 1798, was also Cowper's publisher, and the verso of the final page of *Frost* in the volume contains an advertisement for a new edition of Cowper's *Poems*.

14. *Biographia Literaria*, 1:244–47. See Thomas McFarland, *Coleridge and the Pantheist Tradition* (Oxford: Clarendon Press, 1969), pp. 134–36 (on Coleridge's "translation—or 'plagiarism'—verbatim from Leibniz" in the paragraph), and the review articles by Norman Fruman, "Aids to Reflection on the New *Biographia*," *Studies in Romanticism* 24 (1985): 141–73, esp. pp. 172–73, and McFarland, "So Immethodical a Miscellany: Coleridge's Literary Life," *Modern Philology* 83 (1986): 405–13, esp. pp. 410–12.

15. Fruman, "Aids to Reflection on the New *Biographia*," p. 171.

16. There is an extensive literature on Coleridge's plagiarisms. The most important works of the last two decades are McFarland's *Coleridge and the Pantheist Tradition*, esp. chap. 1, "The Problem of Coleridge's Plagiarisms," pp. 1–52, and excursus note 1, "Coleridge's Indebtedness to A. W. Schlegel," pp. 256–61; Fruman's *Coleridge, the Damaged Archangel*, passim (but specifically chaps. 11, 12, and 14 on Tennemann, Schelling and Steffens, and Schlegel); and the introduction and notes in the Engell–Bate edition of *Biographia Literaria* (esp. Engell's "The German Borrowings and the Issue of Plagiarism," 1:cxiv–cxxvii). McFarland discusses the borrowings from Tetens in "The Origin and Significance of Coleridge's Theory of Secondary Imagination" (1972), reprinted as chap. 4 in his *Originality and Imagination* (Baltimore: Johns Hopkins University Press, 1985), pp. 90–119, esp. pp. 100–105.

17. Thomas De Quincey, "Samuel Taylor Coleridge," *Tait's Edinburgh Magazine*, n.s., 1 (1834): 510–11.

18. James Frederick Ferrier, "The Plagiarisms of S. T. Coleridge," *Blackwood's Edinburgh Magazine* 47 (1840): 287–99; *The Works of Thomas Reid*, ed. Sir William Hamilton (Edinburgh: Maclachlan, Stewart, 1846), p. 890.

19. *Biographia Literaria,* 2nd ed., ed. H. N. Coleridge and Sara Coleridge, 2 vols. (London: William Pickering, 1847). Sara Coleridge's numerous corrections and revisions of the text in this edition (what she described in her diary, 28 October 1848, as "putting in order a literary house that otherwise would be open to censure here or there") constitute yet another kind of collaborative authorship in the Coleridge canon; see Bradford K. Mudge's recent articles, "Burning Down the House: Sara Coleridge, Virginia Woolf, and the Politics of Literary Revision," *Tulsa Studies in Women's Literature* 5 (1986): 230–31, and "Sara Coleridge and 'The Business of Life,' " *The Wordsworth Circle* 19 (1988): 55–64, and his biography, *Sara Coleridge, a Victorian Daughter: Her Life and Essays* (New Haven, Conn.: Yale University Press, 1989), esp. pp. 4, 14, 16, 122–33.

20. René Wellek, *Immanuel Kant in England, 1793–1838* (Princeton, N.J.: Princeton University Press, 1931), pp. 63–135 (quotation from p. 67); "Coleridge's Philosophy and Criticism," in *The English Romantic Poets: A Review of Research,* ed. Thomas M. Raysor (New York: Modern Language Association, 1950), pp. 95–117 (revised in the 2nd ed., ed. Raysor [1956], and further expanded in the 3rd ed., ed. Frank Jordan [1972]); *A History of Modern Criticism: 1750–1950,* vol. 2: *The Romantic Age* (New Haven, Conn.: Yale University Press, 1955), pp. 151–87 (quotation from p. 187).

21. Joseph Warren Beach, "Coleridge's Borrowings from the German," *ELH* 9 (1942): 36–58 (quotation from p. 42).

22. G. N. G. Orsini, *Coleridge and German Idealism: A Study in the History of Philosophy with Unpublished Materials from Coleridge's Manuscripts* (Carbondale: Southern Illinois University Press, 1969), pp. v–vi, 216, 219.

23. John Beer, ed., *Coleridge's Variety: Bicentenary Studies* (London: Macmillan, 1974), p. viii.

24. Max F. Schulz, *Modern Philology* 71 (1974): 453–55.

25. Thomas Lask, "Was He Charlatan or Genius?" *New York Times,* 24 December 1971, p. 22; Cyril Connolly, "Archangel with Feet of Clay," London *Sunday Times,* 17 September 1972, p. 39; Anthony West, "Triumphant," *New Statesman,* 20 October 1972, pp. 566–67; Paul West, "Prometheus at the Supermarket," *Book World,* 26 December 1971, p. 4; Hugh Kenner, "A Portrait of the 'Da Vinci of Literature,' " *Los Angeles Times Book Review,* 23 January 1972, p. 16; Robert E. Spiller, "Hard Evidence about Coleridge," Philadelphia *Sunday Bulletin,* 19 March 1972, sec. 2, p. 3; *Economist,* 23 September 1972, pp. 58–59; "The Deviousness of STC," *Times Literary Supplement,* 1 December 1972, p. 1463; Christopher Ricks, "The Moral Imbecility of a Would-Be Wunderkind," *Saturday Review,* 15 January 1972, pp. 31–33, 49; Geoffrey Hartman, *New York Times Book Review,* 12 March 1972, pp. 1, 36; George Steiner, "S. T. C.," *New Yorker,* 27 August 1973, pp. 77–90.

26. L. C. Knights, "Coleridge: The Wound without the Bow," *New York Review of Books,* 4 May 1972, pp. 25–26; Owen Barfield, "Abysses of Incomprehension," *Nation,* 12 June 1972, pp. 764–65; Roy Park, "Plagiarist," *Listener,* 14 December 1972, pp. 836–37, and his review in *British Journal of Aesthetics* 13 (1973): 301–3; Richard Harter Fogle, "Coleridge in the Dock," *Virginia Quarterly Review* 48 (1972): 477–80; J. B. Beer, *Review of English Studies,* n.s., 24 (1973): 346–53; Elinor Shaffer, *Southern Humanities Review* 8 (1974): 244–46; R. A. Foakes, "Repairing the Damaged Archangel," *Essays in Criticism* 24 (1974): 423–27, referring to Basil Cottle's "Damaged," *Essays in Criticism* 23 (1973): 413–19; Thomas McFarland, "Coleridge's Plagiarisms Once More: A Review Essay," *Yale Review* 63 (1974): 252–86.

27. R. A. Foakes's two-volume edition has since appeared, *Lectures 1808–1819: On Literature* (Princeton, N.J.: Princeton University Press, 1987), with discussion of Coleridge's reading of A. W. Schlegel and the plagiarism charges at 1:lix–lxiv, 172–75. Foakes's initial reference to Fruman (the first of two in the work) revives the meanspirited tone of the early 1970s: "The crude treatment of the matter by Norman Fruman . . . perhaps sufficiently betrays its own inadequacies, which have been demonstrated in the reviews of the book by John Beer . . . and by Thomas McFarland" (1:lxiv n.).

28. See note 24. In a recent essay on one of Coleridge's recurring themes, Schulz pointedly sidesteps the issue of originality: "Since I am making no special claims for the intellectual status of Coleridge's ideas of paradise, I see no need to raise the question of his use of others' writings" ("Coleridge and the Enchantments of Earthly Paradise," in *Reading Coleridge: Approaches and Applications*, ed. Walter B. Crawford [Ithaca, N.Y.: Cornell University Press, 1979], pp. 116–59 [quotation from p. 128 n.]).

29. Dorothy Emmet, "Coleridge on Powers in Mind and Nature," in *Coleridge's Variety*, ed. Beer, p. 167.

30. Alexander Kern, "Coleridge and American Romanticism: The Transcendentalists and Poe," in *New Approaches to Coleridge*, ed. Sultana, pp. 119–20.

31. The situation nicely illustrates Gerald Graff's contention that literary criticism generally in the last three or four decades has become "a technique by which literature is actually protected from criticism," with "perfection of the now-familiar conventions by which explicators could prove and teachers could teach that any literary feature which looks like a defect is actually a virtue": "the literary work is assumed infallible and the only question for the critic is how that infallibility is best described" ("The University and the Prevention of Culture," in *Criticism in the University*, ed. Gerald Graff and Reginald Gibbons [Evanston, Ill.: Northwestern University Press, 1985], pp. 72–73).

32. McFarland, *Originality and Imagination*, p. 22, referring to Harold Bloom's *The Anxiety of Influence: A Theory of Poetry* (New York: Oxford University Press, 1973).

33. Laurence S. Lockridge, *Coleridge the Moralist* (Ithaca, N.Y.: Cornell University Press, 1977), esp. pp. 270–74 and the appendix on Coleridge's plagiarisms, pp. 279–83. See also Lockridge's clearheaded "Explaining Coleridge's Explanation: Toward a Practical Methodology for Coleridge Studies," in *Reading Coleridge*, ed. Crawford, pp. 23–55.

34. Jerome Christensen, *Coleridge's Blessed Machine of Language* (Ithaca, N.Y.: Cornell University Press, 1981), chap. 3, "The Marginal Method of the *Biographia Literaria*," pp. 96–117 (quotations from pp. 100—the entry from Coleridge's notebook—and 105); the earlier version appeared in *PMLA* 92 (1977): 928–40.

35. *Biographia Literaria*, 1:lviii. See also Bate's sympathetic treatment of the plagiarisms in *Coleridge* (New York: Macmillan, 1968), pp. 131–38.

36. Daniel Mark Fogel, "A Compositional History of the *Biographia Literaria*," *Studies in Bibliography* 30 (1977): 219–34; Fruman, "Aids to Reflection on the New *Biographia*," pp. 160–65.

37. Fruman, *Coleridge, the Damaged Archangel*, p. 214.

38. More recently, Fruman and McFarland again appear together in the Fall 1986 *Studies in the Literary Imagination*, an issue devoted to "Coleridge's Theory of Imagination as Critical Method Today."

39. Rosemary Ashton, *The German Idea: Four English Writers and the Reception of German Thought, 1800–1860* (Cambridge: Cambridge University Press, 1980), pp. 27–66 (quotations from p. 28).

40. Kathleen M. Wheeler, *Sources, Processes and Methods in Coleridge's "Biographia Literaria"* (Cambridge: Cambridge University Press, 1980), pp. 43–44, 81–106, 191–93 (quotation from p. 193); Paul Hamilton, *Coleridge's Poetics* (Oxford: Basil Blackwell, 1983), p. 119.

41. Trevor H. Levere, *Poetry Realized in Nature: Samuel Taylor Coleridge and Early Nineteenth-Century Science* (Cambridge: Cambridge University Press, 1981), pp. 7, 224. Cf. Fruman, *Coleridge, the Damaged Archangel*, pp. 121–34.

42. Catherine Miles Wallace, *The Design of "Biographia Literaria"* (London: George Allen and Unwin, 1983), pp. 2, 150, 159, 69.

43. Anthony John Harding, *Coleridge and the Inspired Word* (Kingston and Montreal: McGill-Queen's University Press, 1985), pp. 65, 69, 70. Everyone, I suppose, should agree that Schelling's own words (even in translation) are "Schellingian."

44. Raimonda Modiano, *Coleridge and the Concept of Nature* (London: Macmillan, 1985), pp. 100, 231.

6. *Pound's* Waste Land

1. See the Wordworths' *Letters: The Early Years*, pp. 452, 464, 573, 607.

2. H. W. Garrod, *Wordsworth: Lectures and Essays* (Oxford: Clarendon Press, 1923), pp. 29–30; Fruman, *Coleridge, the Damaged Archangel*, chaps. 19–20, esp. pp. 265–69, 280, 300 (quotation from p. 268); McFarland, *Romanticism and the Forms of Ruin*, chap. 1, "The Symbiosis of Coleridge and Wordsworth," pp. 56–103; Magnuson, *Coleridge and Wordsworth: A Lyrical Dialogue*. Scholars have usually promoted one writer at the expense of the other. As a recent instance of overshadowing by accident, consider Rosemary Ashton's essay "How to Deal with Wordsworth," *Times Literary Supplement*, 26 August 1983, p. 913: no one could guess from the title (in forty-eight-point letters) that the piece is about Coleridge, a review of the Engell–Bate edition of *Biographia Literaria!*

3. *"The Waste Land": A Facsimile and Transcript of the Original Drafts including the Annotations of Ezra Pound*, ed. Valerie Eliot (New York: Harcourt Brace Jovanovich, 1971), hereafter cited as *Facsimile*. The manuscripts were first made public in an exhibition at the New York Public Library in November 1968 and were first described in detail in Donald Gallup's "The 'Lost' Manuscripts of T. S. Eliot," *Times Literary Supplement*, 7 November 1968, pp. 1237–40.

4. Florence Marsh, "The Ocean-Desert: *The Ancient Mariner* and *The Waste Land*," *Essays in Criticism* 9 (1959): 126–33 (quotation from p. 126). Marsha Anne McCreadie surveys likenesses in other poems by Eliot and Coleridge in "T. S. Eliot and the Romantic Poets: A Study of the Similar Poetic Themes and Methods Used by Eliot and Wordsworth, Coleridge, Keats, Byron, and Shelley" (Ph.D. diss., University of Illinois at Urbana-Champaign, 1973), chap. 3, "Coleridge and Eliot: Self-Inquiry and Paralysis," pp. 44–84. For general treatment of Eliot's nearly lifelong interest in Coleridge, see Carlos Baker, *The Echoing Green: Romanticism, Modernism, and the Phenomena of Transference in Poetry* (Princeton, N.J.: Princeton University Press, 1984), pp. 265–76.

5. Quoted in Kathleen Coburn's introduction to *Coleridge: A Col* *cal Essays* (Englewood Cliffs, N.J.: Prentice-Hall, 1967), p. 1.

6. Eliot, *The Use of Poetry and the Use of Criticism: Studies in the* *Criticism to Poetry in England* (London: Faber and Faber, 1933), pp. 68–6!

7. Peter Ackroyd, *T. S. Eliot: A Life* (New York: Simon and Schuster, 256, citing Woolf's diary entry for 25 May 1940.

8. Eliot, "The Literature of Politics" (1955), in *To Criticize the Critic and Other Writings* (New York: Farrar, Straus and Giroux, 1965), p. 138.

9. *Collected Letters of Samuel Taylor Coleridge*, 2:775. Curiously, Coleridge's "three persons . . . but one God" is the basis—via Alois Brandl's translation into German (1886), Lady Eastlake's mistranslation of Brandl's German back into English (1887), and a further slight alteration by subsequent scholars—for the frequently repeated statement that William and Dorothy Wordsworth and Coleridge were "three persons and one soul" (see Ruth I. Aldrich, "The Wordsworths and Coleridge: 'Three Persons,' but *Not* 'One Soul,' " *Studies in Romanticism* 2 [1962]: 61–63).

10. Eliot, *The Use of Poetry and the Use of Criticism,* pp. 70, 75.

11. For chronology and descriptions of the manuscripts and of Pound's and Eliot's revisions, the most useful works are Valerie Eliot's introduction and notes in *Facsimile;* Grover Smith, "The Making of *The Waste Land,*" *Mosaic* 6, no. 1 (Fall 1972): 127–41 (revised in Smith's *T. S. Eliot's Poetry and Plays: A Study in Sources and Meaning,* 2nd ed. [Chicago: University of Chicago Press, 1974], pp. 300–314); Glauco Cambon, "*The Waste Land* as Work in Progress," *Mosaic* 6, no. 1 (Fall 1972): 191–200; Hugh Kenner, "The Urban Apocalypse," in *Eliot in His Time: Essays on the Occasion of the Fiftieth Anniversary of "The Waste Land,*" ed. A. Walton Litz (Princeton, N.J.: Princeton University Press, 1973), pp. 23–49; Richard Ellmann, "The First *Waste Land,*" in *Eliot in His Time,* pp. 51–66; Helen Gardner, "*The Waste Land:* Paris 1922," in *Eliot in His Time,* pp. 67–94; Lyndall Gordon, *Eliot's Early Years* (Oxford: Oxford University Press, 1977), chap. 5, "The Waste Land Traversed," pp. 86–119, and appendix 2, "Dating *The Waste Land* Fragments," pp. 143–46; Peter Barry, "The *Waste Land* Manuscript: Picking up the Pieces—in Order," *Forum for Modern Language Studies* (University of St. Andrews) 15 (1979): 237–48; and Wayne Koestenbaum, "*The Waste Land:* T. S. Eliot's and Ezra Pound's Collaboration on Hysteria," *Twentieth Century Literature* 34 (1988): 113–39 (revised in Koestenbaum's *Double Talk: The Erotics of Male Literary Collaboration* [New York: Routledge, 1989], pp. 112–39, 189–92). This last is especially valuable in drawing on unpublished correspondence (at Yale) of Pound, Eliot, and others.

12. *The Letters of T. S. Eliot,* ed. Valerie Eliot (London: Faber and Faber, 1988–), 1:344, 351, 451; Ackroyd, *T. S. Eliot,* p. 110.

13. Eliot's *Letters,* 1:572.

14. The most recent example is Louis Auchincloss, "The Waste Land without Pound," *New York Review of Books,* 11 October 1984, p. 46.

15. Barry suggests that the pencil canceling the page may actually have been Pound's rather than Eliot's ("The *Waste Land* Manuscript," p. 246).

16. Eliot's *Letters,* 1:504, 505.

17. Eliot's *Letters,* 1:497, 504.

18. Eliot's *Letters,* 1:572. Eliot goes on to say, in the same letter, "Naturally, I hope that the portions which I have suppressed will never appear in print. . . . You will find [in the papers] a great many sets of verse which have never been printed and which

I am sure you will agree never ought to be printed, and in putting them in your hands, I beg you fervently to keep them to yourself and see that they never are printed."

19. Eliot, "On a Recent Piece of Criticism," *Purpose* 10, no. 2 (April/June 1938): 92–93.

20. Eliot, "Ezra Pound," *Poetry* 68 (1946): 330.

21. Timothy Wilson, "The Wife of the Father of *The Waste Land*," *Esquire*, May 1972, p. 44.

22. Gertrude Patterson, " 'The Waste Land' in the Making," *Critical Quarterly* 14 (1972): 270–71; Smith, first version of "The Making of *The Waste Land*," pp. 128, 140; D. E. S. Maxwell, " 'He Do the Police in Different Voices,' " *Mosaic* 6, no. 1 (Fall 1972): 178; Richard Sheppard, "Cultivating the Waste Land," *Journal of European Studies* 2 (1972): 188; Denis Donoghue, " 'The Word within a Word,' " in "*The Waste Land*" *in Different Voices: The Revised Versions of Lectures Given at the University of York in the Fiftieth Year of "The Waste Land*," ed. A. D. Moody (London: Edward Arnold, 1974), p. 185; Gareth Reeves, "The Obstetrics of *The Waste Land*," *Critical Quarterly* 17 (1975): 35, 50, 51; Ruth Pulik, "Pound and 'The Waste Land,' " *Unisa English Studies* 15, no. 2 (September 1977): 16; Ronald Bush, *T. S. Eliot: A Study in Character and Style* (New York: Oxford University Press, 1983), pp. 71, 72; Harriet Davidson, *T. S. Eliot and Hermeneutics: Absence and Interpretation in "The Waste Land*" (Baton Rouge: Louisiana State University Press, 1985), pp. 101, 102.

23. Cambon, "*The Waste Land* as Work in Progress," pp. 192, 195, 194; Bernard Bergonzi, *T. S. Eliot* (New York: Macmillan, 1972), p. 100; Russell Kirk, "The Waste Land Lies Unredeemed," *Sewanee Review* 80 (1972): 471; Lewis Turco, "*The Waste Land* Reconsidered," *Sewanee Review* 87 (1979): 294 (the essay is reprinted in revised form, with the title "*The Waste Land* Revisited," in Turco's *Visions and Revisions of American Poetry* [Fayetteville: University of Arkansas Press, 1986], pp. 85–94).

24. Grover Smith, *The Waste Land* (London: George Allen and Unwin, 1983), pp. 81, 83; Ackroyd, *T. S. Eliot*, pp. 119–20; Nina Baym, in *The Norton Anthology of American Literature*, 2nd ed., ed. Baym et al. (New York: Norton, 1985), 2:1194; 3rd ed. (1989), 2:1266.

25. Smith speculates interestingly on how the poem might have developed without Pound (the possibilities include ending up with "no poem at all") (*The Waste Land*, pp. 81–83).

26. Ackroyd, *T. S. Eliot*, p. 120.

27. Eliot, *On Poetry and Poets* (London: Faber and Faber, 1957), p. 98.

7. *American Novels: Authors, Agents, Editors, Publishers*

1. The best general study of the development of a mass audience remains Richard D. Altick's *The English Common Reader: A Social History of the Mass Reading Public, 1800–1900* (Chicago: University of Chicago Press, 1957). On concurrent changes in the profession of authorship, see Victor Bonham-Carter, *Authors by Profession* (Los Altos, Calif.: William Kaufmann, 1978), which focuses on British writers; William Charvat, *The Profession of Authorship in America, 1800–1870*, ed. Matthew J. Bruccoli (Columbus: Ohio State University Press, 1968); and James L. W. West III, *American Authors and the Literary Marketplace since 1900* (Philadelphia: University of Pennsylvania Press, 1988).

2. J. A. Sutherland, *Victorian Novelists and Publishers* (Chicago: University of Chicago Press, 1976), pp. 2, 27, 30, 104–16, 124–26, 180–87.

3. Engel's Book Creations, Inc., is discussed as the most successful of the "fiction factories" in Lewis A. Coser, Charles Kadushin, and Walter W. Powell, *Books: The Culture and Commerce of Publishing* (New York: Basic Books, 1982), chap. 10, "Books without Authors," pp. 263–64.

4. Emily Toth, *Inside Peyton Place: The Life of Grace Metalious* (Garden City, N.Y.: Doubleday, 1981), pp. 96–109 (principal quotations from pp. 98, 99, 103, 105, 109).

5. Barbara Seaman, *Lovely Me: The Life of Jacqueline Susann* (New York: Morrow, 1987), pp. 239–40.

6. Seaman, *Lovely Me,* p. 285. My subsequent quotations from the readers' reports and particulars of the editing of the novel are taken from pp. 286, 287, 298. For similar details concerning work on Susann's draft of *The Love Machine* (1969) by "the Simon and Schuster editorial team," Jonathan Dolger and Michael Korda—"[We] did a terrific job of editing that book. . . . We tore it to pieces and put it back together again"—see p. 375.

7. In both my chapter title and the bulk of my examples, I am focusing on American fiction primarily as a matter of practical convenience: a considerable body of material has been made available concerning the composition procedures and editing of American writers of the last hundred years, seemingly much more than that available for British writers of the same period. Harry E. Maule, an editor of Sinclair Lewis first at Doubleday and then at Random House, says that "in America editors do a great deal more editing than they do in England" (in his contribution to *Editors on Editing,* ed. Gerald Gross [New York: Grosset and Dunlap, 1962], p. 122). If this is so, there are several possible reasons, among which might be the greater commercial ambitions of even "serious" authors in the United States.

8. Seaman, *Lovely Me,* p. 271.

9. A. Scott Berg, *Max Perkins: Editor of Genius* (New York: Dutton, 1978). The other principal sources of information about Perkins are *Editor to Author: The Letters of Maxwell E. Perkins,* ed. John Hall Wheelock (New York: Scribner's, 1950); *Dear Scott/Dear Max: The Fitzgerald–Perkins Correspondence,* ed. John Kuehl and Jackson R. Bryer (New York: Scribner's, 1971); and *Ring around Max: The Correspondence of Ring Lardner and Max Perkins,* ed. Clifford M. Caruthers (DeKalb: Northern Illinois University Press, 1973).

10. Berg, *Max Perkins,* p. 237. Wolfe refers to their joint effort as "collaboration" ("our work—perhaps I could better say our collaboration, although that term, I know, would embarrass [Perkins]") in the typescript version of *The Story of a Novel* (1936), which opens with description of "the work that both of us were doing, the transaction that occurred, the whole stroke and catch, the flow, the stop, the cut, the molding, the whole ten thousand meetings, gratings, changings, surrenders, triumphs, and agreeings that went into the making of the book" (see David Herbert Donald, *Look Homeward: A Life of Thomas Wolfe* [Boston: Little, Brown, 1987], p. 350, and the text of *Story* published as the first part of Wolfe's *The Autobiography of an American Novelist,* ed. Leslie Field [Cambridge, Mass.: Harvard University Press, 1983], pp. 71, 3). It is perhaps worth mentioning that Wolfe's *Story* was substantially revised and cut by Elizabeth Nowell, his agent, and was given its title by George Stevens, a friend of his who worked at the *Saturday Review* (Donald, *Look Homeward,* pp. 352–53). The printed text of 1936 omits entirely the short paragraph about "our collaboration" and,

among several alterations in the text of the other passage just quoted, omits "the transaction that occurred" and revises "ten thousand meetings" to "ten thousand fittings."

11. Berg, *Max Perkins,* p. 328.

12. See Leslie Field, *Thomas Wolfe and His Editors: Establishing a True Text for the Posthumous Publications* (Norman: University of Oklahoma Press, 1987), and my review of Field's work in *Journal of English and Germanic Philology* 88 (1989): 146–48.

13. See, for example, Perkins's letter to Marjorie Rawlings, 20 September 1940, concerning the manuscript of *Cross Creek* (1942), and that to Marcia Davenport, 28 April 1947, concerning *East Side, West Side* (1947), in *Editor to Author,* pp. 175–80, 286–94.

14. Berg, *Max Perkins,* p. 404.

15. Berg, *Max Perkins,* p. 303; Milton R. Stern, *"Tender Is the Night:* The Text Itself," in *Critical Essays on F. Scott Fitzgerald's "Tender Is the Night,"* ed. Stern (Boston: Hall, 1986), pp. 21–31.

16. *Dear Scott/Dear Max,* pp. 83–84, 85, 89.

17. Berg, *Max Perkins,* pp. 133–34.

18. Berg, *Max Perkins,* pp. 6, 123. Wheelock lists among Perkins's editorial qualities "a self-effacement . . . almost feminine in character" in his introduction to *Editor to Author* (pp. 3–4), and Berg mentions "Perkins's pathological self-effacement" (*Max Perkins,* p. 421).

19. The best sources of information about Commins are Dorothy Commins, *What Is an Editor? Saxe Commins at Work* (Chicago: University of Chicago Press, 1978), and *"Love and Admiration and Respect": The O'Neill–Commins Correspondence,* ed. Dorothy Commins (Durham, N.C.: Duke University Press, 1986).

20. Commins, *What Is an Editor,* pp. 90–92. For Saxe Commins's ghosting of Parker Morell's *Lillian Russell: The Era of Plush* (1940), see the same work, pp. 153–69.

21. Commins, *What Is an Editor,* pp. 225–26 (and on Saxe Commins and Faulkner more generally, pp. 194–228).

22. These editors (with others) figure prominently in Gerald Gross's *Editors on Editing,* either in the original edition of 1962 or in the revised edition of 1985 (New York: Harper & Row).

23. Herbert Mitgang, "Imprint" (a profile of Helen Wolff), *New Yorker,* 2 August 1982, pp. 67–68.

24. Edwin McDowell, " 'Catch-22' Sequel by Heller," *New York Times,* 8 April 1987, p. C19. Gottlieb was responsible for the title of *Catch-22,* which in Heller's original version was "Catch-18."

25. *Editors on Editing,* ed. Gross, rev. ed. (1985), pp. 40, 41, 66, 106, 114, 137, 193, 204.

26. Barbara Probst Solomon, "Where's Papa?" *New Republic,* 9 March 1987, pp. 30–34.

27. See Donald, *Look Homeward,* pp. 291, 352–53, 366–67, 407–9, 445, 549 (note to 407/35).

28. See Faulkner's *Flags in the Dust,* ed. Douglas Day (New York: Random House, 1973); Joseph Blotner, "William Faulkner's Essay on the Composition of *Sartoris,"* *Yale University Library Gazette* 47 (1973): 121–24; and George F. Hayhoe, "William Faulkner's *Flags in the Dust," Mississippi Quarterly* 28 (1975): 370–86.

29. Janice Thaddeus, "The Metamorphosis of Richard Wright's *Black Boy,"*

American Literature 57 (1985): 199–214. The rest of the autobiography was published seventeen years after Wright's death as *American Hunger,* afterword by Michel Fabre (New York: Harper & Row, 1977).

30. Sherry Lutz Zivley, "A Collation of John Barth's *Floating Opera,*" *Papers of the Bibliographical Society of America* 72 (1978): 201–12. After establishing his reputation as a novelist, Barth restored much of his original text in a revised edition of 1967.

31. See Edwin McDowell, "Publishing: 'Clockwork Orange' Regains Chapter 21," *New York Times,* 31 December 1986, p. C16.

32. *Correspondence of F. Scott Fitzgerald,* ed. Matthew J. Bruccoli and Margaret M. Duggan (New York: Random House, 1980), pp. 193–96. See Frederic J. Svoboda, *Hemingway and "The Sun Also Rises": The Crafting of a Style* (Lawrence: University Press of Kansas, 1983), esp. pp. 97–110, and Michael S. Reynolds, "False Dawn: A Preliminary Analysis of *The Sun Also Rises'* Manuscript," in *Hemingway: A Revaluation,* ed. Donald R. Noble (Troy, N.Y.: Whitston, 1983), pp. 115–34.

33. *Sister Carrie,* The Pennsylvania Edition, ed. James L. W. West III et al. (Philadelphia: University of Pennsylvania Press, 1981). I do not mean to suggest that my other examples in this chapter are not controversial. As early as 1936, reviewing Wolfe's *The Story of a Novel,* Bernard De Voto expressed great indignation over the lack of integrity in works "in which not the artist but the publisher has determined where the true ends and the false begins," placing the blame, in Wolfe's case, on "Mr. Perkins and the assembly line at Scribners' " ("Genius Is Not Enough," *Saturday Review of Literature,* 25 April 1936, pp. 3–4, 14–15). Scholars continue to argue over which is the "real" *Tender Is the Night* (see Stern, *"Tender Is the Night:* The Text Itself"), and some think that Perkins gave Fitzgerald bad advice for *Gatsby.* Questions have been raised about the textual principles underlying Noel Polk's editing of Faulkner from holograph manuscripts and typescripts rather than from printed texts—for example, the four novels in *William Faulkner: Novels 1930–1935* (New York: Library of America, 1985) (see Karl F. Zender in *American Literary Scholarship: An Annual/1985* [Durham, N.C.: Duke University Press, 1987], pp. 147–49). I have already referred to Barbara Probst Solomon's dismay at Scribner's handling of Hemingway's posthumous *The Garden of Eden.*

34. The most helpful sources concerning the composition and revision of *Sister Carrie* are the Pennsylvania edition, esp. the section *"Sister Carrie:* Manuscript to Print," pp. 503–41; Donald Pizer's review of this edition, *American Literature* 53 (1982): 731–37; James L. W. West III's *A "Sister Carrie" Portfolio* (Charlottesville: University Press of Virginia, 1985); and two articles by Stephen C. Brennan: "The Composition of *Sister Carrie:* A Reconsideration," *Dreiser Newsletter* 9, no. 2 (Fall 1978): 17–23, and "The Publication of *Sister Carrie:* Old and New Fictions," *American Literary Realism, 1870–1910* 18 (1985): 55–68. The details in Richard Lingeman's new biography, *Theodore Dreiser: At the Gates of the City, 1871–1907* (New York: Putnam, 1986), pp. 241–97 passim, are drawn mainly from the Pennsylvania edition.

35. At Dreiser's request, Henry alone made further cuts for the first British edition of *Sister Carrie,* in Heinemann's Dollar Library of American Fiction series (1901). Henry condensed the first 195 pages to about 90 (see the Pennsylvania edition, pp. 529–30).

36. The seminal essays, much referred to, interpreted, and disputed, are W. W. Greg, "The Rationale of Copy-Text" (1949), and Fredson Bowers, "Current Theories of Copy-Text, with an Illustration from Dryden" (1950). The Greg–Bowers theory of copy-text is discussed (and documented) in the final section of Chapter 9. Bowers has

238   *Notes*

extended the theory to the editing of American fiction in, among other writings, "A
Preface to the Text," in *The Scarlet Letter*, vol. 1 of the Centenary Edition of the Works
of Nathaniel Hawthorne (Columbus: Ohio State University Press, 1962), esp. pp.
xxxiii–xxxvi, and "Some Principles for Scholarly Editions of Nineteenth-Century
American Authors," *Studies in Bibliography* 17 (1964): 223–28.

    37. Pizer, review of the Pennsylvania edition of *Sister Carrie*, pp. 733, 736. Pizer
has also commented valuably on the editorial problems of *Sister Carrie* in "Self-
Censorship and Textual Editing," in *Textual Criticism and Literary Interpretation*, ed.
Jerome J. McGann (Chicago: University of Chicago Press, 1985), pp. 144–61, 227.

8. *Plays and Films: Authors, Auteurs, Autres*

    1. The evidence is a letter from Dryden to Elizabeth Steward, 4 March 1699:
"This Day was playd a reviv'd Comedy of Mr Congreve's calld the Double Dealer. . . .
in the play bill was printed,—Written by Mr Congreve. . . . the printing an Authours
name, in a Play bill, is a new manner of proceeding, at least in England" (*The Letters of
John Dryden*, ed. Charles E. Ward [Durham, N.C.: Duke University Press, 1942], pp.
112–13).

    2. My text is Nahum Tate's *The History of King Lear*, ed. James Black (Lincoln:
University of Nebraska Press, 1975).

    3. *The Works of Charles and Mary Lamb*, ed. Thomas Hutchinson (London:
Oxford University Press, 1934), 1:134; Mel Gussow, "Theatre: Tate's 'Lear' at Riverside," *New York Times*, 13 March 1985, p. C21.

    4. Charles H. Shattuck has made many distinguished contributions to the perfor-
mance history of Shakespeare's plays. In this and the next five paragraphs I have drawn
freely on the most compact and accessible of them, "Shakespeare's Plays in Performance from 1660 to the Present," in *The Riverside Shakespeare*, ed. G. B. Evans et al.
(Boston: Houghton Mifflin, 1974), pp. 1799–1825 (bibliography on pp. 1896–97). A
standard earlier work is Hazelton Spencer's *Shakespeare Improved: The Restoration
Versions in Quarto and on the Stage* (Cambridge, Mass.: Harvard University Press,
1927).

    5. *The Dramatic Works of Sir William D'Avenant*, 5 vols. (Edinburgh: William
Paterson; London: H. Sotheran, 1872–74), 5:334, 338, 387–88. In Shakespeare's text,
the references are 1.7.60, 2.2.34, and 5.5.19–23.

    6. *The London Stage, 1660–1800: A Calendar of Plays, Entertainments and After-
pieces*, ed. William Van Lennep et al. (Carbondale: Southern Illinois University Press,
1960–68), part 1, p. cxl.

    7. Shattuck, "Shakespeare's Plays in Performance," pp. 1805–6.

    8. Shattuck, "Shakespeare's Plays in Performance," p. 1822.

    9. A number of these studies are conveniently reprinted and summarized in
David V. Erdman and Ephim G. Fogel, eds., *Evidence for Authorship: Essays on
Problems of Attribution* (Ithaca, N.Y.: Cornell University Press, 1966), pp. 146–228,
427–94.

    10. Cyrus Hoy, "The Shares of Fletcher and His Collaborators in the Beaumont
and Fletcher Canon," *Studies in Bibliography* 8 (1956): 129–46; 9 (1957): 143–62; 11
(1958): 85–106; 12 (1959): 91–116; 13 (1960): 77–108; 14 (1961): 45–67; 15 (1962): 71–
90. The first part of the series is reprinted in *Evidence for Authorship*, ed. Erdman and
Fogel, pp. 204–23.

11. Gerald Eades Bentley, *The Profession of Dramatist in Shakespeare's Time, 1590–1642* (Princeton, N.J.: Princeton University Press, 1971), p. 199.

12. Bentley, *The Profession of Dramatist in Shakespeare's Time,* chaps. 8 ("Collaboration") and 9 ("Revision"), pp. 197–263 passim.

13. See the summaries in *Evidence for Authorship,* ed. Erdman and Fogel, pp. 454–78, 480–94. The passages of *Sir Thomas More* ascribed to Shakespeare are given in both old and modernized spelling, along with photographs of the manuscript, in *The Riverside Shakespeare,* ed. Evans et al., pp. 1683–1700.

14. Bentley, *The Profession of Dramatist in Shakespeare's Time,* p. 262.

15. Alfred Harbage, *Shakespeare without Words and Other Essays* (Cambridge, Mass.: Harvard University Press, 1972), p. 3.

16. My main source in this and the next three paragraphs is Philip Gaskell's *From Writer to Reader: Studies in Editorial Method* (Oxford: Clarendon Press, 1978), pp. 245–62. *Travesties* was published in London by Faber and in New York by the Grove Press, both editions in 1975. Stoppard comments on some of the changes made in the production of the play in two interviews published in Ronald Hayman's *Tom Stoppard* (London: Heinemann, 1977), pp. 1–13, 139–40. Gaskell has also made a similar study of Stoppard's next full-length play, *"Night and Day:* The Development of a Play Text," in *Textual Criticism and Literary Interpretation,* ed. McGann, pp. 162–79, 227–28.

17. Hayman, *Tom Stoppard,* pp. 8–9.

18. William Gibson, *The Seesaw Log: A Chronicle of the Stage Production, with the Text, of "Two for the Seesaw"* (New York: Knopf, 1959), pp. 30, 4. Subsequent references are given parenthetically in the text. Gibson's reading version of the play (pp. 143–273), the only one in print, is a composite of preproduction script, some (but by no means all) of the revisions made during rehearsals and performances, and still later revisions made solely for this published text.

19. Here are some of the New York reviewers' comments specifically about Gibson: "Author William Gibson has a deft, buoyant, rapid-fire flair for dialogue . . . and his eye for accurately observed detail is excellent" (Walter Kerr in the *Herald Tribune*); "Gibson has made . . . a tricky task look as easy as pie" (John Chapman in the *New York Daily News*); "Gibson knows what makes people tick, and how to project it. He has a flair for speech that is accurate and flavorsome" (Robert Coleman in the *New York Mirror*); "The author has constructed his story well. . . . Mr. Gibson can really write" (John McClain in the *New York Journal American*); "It is clear that this new dramatist is both an expert craftsman and an honest and compassionate observer, with an engaging sense of humor" (Richard Watts in the *New York Post*)—all quoted from Gibson's *The Seesaw Log,* pp. 127, 128, 130, 133, 135.

20. Woody Allen, "True Colors," *New York Review of Books,* 13 August 1987, p. 38.

21. These details are taken from Patrick McGilligan's introduction to the screenplay, *Yankee Doodle Dandy,* ed. McGilligan (Madison: University of Wisconsin Press, 1981). See also Julius Epstein's comments quoted in McGilligan's *Backstory: Interviews with Screenwriters of Hollywood's Golden Age* (Berkeley: University of California Press, 1986), pp. 183–85.

22. Michael Carpenter, *Corporate Authorship: Its Role in Library Cataloging* (Westport, Conn.: Greenwood Press, 1981), regards films as the epitome of "multiple and diffuse authorship" (pp. 135, 138).

23. See Hal Wallis and Charles Higham, *Starmaker: The Autobiography of Hal Wallis* (New York: Macmillan, 1980), pp. 83–92 (also the interoffice memos on pp.

208–12); Howard Koch, *As Time Goes By: Memoirs of a Writer* (New York: Harcourt Brace Jovanovich, 1979), pp. 76–84; Rudy Behlmer, ed., *Inside Warner Bros. (1935–1951)* (New York: Viking, 1985), pp. 194–221; and McGilligan, *Backstory,* pp. 185–87. Casey Robinson also contributed to the writing of *Casablanca* (*Inside Warner Bros.,* ed. Behlmer, pp. 206–7, 213; McGilligan, *Backstory,* pp. 306–8).

24. Among many possible sources for the generalizations about screenwriters here and in the next three paragraphs, I have made most use of McGilligan's *Backstory;* John Brady's *The Craft of the Screenwriter: Interviews with Six Celebrated Screenwriters* (New York: Simon and Schuster, 1981); and Mark Litwak's *Reel Power: The Struggle for Influence and Success in the New Hollywood* (New York: Morrow, 1986), esp. chap. 9, "Writers," pp. 173–95.

25. Robert L. Carringer, *The Making of "Citizen Kane"* (Berkeley: University of California Press, 1985), quotes the waiver in Herman Mankiewicz's contract for work on the script of *Citizen Kane:* "All material composed, submitted, added or interpolated by you under this employment agreement, and all results and proceeds of all services rendered or to be rendered by you under this employment agreement, are now and shall forever be the property of Mercury Productions, Inc., who, for this purpose, shall be deemed the author and creator thereof, you having acted entirely as its employee" (p. 32).

26. McGilligan, *Backstory,* p. 182.

27. Litwak, *Reel Power,* p. 195.

28. McGilligan, *Backstory,* p. 223. On film censorship generally, see Leonard J. Leff and Jerold L. Simmons, *The Dame in the Kimono: Hollywood, Censorship, and the Production Code from the 1920s to the 1960s* (New York: Grove Weidenfeld, 1990).

29. McGilligan, *Backstory,* pp. 341–42.

30. Andrew Sarris's landmark essay, frequently cited as the beginning of the American auteur movement, is "Notes on the Auteur Theory in 1962," *Film Culture* 27 (Winter 1962/63): 1–8; but Sarris and Archer had been publishing auteur criticism in the journal since the mid-1950s.

31. As in Patrick McGilligan's *Cagney: The Actor as Auteur,* rev. ed. (San Diego: Barnes, 1982), esp. chap. 12, "The Actor as Auteur," pp. 261–75.

32. Roy Fowler, *Orson Welles: A First Biography* (London: Pendulum, 1946), quoted by Carringer at the beginning of his preface to *The Making of "Citizen Kane,"* p. ix.

33. Carringer also sent Welles an earlier version of his chap. 4, "Cinematography," published as "Orson Welles and Gregg Toland: Their Collaboration on *Citizen Kane," Critical Inquiry* 8 (1982): 651–74, and was able to incorporate Welles's responses into his book. In addition, Carringer has published a fuller account of the successive drafts of *Citizen Kane* in "The Scripts of *Citizen Kane," Critical Inquiry* 5 (1978): 369–400, and a condensed version of his chap. 2, "Scripting," as "Who Really Wrote *Citizen Kane?" American Film,* September 1985, pp. 42–49, 70. I am much indebted to all these publications.

34. Carringer, *The Making of "Citizen Kane,"* p. 35.

35. See the review of Carringer's book by Richard M. Gollin, "Collaborative Auteurism," *Quarterly Review of Film Studies* 10 (1985): 271–75.

36. Carringer, *The Making of "Citizen Kane,"* p. 134.

37. Donald Spoto, *The Dark Side of Genius: The Life of Alfred Hitchcock* (Boston: Little, Brown, 1983), esp. pp. 108–9; Leonard J. Leff, *Hitchcock and Selznick:*

The Rich and Strange Collaboration of Alfred Hitchcock and David O. Selznick in Hollywood (New York: Weidenfeld and Nicolson, 1987).

9. *Implications for Theory*

1. At one point in his tribulations, the playwright William Gibson (see Chapter 8) tells that he "visited a painter's studio, and envied her; she was working in a medium where she alone could ruin it. This seemed to me a definition of art" (*The Seesaw Log*, p. 43). But Gibson is romanticizing: at the very least, painters are constrained by the size, shape, and materials of their various media, not to mention the tastes and whims of critics, patrons, and prospective purchasers.

2. The distinction between "creative or literary" and "popular fare" occurs in West's *American Authors and the Literary Marketplace since 1900*, p. 60. One sees the result of this kind of thinking in West's opinion that Ripley Hitchcock's wholesale editorial rewriting of Edward Noyes Westcott's *David Harum* (producing a famous best-seller) was nothing short of brilliant, while revision of Dreiser's *Jennie Gerhardt* (now canonized among the "serious" works of American literature) "blunted" the religious ideas, "muted" the philosophy, and rendered Dreiser's prose "more conventional" (cf. pp. 53 and 55).

3. Fredson Bowers, "Textual Criticism," in *The Aims and Methods of Scholarship in Modern Languages and Literatures,* ed. Thorpe, p. 24. My point about the purity of an unread manuscript has been partly anticipated by Jerome McGann: "An author's work possesses autonomy only when it remains an unheard melody. As soon as it begins its passage to publication it undergoes a series of interventions which some textual critics see as a process of contamination, but which may equally well be seen as a process of training the poem for its appearances in the world" (*A Critique of Modern Textual Criticism*, p. 51).

4. W. J. T. Mitchell, ed., *Against Theory: Literary Studies and the New Pragmatism* (Chicago: University of Chicago Press, 1985), p. 2.

5. We all share this kind of knowledge. On the day after President Bush's inauguration, for example, the *New York Times* carried an article about Peggy Noonan, a writer of major speeches for both Reagan and Bush (Maureen Dowd, "A Stirring Breeze Sparks Feelings, Then Words for a President's Vision," 21 January 1989, p. 10). The speech by Noonan that Bush delivered when he accepted his party's nomination at the Republican National Convention in August 1988 "was widely hailed as the best of his career and the one that helped change the tide for his lagging campaign." Nevertheless, in this first year of the new presidency, there is continual public reference to now-clichéd phrases from the campaign and inaugural rhetoric—"read my lips" (taken over from a Clint Eastwood film), "kinder, gentler nation," "a new breeze is blowing"—as if they had originated with Bush rather than with Noonan and her sources. Noonan describes her speechwriting in *What I Saw at the Revolution: A Political Life in the Reagan Era* (New York: Random House, 1990).

6. Readers also have to *believe* in the reality of the nominal authors. As an illustration, consider this comment by John Franklin Jameson, in *The History of Historical Writing in America* (Boston: Houghton, Mifflin, 1891), concerning the thirty-four-volume *History of the Pacific States of North America* published between 1882 and 1890 under the nominal authorship of Hubert Howe Bancroft: "It is obvious that a work of

such magnitude, carried through in so few years, could not possibly be written by a single hand. In fact, the books were first written by the various members of the cohort of assistants, and the person whose name they bear has simply revised, as a sort of managing editor, the productions of this highly-organized staff. Valuable as the work proves to be, some of the faults of such a plan are evident. There can be no fixing of responsibility. No one knows whom to criticise. No one can know whether the authority of this or that part of the book, or of the whole, should be much or little" (pp. 153–54). There is of course no end to the possibilities for documenting the importance of authorial identity. A novel example concerns the recent publication in facsimile of the manuscript of André Breton and Philippe Soupault's *Les Champs magnétique* (1920), the first piece of Surrealist *écriture automatique,* described by Louis Aragon as "the work of a single author with two heads." In a letter to the *New York Review of Books,* Mary Ann Caws remarks, with evident satisfaction, "The individual parts of the text were not ascribed to one or the other of the authors when it was first published, but now the different handwritings distinguish the authors" ("Automatic Writing Is Born," 16 March 1989, p. 45).

7. I am of course not alone in this opinion. Cf. Barthes, "The Death of the Author," in *Image—Music—Text:* "Once the Author is removed, the claim to decipher a text becomes quite futile. . . . Hence there is no surprise in the fact that, historically, the reign of the Author has also been that of the Critic" (p. 147).

8. Cited in Chapter 1, note 9. My quotations here and in the next paragraph are from the text in Wimsatt's *The Verbal Icon,* pp. 3–5.

9. Wimsatt, "Genesis: A Fallacy Revisited," in *The Disciplines of Criticism,* ed. Demetz et al., p. 222 (italics added). For Beardsley's later statements, see his *Aesthetics: Problems in the Philosophy of Criticism* (New York: Harcourt, Brace & World, 1958), esp. pp. 457–61, and "Textual Meaning and Authorial Meaning," *Genre* 1 (1968): 169–81, revised in Beardsley's *The Possibility of Criticism* (Detroit: Wayne State University Press, 1970), "The Authority of the Text," pp. 16–37.

10. *On Literary Intention: Critical Essays,* ed. David Newton-De Molina (Edinburgh: Edinburgh University Press, 1976). The two most cogent essays are Frank Cioffi's "Intention and Interpretation in Criticism," pp. 55–73, 260 (reprinted from *Proceedings of the Aristotelian Society,* n.s., 64 [1963–64]: 85–106), and Alastair Fowler's "Intention Floreat," pp. 242–55 (written especially for Newton-De Molina's volume).

11. E. D. Hirsch, Jr., *Validity in Interpretation,* pp. 4, 3, 5, 26–27. Hirsch has restated his position on many subsequent occasions. See, for a gathering of instances, *The Aims of Interpretation* (Chicago: University of Chicago Press, 1976). The flinty minded refinement of Hirsch's system in P. D. Juhl's *Interpretation: An Essay in the Philosophy of Literary Criticism* (Princeton, N.J.: Princeton University Press, 1980) aspires to be another landmark in the debate, but Juhl undermines himself in the first two sentences of his preface: "This book is an attempt to provide and defend an analysis of our concept of the meaning of a literary work. In undertaking to do this I am assuming that we in fact share one such concept, that one such concept underlies the practice of literary interpretation." Juhl's assumption, which in effect renders the rest of the book a tautology, is demonstrably unjustified.

12. An early example is the July 1968 issue of *Genre* (vol. 1, no. 3), "A Symposium on E. D. Hirsch's *Validity in Interpretation,*" in which all eight authors, starting with Beardsley ("Textual Meaning and Authorial Meaning"), find fault with one or another aspect of Hirsch's work. The editor of the issue comments that "the objections

of our contributors are inconsistent with one another: one critic objects to a position that another accepts."

13. Steven Knapp and Walter Benn Michaels, "Against Theory," *Critical Inquiry* 8 (1982): 723–42. My quotations are from the reprint in *Against Theory*, ed. Mitchell, pp. 11–30.

14. These are all reprinted in Mitchell's *Against Theory*. Subsequently, Knapp and Michaels have added "Against Theory 2: Hermeneutics and Deconstruction" to the fray (*Critical Inquiry* 14 [1987]: 49–68); it begins and concludes with the same refrain of their earlier piece: "a text means what its author intends it to mean."

15. William R. Schroeder, "A Teachable Theory of Interpretation," in *Theory in the Classroom*, ed. Cary Nelson (Urbana: University of Illinois Press, 1986), pp. 9–44.

16. *Literature and the Question of Philosophy*, ed. Anthony J. Cascardi (Baltimore: Johns Hopkins University Press, 1987), pp. 206 (Dutton) and 214–15, 221 (Rosen). Nehamas's earlier essay "The Postulated Author: Critical Monism as a Regulative Ideal" is cited in Chapter 1, note 17.

17. David H. Hirsch, "Penelope's Web," *Sewanee Review* 90 (1982): 124.

18. The one exception that I know of is Wimsatt, who in the 1968 "Genesis: A Fallacy Revisited" cites James Thorpe's disclosures about editorial and compositorial revision of works as a further argument against intentional reading: "it is possible and, as [Thorpe] shows, frequently is the fact that a designed work is the design of more than one head. A second completes the work of the first" (*The Disciplines of Criticism*, ed. Demetz et al., p. 206). Wimsatt cites Thorpe's "The Aesthetics of Textual Criticism," *PMLA* 80 (1965): 465–82, the essay that became, after further revision, chap. 1 of Thorpe's *Principles of Textual Criticism*.

19. *Autobiography and Literary Essays*, in *Collected Works of John Stuart Mill*, 1:34.

20. David H. Hirsch, "Penelope's Web," p. 125.

21. For example, G. Thomas Tanselle, "Textual Scholarship," in *Introduction to Scholarship in Modern Languages and Literatures*, ed. Joseph Gibaldi (New York: Modern Language Association, 1981), esp. pp. 30, 31, 37, and William Proctor Williams and Craig S. Abbott, *An Introduction to Bibliographical and Textual Studies* (New York: Modern Language Association, 1985), esp. pp. 57–58.

22. W. W. Greg, "The Rationale of Copy-Text," *Studies in Bibliography* 3 (1950–51): 19–36 (first presented as a paper at the English Institute in September 1949), reprinted in Greg's *Collected Papers*, ed. J. C. Maxwell (Oxford: Clarendon Press, 1986), pp. 374–91; Fredson Bowers, "Current Theories of Copy-Text, with an Illustration from Dryden," *Modern Philology* 48 (1950): 12–20, and numerous subsequent publications. Several of G. Thomas Tanselle's essays in *Studies in Bibliography* have a bearing on the Greg–Bowers theory; see his two collections, *Selected Studies in Bibliography* (Charlottesville: University Press of Virginia, 1979) and *Textual Criticism since Greg: A Chronicle, 1950–1985* (Charlottesville: University Press of Virginia, 1987), esp. "Greg's Theory of Copy-Text and the Editing of American Literature" (1975), reprinted in both *Selected Studies in Bibliography*, pp. 245–307, and *Textual Criticism since Greg*, pp. 1–63.

23. *Little Dorrit*, ed. Harvey Peter Sucksmith (Oxford: Clarendon Press, 1979). See my review in *Nineteenth-Century Fiction* 35 (1981): 543–47.

24. *The Blithedale Romance* and *The Marble Faun*, vols. 3 and 4 of the Centenary Edition of the Works of Nathaniel Hawthorne, ed. Fredson Bowers (Columbus: Ohio State University Press, 1964, 1968). There is also (just as in interpretive theory) a vast

literature on the place of authorial intention in editing. The most frequently cited work is Tanselle's "The Editorial Problem of Final Authorial Intention," *Studies in Bibliography* 29 (1976): 167–211 (reprinted in *Selected Studies in Bibliography,* pp. 309–53).

25. For an early account of seven of the versions, see I. A. Gordon, "The Case-History of Coleridge's *Monody on the Death of Chatterton,"* *Review of English Studies* 18 (1942): 49–71.

26. A recent typical example is the Northwestern/Newberry edition of *Moby-Dick,* ed. Harrison Hayford et al. (Evanston, Ill.: Northwestern University Press, 1988). See Peter Shillingsburg, "The Three *Moby-Dicks,"* *American Literary History* 2 (1990): 119–30.

27. Thorpe, "The Aesthetics of Textual Criticism." My quotations are from the expanded version in Thorpe's *Principles of Textual Criticism,* pp. 35, 47.

28. Donald Pizer, "On the Editing of Modern American Texts," *Bulletin of the New York Public Library* 75 (1971): 147–53 (quotations from p. 149) (see also Pizer's later writings: review of the Pennsylvania edition of *Sister Carrie,* in *American Literature;* "Self-Censorship and Textual Editing"); Zeller, "A New Approach to the Critical Constitution of Literary Texts"; Philip Gaskell, *A New Introduction to Bibliography* (New York: Oxford University Press, 1972), p. 339, and *From Writer to Reader: Studies in Editorial Method,* p. vii (with mention of versions on pp. 3, 76, 139); McGann, *A Critique of Modern Textual Criticism;* James McLaverty, "The Concept of Authorial Intention in Textual Criticism," *Library,* 6th ser., 6 (1984): 121–38.

29. McGann, *A Critique of Modern Textual Criticism,* pp. 8, 100, 54.

30. Thorpe, *Principles of Textual Criticism,* p. 185. The subjectivity of "changed aesthetic effect" is rather like Tanselle's distinction between "vertical" and "horizontal" revisions ("The Editorial Problem of Final Authorial Intention," in *Selected Studies in Bibliography,* pp. 334–36) and open to the same objections.

31. Reiman, *Romantic Texts and Contexts,* chap. 10, " 'Versioning': The Presentation of Multiple Texts," pp. 167–80; Peter L. Shillingsburg, "An Inquiry into the Social Status of Texts and Modes of Textual Criticism," *Studies in Bibliography* 42 (1989): 55–79. See also Shillingsburg's discussion of versions in *Scholarly Editing in the Computer Age: Theory and Practice* (Athens: University of Georgia Press, 1986), pp. 44–55, 99–106. Stephen Parrish's recent "The Whig Interpretation of Literature" (cited in Chapter 4, note 30) is, in part at least, an eloquent defense of "the autonomy and the validity of each steady state of the text [of a work] as it changes in confused, unpredictable ways, through patterns which the author may never have foreseen, let alone 'intended' " (p. 349).

32. W. J. T. Mitchell, ed., *The Politics of Interpretation* (Chicago: University of Chicago Press, 1983), reprinting articles from *Critical Inquiry* (1982–83), and Stanley Rosen, *Hermeneutics as Politics* (New York: Oxford University Press, 1987). Rosen's book contains a revised version of his essay first published in *Literature and the Question of Philosophy,* ed. Cascardi.

Index

Stone, Irving, 211
Stoppard, Tom, 181; *Night and Day,* 239 n.16; *Travesties,* 170–71
Strauss, Harold, 152
Styron, William, *Lie Down in Darkness,* 212
Susann, Jacqueline, 212; *The Love Machine,* 235 n.6; *Valley of the Dolls,* 141, 143–45
Sussman, Aaron, 142
Sutherland, J. A., 140–41, 204, 235 n.2
Svoboda, Frederic J., 237 n.32
Swedenborg, Emanuel, 185

Tanselle, G. Thomas, 195, 243 nn.21, 22, 244 n.30
Targ, William, 153
Tate, Allen, 145
Tate, Nahum, 164–65, 167, 169
Tati, Jacques, 174
Taylor, Helen, 52, 67
Taylor, John (Keats's publisher), 22–23, 27, 29–30, 34, 37–38, 40–41, 43–46, 205, 219 n.14
Taylor, John (first husband of Harriet Mill), 59–60
Taylor, Sam, 168
Tennemann, Wilhelm Gottlieb, 105, 110, 229 n.16
Tetens, Johann Nicolai, 105, 119, 229 n.16
Thackeray, William Makepeace, *Henry Esmond,* 140
Thaddeus, Janice, 211, 236–37 n.29
Thomas, D. M., *The White Hotel,* 207
Thomas, Jo, 207
Thomas, W. K., 217 n.15
Thomason, John W., Jr., *Jeb Stuart,* 148
Thorpe, James, 48, 94, 198, 199, 200, 204, 219 n.20, 227 n.39, 243 n.18, 244 nn.27, 30

Toklas, Alice B., 209
Toland, Gregg, 180
Toth, Emily, 141, 142–43, 212, 235 n.4
Train, Arthur, *The World and Thomas Kelly,* 148
Tree, Herbert Beerbohm, 167
Trelawny, Edward John, *Adventures of a Younger Son,* 205
Trollope, Anthony, *Barchester Towers,* 140, 206
Truffaut, François, 178
Turco, Lewis, 134–35, 234 n.23
Twain, Mark, 208, 227 n.38

Updike, John, *Rabbit, Run,* 212

Van Dine, S. S., 145, 148
Vaughan, Samuel S., 153
Versions, theory of, 94–95, 197–200
Vincent, Howard P., 208
Vittoz, Dr. Roger, 126
Vonnegut, Kurt, Jr., 212

Waldron, Randall H., 213
Walker, Eric C., 223 n.9
Wallace, Catherine Miles, 118, 232 n.42
Wallace, Lew, 208
Wallace, Mike, 143
Wallace, Susan Arnold, 208
Wallis, Hal B., 174, 175, 239 n.23
Walton, Kendall L., 16, 217 n.17
Warner, Charles Dudley, 208
Warren, Austin, 134
Warton, Thomas, 10
Wasson, Ben, 156
Watts, Richard, 239 n.19
Weeks, Edward, 153
Wellek, René, 106–7, 113, 230 n.20
Welles, Orson, 178–80, 240 n.33
West, Anthony, 110, 230 n.25
West, James L. W., III, 204, 234 n.1, 237 nn.33, 34, 241 n.2

200 904496